**WOMEN IN THE DEVELOPMENT PROCESS:
A SELECT BIBLIOGRAPHY ON WOMEN IN
SUB-SAHARAN AFRICA AND LATIN AMERICA**

WOMEN IN THE DEVELOPMENT PROCESS: A Select Bibliography on Women in Sub-Saharan Africa and Latin America
by Suzanne Smith Saulniers and
Cathy A. Rakowski

A Special Publication of the
Institute of Latin American Studies
The University of Texas at Austin

INSTITUTE OF LATIN AMERICAN STUDIES
William P. Glade, *Director*
Lawrence S. Graham, *Associate Director*

Cover design by Stephen Frels

International Standard Book Number 0-292-79010-4
Library of Congress Card Catalogue Number 77-90888
© 1977 by the Institute of Latin American Studies,
The University of Texas at Austin. All rights reserved.

PRINTED BY THE UNIVERSITY PRINTING DIVISION OF
THE UNIVERSITY OF TEXAS AT AUSTIN
MANUFACTURED IN THE UNITED STATES OF AMERICA

Distributed for the Institute of Latin
American Studies by:
    University of Texas Press
    P. O. Box 7819
    Austin, Texas 78712

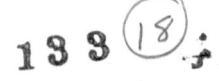

CONTENTS

PREFACE xiii

INTRODUCTION xvii

Chapter I: WOMEN AND SOCIETY 3

  A. STATUS 4
     Africa--General 4
     West Africa 5
     Central Africa 7
     East Africa 7
     Southern Africa 7

     Latin America--General 8
     Mexico and Central America 8
     Caribbean 10
     Andean Region 10
     Chile and the Platine 11
     Brazil 12

  B. SOCIAL ROLES (contains "Rural Only" subsections) 13
     Africa--General 13
     West Africa 17
     Central Africa 21
     East Africa 23
     Southern Africa 24

     Latin America--General 25
     Mexico and Central America 26
     Caribbean 28
     Andean Region 29
     Chile and the Platine 32
     Brazil 33

  C. SOCIAL ASPECTS (includes feminine culture and
    values, stereotypes, social conditions, and
    alternative lifestyles) 34
     Africa--General 34
     West Africa 36
     Central Africa 38
     East Africa 39
     Southern Africa 40

Latin America--General	41
Mexico and Central America	43
Caribbean	46
Andean Region	47
Chile and the Platine	49
Brazil	50

Chapter II: WOMEN AND THE LAW 53

A. CIVIL AND LEGAL STATUS 53

Africa--General	53
West Africa	54
Central Africa	56
East Africa	57
Southern Africa	58
Latin America--General	58
Mexico and Central America	59
Caribbean	61
Andean Region	62
Chile and the Platine	64
Brazil	65

B. LABOR AND CONTRACTUAL LEGISLATION 66

Africa--General	66
West Africa	66
Latin America--General	67
Mexico and Central America	67
Caribbean	68
Andean Region	69
Chile and the Platine	70
Brazil	71

Chapter III: WOMEN AND THE FAMILY 72

A. FAMILIAL ROLES AND STATUSES (includes wife and maternal roles, status in family structure, brideprice literature; contains "Rural Only" subsections) 73

Africa--General	73
West Africa	74
Central Africa	77
East Africa	78
Southern Africa	79
Latin America--General	79
Mexico and Central America	80
Caribbean	82

Andean Region	83
Chile and the Platine	85
Brazil	86

B. THE SINGLE MOTHER 88
   Latin America--General 88
   Mexico and Central America 88
   Caribbean 89
   Andean Region 89
   Chile and the Platine 89
   Brazil 90

Chapter IV: WOMEN AND RELIGION 91

   Africa--General 91
   West Africa 92
   Central Africa 93
   East Africa 93
   Southern Africa 93

   Latin America--General 93
   Andean Region 94
   Chile and the Platine 94
   Brazil 94

Chapter V: WOMEN AND EDUCATION 95

A. GENERAL TOPICS 96
   Africa--General 96
      Education of Women 96
      Education of Girls 97
   West Africa 98
      Education of Women 98
      Education of Girls 99
   Central Africa 101
      Education of Women 101
      Education of Girls 102
   East Africa 103
      Education of Women 103
      Education of Girls 104
   Southern Africa 105

   Latin America--General 105
   Mexico and Central America 106
   Caribbean 107
   Andean Region 107
   Chile and the Platine 108
   Brazil 109

B. SPECIALIZED TRAINING (includes rural, technical, literary, professional, and political education) 109
Africa-general 109
West Africa 111
Central Africa 112
East Africa 113
Southern Africa 115

Latin America--General 116
Mexico and Central America 116
Caribbean 117
Andean Region 118
Chile and the Platine 121
Brazil 122

Chapter VI: WOMEN AND THE POLITY 123

A. VARIOUS TOPICS 124
Africa--General 124
West Africa 124
Central Africa 125
East Africa 126
Southern Africa 126

Latin America--General 127
Mexico and Central America 127
Caribbean 128
Andean Region 129
Chile and the Platine 129
Brazil 131

B. WOMEN IN PUBLIC LIFE AND AS LEADERS 131
Africa--General 131
West Africa 132
Central Africa 133
East Africa 133
Southern Africa 134

Mexico and Central America 134
Caribbean 135
Andean Region 135
Chile and the Platine 135
Brazil 136

C. WOMEN IN REVOLUTION AND WARFARE 136
West Africa 136
Central Africa 136
East Africa 136

	Latin America--General	137
	Mexico and Central America	137
	Caribbean	137
	Andean Region	139
	Chile and the Platine	139

Chapter VII: WOMEN AND ORGANIZATIONS 140

A. ORGANIZATIONS, VOLUNTARY ASSOCIATIONS AND
   SOCIETIES 140
   Africa--General 140
   West Africa 141
   Central Africa 142
   East Africa 143
   Southern Africa 144

   Latin America--General 144
   Mexico and Central America 145
   Caribbean 145
   Andean Region 145
   Chile and the Platine 146

B. FEMINIST MOVEMENTS 146
   Africa--General 146
   West Africa 147
   Central Africa 148
   East Africa 148
   Southern Africa 149

   Latin America--General 149
   Mexico and Central America 150
   Caribbean 151
   Andean Region 151
   Chile and the Platine 152
   Brazil 153

Chapter VIII: WOMEN AND THE ECONOMY 154

A. THE POLITICAL ECONOMY OF WOMEN'S ROLES 155
   Africa--General 155
   West Africa 156
   Central Africa 156
   East Africa 157
   Southern Africa 157

   Latin America--General 157
   Mexico and Central America 158
   Andean Region 158
   Brazil 158

B. THE INFORMAL SECTOR (includes home labor,
   handicrafts, rural participation, prostitution,   158
   and domestic service)   158
   Africa--General   158
   West Africa   160
   Central Africa   163
   East Africa   164
   Southern Africa   165

   Latin America--General   166
   Mexico and Central America   167
   Caribbean   170
   Andean Region   171
   Chile and the Platine   174
   Brazil   175

C. MARKETING AND COMMERCE   176
   West Africa   176
   Central Africa   179

   Latin America--General   179
   Mexico and Central America   179
   Caribbean   180
   Andean Region   180

D. THE FORMAL SECTOR (includes women in industry
   and the professions)   180
   Africa--General   180
   West Africa   182
   Central Africa   184
   East Africa   185
   Southern Africa   187

   Latin America--General   187
   Mexico and Central America   190
   Caribbean   193
   Andean Region   195
   Chile and the Platine   197
   Brazil   199

E. SOCIAL ASPECTS OF WOMEN'S LABOR   201
   Africa--General   202
   West Africa   202
   Central Africa   202
   East Africa   202
   Southern Africa   203

   Latin America--General   203
   Mexico and Central America   204
   Caribbean   205

Andean Region	205
Chile and the Platine	206
Brazil	207

Chapter IX: WOMEN AND SOCIAL CHANGE 209

Africa--General	209
West Africa	214
Central Africa	216
East Africa	218
Southern Africa	220
Latin America--General	220
Mexico and Central America	221
Caribbean	223
Andean Region	225
Chile and the Platine	226
Brazil	227

Chapter X: WOMEN AND DEVELOPMENT (contains "Rural Only" subsections for Africa) 228

Africa--General	228
West Africa	233
Central Africa	235
East Africa	236
Southern Africa	237
Latin America--General	238
Mexico and Central America	239
Caribbean	240
Andean Region	240
Chile and the Platine	241
Brazil	241

APPENDICES 243

Appendix A: SUPPLEMENTARY RESEARCH ON WOMEN AND THE DEVELOPMENT PROCESS 247

1. GENERAL REFERENCES 247
2. SPECIAL JOURNAL ISSUES RELATED TO THE TOPIC OF WOMEN IN THE DEVELOPMENT PROCESS 258

Appendix B: SOURCES CONSULTED 262

1. SOURCES CONSULTED FOR AFRICAN CITATIONS 262
   a. Bibliographies 262

b. Serial Abstracts, Guides, and Indexes	267
c. Library Card Catalogs and Acquisition Lists	269
2. SOURCES CONSULTED FOR LATIN AMERICAN CITATIONS	269
a. Bibliographies	269
b. Serial Abstracts, Guides, and Indexes	270
c. Library Card Catalogs and Acquisition Lists	271
Appendix C: NAME AND PLACE OF PUBLICATION OF SELECTED REFERENCES INCLUDED IN AFRICAN AND LATIN AMERICAN CITATIONS	273
1. PUBLICATIONS INCLUDED IN AFRICAN CITATIONS	273
2. PUBLICATIONS INCLUDED IN LATIN AMERICAN CITATIONS	279

PREFACE

The 1970s have been years characterized by an increasing recognition of the importance of women's roles in developing nations and the impact of technological and social change on women. The declaration of 1975 as International Women's Year served to intensify interest in the study of women in national development planning and programs. International development agencies have also fostered interest in the study of roles of women in the evaluation of projects funded through these agencies. Our bibliography, coming at the time of this heightened world-wide interest, has as its purpose to draw together references that can be used to evaluate women's actual and potential roles in institutional settings and in societal development in both Sub-Saharan Africa and Latin America. It is hoped that by compiling source materials in these two regions we will encourage comparative research on women's roles in development.

We owe our initial efforts and collaboration to Dr. William Glade, director of the Institute of Latin American Studies at the University of Texas at Austin. He approached both of us in the summer of 1976 with the idea of compiling a bibliography on women, its publication to coincide with the joint national meetings of the African Studies Association and the Latin American Studies Association in Houston, Texas, November 2-5, 1977. Dr. Saulniers was asked to compile materials on women in Africa and to coordinate the project; Ms. Rakowski was asked to compile materials on women in Latin America.

The role and status of women in the development process is our main focus. It is our conviction that societies are in a state of continual change — change that is not only economic but also social, technological, institutional, and psychological. Women's roles at one point in time may therefore be more easily understood in the context of roles at other points in time.

We hope to present the user with materials that show the shifting orientations and focuses of researchers from 1900 to the present. What the researcher considers important for study says as much about the researcher, the academic field, a perceived problem of the era, and the problems of studying the female sex as it does about the subject under investigation. Source materials may also provide the user with clues as to how, when, and where women have been considered part of the process of development.

The selection of sources to be included was not always as systematic or as complete as we had intended originally. Our search was constrained by our respective access to library resources and by the time necessary to meet other academic commitments. We were also limited to working in the four languages in which we are competent--English, French, Portuguese, and Spanish. Those writings on women in Africa by Swedish, German, Italian, or Flemish-speaking researchers are unfortunately omitted unless the materials were translated into one of the above four languages. Also omitted are references to works written in native African languages.

Most of our entries come from library materials at the University of Michigan and the University of Texas at Austin. Other entries come from inter-library loans or correspondence with researchers or bibliographers working in the same area. Because of our dependence on secondary sources, citations given are not always complete. The decision was made to include only those incomplete entries that provide information sufficient to indicate the type of research within a particular area or draw associations between names of researchers and areas of research.

Further, we did not include the following topics: fertility and family planning; female physiology; biographies of famous women unless they provided information on women's political or leadership potential in Africa; fiction; or detailed descriptions of dress and rituals. Although literary works such as novels and poetry may provide very accurate pictures of the lives of women, we were primarily interested in compiling sources using socio-scientific approaches to women's roles and statuses. We chose not to include a chapter on women and fertility or family planning because this topic is sufficient for a bibliography in itself; moreover, there are numerous comprehensive bibliographies in this field that our efforts would only duplicate.

We have neither annotated nor provided an index. The decision not to annotate was based on the incomplete accessibility of the reference materials in our geographical location and the time required to make extensive use of inter-library loans. The decision to forego an index at this time was based on a commitment to have the bibliography completed by the time of the joint national meetings of the African Studies Association and the Latin American Studies Association.

We recognize that there may be errors in categorizing articles and in unintentionally duplicating entries. We hope these problems are minimal and will not detract from the usefulness of this bibliography.

A special note of thanks goes to two students who assisted us in the final stages of research: Katherine Murray, a graduate student at the Institute of Latin American Studies, who volunteered several weeks of her time to pore over materials on Latin America (and who also was responsible for a good deal of typing), and John W. Davis, a student at Huston-Tillotson College, who spent several months searching for additional materials on Latin America and rechecking incomplete entries in both sections.

We are indebted to the many individuals and organizations both in the United States and abroad who volunteered bibliographies, photocopied card catalog listings, sent copies of unpublished papers, and referred us to others involved in the study of women in developing countries. We especially want to express our gratitude to Meri Knaster, who provided counsel, guidance, and assistance for the initial search of Latin American sources; to several officials of the Agency for International Development who took upon themselves the tasks of gathering references and copies of papers and booklets and sending them to us for perusal, and to officials of the United Nations and its affiliated divisions, especially UNICEF, for their generous donation of bibliographies, papers, and reports for our inspection. Other individuals or organizations who contributed to our effort are too numerous to mention, but we wish to express our appreciation for their responses to requests for assistance and copies of papers.

We must also thank the staff of the Institute of Latin American Studies for advice and assistance in the organization and publication of the bibliography. They devoted considerable time and suffered untold frustrations during the preparation of the manuscript. We do appreciate all they put into the finished product.

Finally, Susie would like to thank her husband, Al Saulniers, for his sacrifice and tried patience, while Cathy would like to thank her two young daughters for accepting the absence and inattention of their mother for lengthy periods of time.

Suzanne Smith Saulniers
Cathy A. Rakowski

October, 1977

INTRODUCTION

The purpose of this bibliography is to draw together books, articles, conference papers, pamphlets, and unpublished documents written between 1900 and 1976 on women in Sub-Saharan Africa and Latin America. It expands on previous work about women by combining articles written in both regions and by classifying articles into those that deal with change in roles and status and development and those that describe or analyze roles and status within institutional settings. Particular attention has been given to compiling references using sociological and anthropological perspectives. For Latin America, feminist perspectives also have been incorporated. The list of entries is by no means complete or definitive; rather, it is an attempt to provide a minimal compendium of research materials. In addition, this bibliography strives to produce an awareness of complementary research on women on both continents and suggestions for further research, particularly that taking a comparative approach toward the problem of women and their integration in the development process.

Works Consulted

The initial search for materials was carried out individually by each compiler. As a result of this, the entries reflect different bibliographical styles and different approaches to the topic of women and development. In this section we outline the variety of sources used and explain our respective approaches.

Both sections of the bibliography were compiled from standard bibliographical materials. These include bibliographies, abstracts and indexes of dissertations and theses; indexes of periodicals; serial abstracts, printed catalogs, and acquisition lists from general libraries and special collections on Africa and Latin America; general guides to reference works; and miscellaneous sources, such as monography publications, conference papers, and footnotes in books and articles.

African entries were principally extracted from indexes, serial abstracts, bibliographies, and printed library acquisition lists or card catalogs of various libraries. Source materials accessible in the University of Michigan libraries during the summer of 1976 provided the major proportion of entries.

The following three are among the indexes consulted: <u>Africa South of the Sahara, Index to Periodical Literature</u> and its first supplement; <u>An International Bibliography of Sociology/ Bibliographie Internationale de Sociologie</u>; and <u>A Guide to Periodical Literature in the Social Sciences and Humanities Index</u> and the later publications, <u>Social Science and Humanities Index</u> and <u>Social Science Index</u>. Citations were also drawn from bibliographies and abstracts. Particularly useful were <u>A Current Bibliography on African Affairs</u>; the various bibliographical series on Africa coming out of the Hoover Institution, the International African Institute, and the Program of East African Studies, Syracuse University; and two excellent bibliographies compiled by Christian Chukwunedu Aguolu entitled <u>Ghana in the Humanities and Social Sciences 1900-1971</u> and <u>Nigeria: A Comprehensive Bibliography in the Humanities and Social Sciences, 1900-1971</u>. Printed card catalogs and library acquisition lists, such as those of the Herskovits Library of African Studies at Northwestern University, and the CAMP Catalog also provided data on published materials. Monographs or books that derive special mention for leads to other sources were Denise Paulme (ed.), <u>Women of Tropical Africa</u> and Uma J. Lele, <u>The Design of Rural Development</u>. For a comprehensive list of bibliographical materials used to gather African citations, including years or volumes consulted, see Appendix B, Part 1.

The Latin American section was developed using a slightly different approach. The search began with locating as many current works as possible, especially works not yet cited in published bibliographical materials. This was accomplished through direct correspondence with international organizations, foundations, and individuals who were known to have attended conferences on women or to be working on some current research project involving women. The search then turned to an examination of periodicals, published indexes, and card catalogs or library acquisition lists.

Many Latin American entries were compiled from card searches of the libraries of the University of Texas at Austin from the summer of 1976 to April 1977 and the Center for Research on Economic Development of the University of Michigan in the summer of 1976. A major source of information was published card catalogs of libraries with special Latin American collections, including those of Tulane University, the University of Florida, the

University of London, and the Biblioteca Nacional de Antropología e Historia de México. Additional materials were obtained from recent bibliographies on women in Latin America, such as Ann Pescatello (ed.), Female and Male in Latin America: Essays; Meri Knaster, Women in Spanish America: An Annotated Bibliography; Nelson P. Valdes, "Cuban Women in the Twentieth Century"; and bibliographies found in various periodicals or at the end of published and unpublished papers. The major abstract series and indexes used include Comprehensive Dissertation Index Handbook of Latin American Studies and the Pan American Union's Index to Latin American Periodical Literature and its supplement. A major source of entries came from the collection of Latin American periodicals found in the Nettie Lee Benson Latin American Collection, University of Texas at Austin. These include America Indígena, Boletín Documental sobre las Mujeres, Desarrollo Económico, Latin American Research Review, and sociological and anthropological periodicals from several Latin American countries. A more detailed accounting of sources utilized for the section on Latin America is found in Appendix B, Part 2.

Scope

The scope of the African entries may be characterized in four ways. First, entries are drawn from the 1900-1975 period. This results from a research style emphasizing a review of past trends in topics and methodology. Hence, a large proportion of references was drawn from already published bibliographies on Africa. Citations of recent works primarily come from current journal indexes and conference papers. Second, an uneven distribution across regions and time periods is noted. Thus, citations on women in South Africa are few because many bibliographies excluded entries on South Africa for reasons of politics or regional delimitation from Sub-Saharan Africa. Moreover, many articles on women in Africa have been written in languages other than English, French, Portuguese, and Spanish. This is particularly true of pre-independence literature. A third characteristic is the exclusive use of the female--either girl or woman--as the unit of analysis. Articles on the African family were included only if they provided valuable background materials on women's roles or included a section specific to women. A final attribute of this section is the paucity of entries on labor legislation and the legal status of women. The African compiler was not concerned with this aspect of the development process and did not attempt to compile references in these areas.

The scope of the Latin American entries varies somewhat from that of the African entries. First, the bulk of materials cited is for the post 1930-period. Given the surge of interest about women in Latin America during the current decade, recently written materials were searched first, followed by bibliographic work on earlier periods. Second, the section on women in Latin American organizations is weighted more toward references on women in revolutionary or activist groups, whereas the African section includes entries on this topic but also on women's organizations. Materials on women in revolutions and feminist movements are more specific to Cuba, Bolivia, Chile and Peru, where revolutionary movements have provided greater opportunity to study women in combat than in other countries. Third, many of the Latin American references use the family as the unit of analysis. A concern with machismo as a determinant of interaction between sexes and an emphasis on woman as mother explain the large number of these references. To have limited entries to those with the female as the unit of analysis would have restricted citations to women's roles outside the family or to legislation on women. Finally, a characteristic similar to African citations is that entries are unevenly distributed across countries. More seems to have been written on women in Brazil and Mexico than in any of the other countries. Materials on women in countries such as Costa Rica and Paraguay are extremely scarce.

Format

The bibliography is divided into ten chapters and three appendices. The first chapter contains entries with general descriptions of women's roles and status. The second through eighth chapters provide background materials for understanding potential and actual constraints on change in roles and participation in development that are covered in the ninth and tenth chapters. Decisions were made--at times arbitrarily--about entry placement. For example, an article dealing with a general description of the economic activities of women may be included under the subsection "Social Roles" of chapter I rather than in chapter VIII, "Women and the Economy."

Appendix A includes general materials on women and development. It is intended to supplement area-specific entries and provide a global perspective to the topic of women and development. Appendix B provides a list of sources consulted. Appendix C lists the titles and places of publication of selected periodicals covered by the bibliography.

Countries Included

The African section was restricted to countries commonly classified as Sub-Saharan Africa. This region was then subdivided into four geographical areas. Countries included in each area are as follows:

1. West Africa: Mali, Niger, Senegal, Gambia, Guinea-Bissau, Guinea, Sierra Leone, Liberia, Ivory Coast, Upper Volta, Ghana, Togo, Nigeria, Democratic Republic of Benin, Chad, Cameroons
2. East Africa: Ethiopia, Kenya, Tanzania, Uganda, Mozambique
3. Central Africa: Central African Republic, People's Republic of the Congo, Zaire, Rwanda, Burundi, Angola, Gabon, Sudan
4. Southern Africa: Zambia, Rhodesia, Namibia, Botswana, Basutoland, Nyasaland, Malawi, Lesotho, South Africa

The Latin American section was restricted to Spanish- and Portuguese-speaking countries. These were divided into geographical-cultural areas as follows:

1. Mexico and Central America: Mexico, Guatemala, El Salvador, Honduras, Nicaragua, Costa Rica, Panama
2. Caribbean: Cuba, Dominican Republic, Puerto Rico
3. Andean Region: Venezuela, Colombia, Peru, Ecuador, Bolivia
4. Chile and the Platine: Chile, Argentina, Uruguay, Paraguay
5. Brazil

The Entry

Entries are numbered consecutively. Complete bibliographic information is given whenever possible. Every entry is classified in three ways. First, it is classified by general topic according to its chapter heading. Second, it is categorized by its relationship to subtopics or chapter sections. Third, it is classified by geographical location of research. If an article was specific to a country it was categorized according to the geographical region of the country; otherwise it was placed in the category "Africa--General" or "Latin America--General." Whenever we were unable to determine the country in which the research took place, the entry was also placed in the general categories.

Special classifications were added in chapters I, III, V, and X. In chapters I, III, and X an article that specifically dealt with rural social roles or rural development was separated from general entries and categorized under the subheading "Rural Only." However, if an article dealt with both rural and urban roles or development, it was included with general entries. We felt this would facilitate the use of the bibliography for persons concentrating on rural issues. Another special classification was applied only to African entries in chapter V. An article dealing only with the education of girls was placed under the subheading "Education of Girls;" otherwise it was placed under the subheading "Education of Women." The abundance of articles specific to girls in this topic justified this classification.

An example of an entry included in chapters I, III, and X and the way it is classified appears as follows:

Carre, Shirly Kiborn Desbon. "Women's Position on a Yucatecan Henequin Hacienda." Ph.D. dissertation, Yale University, 1976.

This article appears in chapter I, WOMEN AND SOCIETY; section B., SOCIAL ROLES, Mexico and Central America, "Rural Only."

An example of an entry in chapter V and the way it is classified appears as follows:

Ngonyama, S. "The Education of the African Girl." Nada, v. 31, 1954: 57-58.

This article appears in chapter V, WOMEN AND EDUCATION; Africa--General, "Education of Girls."

Literature Trends

A review of entries reveals several trends in research, some parallel for the two regions, others quite divergent. Specific topics of study have varied by decade. In general, we found the Latin American literature moves from a study of women in the familial context to a study of women outside the family. The concentration of the research effort has shifted from women in urban areas and of middle and upper classes toward women in rural areas and of lower classes. The scientific approach has moved from descriptive and social-psychological to analytical and political-economic.

Within the African literature a similar move from descriptive to analytical appears. In addition, research on rural women has shifted from an ethnocentric (colonial) perspective to an economic-anthropological perspective. A recent emphasis has been placed also on using a conflict rather than a consensus approach to the study of social change and changing values or opportunities for rural and urban women. Finally, the orientation of research has moved from a discussion of opportunities and static roles at the local level to a discussion of emerging roles and opportunities at the national level.

Temporally, the treatment of women and the polity is concentrated in the earlier decades for Latin America and the later decades for Sub-Saharan Africa. Moreover, evidence of greater concern with the civil rights of women appears in the

Latin American literature in the 1930s and 1940s while in the African literature only in the 1960s and 1970s. Participation in community development and social and technological change programs appears to have emerged at the same time in both areas--during the 1960s--with participation in rural development programs gaining importance during the 1970s. Education of women and girls has been of continual interest, but the research focus has changed from a concern with formal education to one of informal education and technical training programs. This shift parallels the growing interest in community development by international agencies and the rapid urbanization in the two regions.

WOMEN IN THE DEVELOPMENT PROCESS:
A SELECT BIBLIOGRAPHY ON WOMEN IN
SUB-SAHARAN AFRICA AND LATIN AMERICA

Chapter I

WOMEN AND SOCIETY

This chapter contains materials that provide a general orientation to the subject of women in society. The references for Africa are predominantly on role activity and perceptions of women's roles in society. They also include general descriptions of female activities and lifestyles. The references for Latin America similarly include descriptions of role activity but many are oriented toward descriptions of ideal behavior and stereotypes of femininity. If a reference for either region includes a description of economic roles but these roles are not the core material of the reference, the entry is included in this chapter rather than in chapter 6, "Women and the Economy."

Although chapter 1 does not deal directly with the issue of women's participation in development, it provides a framework of social and normative factors affecting women's past, present, and future participation in the development process.

Under section B, we found the large volume of references to be somewhat unwieldy for a potential user. Consequently, we separated entries easily identifiable as specific to the rural woman from those either specific to urban woman, to women of both rural and urban areas, or not easily identifiable as specific to women of any area.

A. STATUS

Africa--General

1. Andreski, Iris. <u>Old Wives Tales: Life Stories of African Women</u>. New York: Schocken Books, 1970.

2. Ankrah, E. Maxine. "Has the African Woman Settled for Tokens?" <u>Lutheran World</u>, v. 22 (1), 1975: 22-31.

3. Bledsoe, Caroline. "Women's Strategies in Kpelle Domestic Groups." Paper presented at the American Anthropological Association Annual Meeting, Mexico City, 1974.

4. Durello, G. "The Economic and Social Status of Women in African Countries (abridged extracts from the Report II of the International Labour Organization on the Employment and Conditions of Work of African Women.) <u>Overseas Quarterly</u>, v. 4 (6), June 1965: 176-178.

5. Evans-Pritchard, E. E. "The Position of Women in Primitive Societies and in Our Own." In E. E. Evans-Pritchard, ed., <u>The Position of Women in Primitive Societies and Other Essays</u>. New York: Free Press, 1965.

6. Gollock, Georgina A. <u>Daughters of Africa</u>. Westport: Negro Universities Press, reprint of 1932 edition.

7. "Hommage á la femme noire." <u>Jeune Afrique</u>, v. 496, 7 July 1970, supplément: 27-76.

8. Lembezat, Bertrand. <u>Eve noire</u>. Neuchatel and Paris: Ides and Calendes, 1952.

9. Le Tourneau, C. <u>La Condition de la femme</u>. Paris: V. Giard et E. Briere, 1903. Chapters II, III.

10. McCall, Daniel F., and Elizabeth Colson. "Educated African Women: Their Status and Influence in the Societies South of the Sahara" (summary of a report produced for UNESCO). <u>Overseas Quarterly</u>, v. 1 (2), March 1959: 142-144.

11. Moore, M. P. "Some Economic Aspects of Women's Work and Status in the Rural Areas of Africa and Asia." IDS Discussion Paper No. 43. Mimeo. Brighton, England: University of Sussex, Institute of Development Studies, 1974.

12. Njiiri, Ruth S. "New Roles for Women in Modern Africa." Paper presented to the African-American Scholars Council, Washington, D.C., 10 May 1975.

13. Ojike, Mbonu. "Status of African Women." In Ram DeSai, ed., African Society and Culture. New York: M. W. Lads, 1968: 70-75.

14. Pala, Achola O. "The Role of African Women in Rural Development: Research Priorities." Institute for Development Studies Discussion Paper No. 203. Nairobi, 1975.

15. _____, and Ann Seidman. "A Model of the Status of Women in Africa." Paper presented at the Wellesley Conference on Women and Development, June 1976. Available from Wellesley Center for Research on Women, 828 Washington Street, Wellesley, Massachusetts 02181.

16. Plisnier-Ladame, F. La Condition de l'Africaine en Afrique noire. Brussels: Centre de Documentation Économique et Sociales Africaine. Enquêtes Bibliographiques, No. 7, 1961.

17. Seidman, Ann. "A Proposed Model of the Status of Women in Africa." Unpublished manuscript, 1968.

18. Symons, H. J. "The Status of African Women." In J. M. Peter McEwan, and Robert Sutcliffe, eds., Modern Africa. New York: Crowell, 1965: 326-331.

19. Tillett, Gladys A. "U. N. Status of Women Commission Considers Needs in Africa." U. S. Department of State Bulletin, v. 45, 21 August 1961: 345-349.

20. United Nations Economic and Social Council. Social Welfare Services in Africa. The Status and Role of Women in East Africa. June 1967. United Nations Document # E/CN.14/SWSA/6.

West Africa

21. Adibe, M. L., and A. Tessa. "Position and Problems of the Woman in French-Speaking Africa. II— Gabon." Women Today, v. 6 (3), 1964: 51-53.

22. Bazin, Danielle. Évolution du statut et de l'image de la femme au Mali. Paris: Ecole des Hautes Études, 1971.

23. Beier, Horst Ulrich. "The Position of Yoruba Women." Présence Africaine, v. 1 (1-2), April-July 1955: 39-46.

24. Binet, Jacques. "Le statut des femmes au Cameroun forestier." Recueils Soc. Jean Bodin, v. 11 (1), 1959: 45-62.

25. Burness, H. M. "The Position of Women in Gwandu and Yauri (Nigeria)." Overseas Education, v. 26 (4), January 1955: 143-152.

26. Comhaire-Sylvain, Suzanne. "The Status of Women in Lagos, Nigeria." Pi Lambda Theta Journal, v. 27 (3), March 1949: 158-163.

27. Conservative Commonwealth Council. "Status of Women in West Africa." African Women, v. 1 (3), December 1955: 63-66.

28. Dolbert, Margarita. "The Changing Status of Women in French-Speaking Africa. Two Examples: Dahomey and Guinea." Mimeo. Washington, D.C., American University, 1970.

29. Fumey, W. Ganyo, "Moral Paradoxes and Expatriate Ideas." Ghana Journal of Sociology, v. 5 (1), February 1969: 49-51.

30. Garnier, C. "Africaines 1955." Tropiques, v. 53 (379), 1955: 9-19.

31. Harris, Jack. "The Position of Women in a Nigerian Society." Transactions of the New York Academy of Science, Series II, v. 2 (5), 1939-1940.

32. Jaulin, Robert. "La Distribution des femmes et des biens chez les Mara." Cahiers d'Études Africaines, v. 6 (23), 1966: 419-462.

33. Laurin, G. "La Condition de la femme au Niger." Revue Internationale de l'Education des Adultes et de la Jeunesse, v. 15, 1963: 133-137.

34. _____. "The Status of Women in Niger." International Journal of Adult and Youth Education, v. 15 (3), 1963: 120-124.

35. Little, Kenneth L. "The Position of Women." In Kenneth L. Little, ed., The Mende of Sierra Leone. London: Routledge and Kegan Paul, 1951: 163-174.

36. Ogunbiyi, I. A. "The Position of Muslim Women as Stated by 'Uthmán b. Fúdi'." Odu, v. 2, October 1969: 43-60.

37. Prost, André. "Statut de la femme songhay." Bulletin de l'IFAN, v. 32B (2), April 1970: 486-517.

38. Ransom-Kuti, F. "The Status of Women in Nigeria." Journal of Human Relations, v. 10 (1), Autumn 1961: 67-72.

39. du Sacré-Coeur, Marie-Andrè, Sister. "La Situation de la femme en Afrique noire française." Civilisations, v. 1 (4), 1951: 46-54.

40. Shani, Ma'aji Isa. "The Status of Muslim Women in the Northern States of Nigeria." Journal. Centre Islamic Legal Studies, v. 1 (2), 1967(?): 39-52.

41. Smith, M. G. "The Hausa System of Social Status." Africa, v. 29, 1959: 239-252.

42. "Status of Women in Togoland and the Cameroons." African Women, v. 1 (4), June 1956: 95-98.

43. "Status of Women in West Africa." African Women, v. 1 (3), 1955: 63-66.

Central Africa

44. Carels, H. "La Situation de la femme noire en Afrique centrale." Revue Scientifique, v. 75, February 1937: 61-66.

45. Evans-Pritchard, E. E., ed. Man and Woman among the Azande. New York: Free Press, 1974.

East Africa

46. MacVicar, T. "The Position of Women Among the Wanguru." Primitive Man, v. 7 (2), 1934: 17-22.

47. Mbilinyi, Marjorie J. "The Status of Women in Tanzania." Canadian Journal of African Studies, v. 6 (2), 1972: 371-377.

48. Shepherd, Nancy E. "African Women in Kenya. Education, Present Social Status, and Hopes for the Future." One World, v. 6, August-October 1955: 253-256.

49. United Nations Economic Commission for Africa. Social Development Section. The Status and Role of Women in East Africa. New York: United Nations, 1967. United Nations Document #E/CN/14/SWSA/6.

50. Whiting, Beatrice B. "The Kenyan Career Woman: Traditional and Modern." In Ruth B. Kindsin, ed., The Anatomy of Achievement. New York: William Morrow, 1974.

Southern Africa

51. Bradney, P. J. "The Status of Women Among the Southern Bantu." B. S. thesis, Oxford University, 1950.

52. Simons, H. J. "A Statistical Comment on the Position of Women in Zambia." In Women's Rights in Zambia. Report of a Consultation. Kitwe: Mindolo Ecumenical Foundation, n.d.

53. Wilson, B. M. "The Position of Women in South Africa." <u>The East and the West</u>, v. 14, 1916: 61-68.

Latin America--General

54. Barbieri, M. Teresita de. "La condición de la mujer en América Latina: Su participación social, antecedentes y situación actual." Mimeo. Caracas, 1975. Available from: United Nations Center for Social and Humanitarian Affairs, United Nations Development Programme, New York, N.Y.

55. Interamerican Commission of Women. "Reports to the United Nations Commission on the Status of Women, 1956-1968." Washington, D. C.: Pan American Union, 1956-1968.

56. _____. "Women in Latin America: Past, Present, and Future." Washington, D. C.: Organization of American States, 1973.

57. Lee, Frances M. "The Progress of Women in the American Republics." <u>U.S. Department of State Bulletin</u>, v. 37 (952), 23 September, 1957: 506-508.

58. Orvig de Salazar, Helen de. "El sistema, la mujer y su superación." <u>Boletín Documental sobre las Mujeres</u>, v. 2 (2), 1972.

59. Parra, Teresa de la. <u>Tres conferencias inéditas</u>. Caracas: Ediciones Garrido, 1961.

60. Pena Bustos, Marta Elena. "La condición de la mujer a nivel de los organismos internacionales." <u>Revista Universitaria Nacional de Córdoba</u>, v. 10 (1-2), March-June 1969: 475-522.

61. Villanueva Saavedra, Etelvina. "Afirmando nuestro juicio sobre la posición de la mujer americana." <u>La Voz de Atlántida</u>, November 1947: 13-14.

62. Willard, Mary Jean. "A Study of the Diet and Nutritional Status of Latin American Women." Master's thesis, University of Texas, 1942.

Mexico and Central America

63. Brows, William. "Emancipating Mexico's Women." <u>Mexican-American Review</u>, v. 20 (5), May 1952: 12-14, 32-34.

64. Debayle, Luis Manuel. "The Status of Women in Nicaragua." <u>Mid-Pacific Magazine</u>, March 1933: 237-239.

65. Fisher, Lillian E. "The Influence of the Present Mexican Revolution upon the Status of Mexican Women." Hispanic American Historical Review, v. 22 (1), February 1942: 211-228.

66. Gudjonsson, Petur. "Women in Castro's Cuba." The Progressive, v. 36 (8), 1972: 25-29.

67. Huezo de Espinosa, Justina. La mujer antigua y la mujer moderna. Managua: Ed. La Nueva Prensa, 1946.

68. Jiménez, Liliam. Condiciones de la mujer en El Salvador. Mexico City: Ed. Muñoz, 1962.

69. Langner, T. S. "Psychophysiological Symptoms and the Status of Women in Two Mexican Communities." In J. M. Murphy and A. Leighton, eds., Approaches to Cross-Cultural Psychiatry. Ithaca: Cornell University Press, 1965.

70. Lomnitz, Larissa. "La mujer marginada de México." Diálogos, v. 9 (6), 1973: 29-31.

71. Maynard, Eileen Anne. "The Women of Palin: A Comparative Study of Indian and Ladino Women in a Guatemalan Village." Ph.D. dissertation, Cornell University, 1963.

72. _____. "Guatemalan Women: Life Under Two Types of Patriarchy." In E. G. Matthiason, ed., Many Sisters: Women in Cross-Cultural Perspective. New York: Free Press, 1974: 77-98.

73. Morris, B. "The Status of Women in Mexico." Pamphlet. Washington, D. C.: 1945.

74. Navarrette, Ifigenia M. de. "La mujer en la sociedad moderna." Espejo, v. 3 (7), 1969: 59-83.

75. _____. La mujer y los derechos sociales. Mexico City: Ediciones OASIS, 1969.

76. Ortega de Huezo, Josefa. "La mujer de ayer y la mujer de hoy." Revista Conservadora del Pensamiento Centroamericano, v. 18 (86), November 1967: 75-76.

77. Urrutia, Elena, ed. Imagen y realidad de la mujer. Mexico City: Sep/Setentas, 1975.

Caribbean

78. Bibes Tovar, Federico. The Puerto Rican Woman: Her Life and Evolution Throughout History. New York: Plus Ultra Educational Publishers, 1972.

79. Comisión de Derechos Civiles. "La igualdad de los derechos y oportunidades de la mujer puertorriqueña." San Juan, Puerto Rico, 1972.

80. De la Torre, Silvio. Mujer y Sociedad. Havana: Ed. Universitaria, 1965.

81. Randall, Margaret. Las mujeres. Mexico City: Siglo Veintiuno, 1970.

Andean Region

82. Abelli, Lurs de. "The Status of Women in Bolivia." Mid-Pacific Magazine, v. 44 (6), December 1932: 550-552.

83. Bazán Montenegro, Dora. La mujer en las "Tradiciones peruanas." Madrid: Artes Gráficas Maribel, 1967.

84. Buitrón, Aníbal. "Situación económica, social y cultural de la mujer en los países andinos." América Indígena, v. 16 (2), April 1956: 83-92.

85. Centro de Estudios Sociales con AITEC. "The Effects of Employment and Education on the Status of Women in Venezuela. A Progress Report." Paper presented at the 8th World Congress of the Committee on Family Research, International Sociological Association, 1975. Available from CES, Apartado 14.385, Caracas, Venezuela.

86. Echocopar, H. Carlos. "The Civil and Political Status of Women in Peru." Bulletin of the Pan American Union, v. 72, August 1938: 462-464.

87. Escobar M., Gabriel; R. P. Schaedel; and O. Núñez del Prado. Organización social y cultural del sur del Perú. Serie: Antropología Social 7, Mexico City: Instituto Indigenista Interamericano, 1967.

88. Fernández, Gumersinda, and Norma Sevillano. "Bolivia: Análisis de la situación actual y general de la mujer." Boletín Documental sobre las Mujeres, v. 1 (2), 1970: 60-63.

89. La Fosse, Violeta Sara. "Condición jurídica y social de la mujer y crecimiento demográfico." Boletín Documental sobre las mujeres, v. 4 (1), 1974.

90. Moretta Clavijo, Fabiola. "Ecuador: Falta la investigación sobre la situación actual de la mujer." Boletín Documental sobre las Mujeres, v. 1 (1), 1971: 52-56.

91. Oliveira, Rosiska Darcy de, et al. Discusiones sobre la liberación de la mujer. Medellín, Colombia: Ed. La Pulga, 1975.

92. Ortíz de Castro, Blanca. "Consideraciones sobre la mujer indígena colombiana." América Indígena, v. 32 (4), 1972: 1233-1236.

93. Pantelis, Fanny G. de. "Equality--Not Yet a Dream for Most Bolivian Women." Response, v. 5 (5), May 1973: 6-10.

94. _____. "¿La igualdad? Ni un sueño para las bolivianas." Boletín Documental sobre las Mujeres, v. 4 (3), 1974: 26-31.

95. Portugal, Ana María. "La peruana, ¿tapada sin manto?" Mundo Nuevo, v. 46, 1970: 20-27.

96. Ramírez Canseco, Teresa. "La mujer campesina en Bolivia." América Indígena, v. 32 (3), 1972: 1025-1027.

97. Ungaro de Fox, Lucía. "La tapada." Américas, v. 21 (2), February 1969: 2-7.

98. Velásquez, Lucila. "Proceso y evaluación de la evolución de la mujer en Venezuela." El Farol, No. 237, 1971.

99. Villalobos de Urrutia, Gabriela. "Diagnóstico de la situación social y económica de la mujer peruana: Documento de trabajo." Lima: Centro de Estudios de Población y Desarrollo, 1975.

100. Zolezzi Chocano, Mario. "La revaloración de la mujer en el Perú: Análisis y perspectivas." Convergence, v. 8 (1), 1975: 41-48.

Chile and the Platine

101. Fabbri, Enrique E. "La mujer joven: Presente y futuro." Criterio, v. 42 (1569), 10 April 1969: 206-211.

102. Faron, Louis C. The Mapuche Indians of Chile. New York: Rinehart and Winston, 1968.

103. Madrid, Francisco. "Afirmación de la mujer argentina." Norte, January 1946: 13-64.

104. Mattelart, Armand, and Michele Mattelart. La mujer chilena en una nueva sociedad. Santiago: Ed. del Pacífico, 1968.

105. Ocampo, Victoria. "Pasado y presente de la mujer." La Nación, v. 9, January 1966.

106. Partido Comunista de la Argentina. Sección Nacional de Educación. "Problemas y luchas de las mujeres." Pamphlet. Buenos Aires: Ed. Anteo, 1967.

107. Peralta, Anselmo Jover. "Condición de la mujer en el Paraguay." Vida Femenina, November-December 1941: 6-8.

108. Tappen, K. B. "The Status of Women in Argentina." Washington, D.C.: 1944.

109. _____. "The Status of Women in Chile." Washington, D.C.: 1944.

Brazil

110. Horta, Elisabeth Vorcaro. A mulher na cultura brasileira. Belo Horizonte: Ed. Itatiaia, 1975.

111. Lopes de Almeida, Julia. Maternidade. Rio de Janeiro: Ed. Olivia Herdy de Cabral Peixoto, 1925.

112. Moraes, Tancredo. Pela emancipação integral da mulher. Rio de Janeiro: Ed. Pongetti, 1971.

113. Morais, Vamberto. A emancipação da mulher; as raizes do preconceito anti femenino e seu declínio. São Paulo: Ed. Cital, 1968.

114. Mulheres do Brasil (pensamento e ação). 2 vols. Fortaleza: Ed. Henriqueta Galeno, 1971.

115. Neotti, Ana. A mulher no mundo em conflicto. Ponta Grossa, Brazil: Universidade Estadual de Ponta Grossa, 1973.

116. Raphael, Alison. "Observations on Women in Brazil." Department of State Newsletter, AR-1, December 1975.

117. Rissone, Nice. "Quem libertou a mulher negra?" <u>Cadernos Brasileiros</u>, v. 10 (47), May-June 1968: 139-148.

118. Rosa e Silva, Odette. "Status e papais da mulher." In Maria Isaura Pereira de Queiroz, ed., <u>Campesinato Brasileiro</u>. São Paulo: 1973.

119. Rosemberg, Fulvia; Guiomar Namo de Mello; and Marta Kohl de Oliveira. "Levantamiento bibliográfico preliminar sobre a situação da mulher brasileira." Mimeo. São Paulo: Departamento de Pesquisas Educacionais, Fundação Carlos Chagas, 1976.

120. Sá, Irene Tavares de. "A condição da mulher." <u>Síntese Política Econômica Social</u>, v. 8 (29), January-March 1966: 24-31.

121. Saffioti, Heleieth Iara. "Status of Women in Brazil." In R. R. Leavitt, ed., <u>Cross-Cultural Perspectives on the Women's Movement and Women's Status</u>. The Hague: Mouton, 1976.

122. Tabak, Fanny. "O status da mulher no Brasil: Vitórias e preconceitos." <u>Cadernos da PVC</u>, August 1971: 165-201.

B. SOCIAL ROLES

Africa--General

123. Afro-Asian People's Solidarity Organization. <u>Women in Africa and Asia Today</u>. Cairo: 1972.

124. André, P. J. "Est-que la femme a desórmais un rôle à jouer en Asia et en Afrique." <u>Cahiers Économiques et de Liaison des Comités Eurofrique</u>, special no., 1961: 79-81.

125. Andreski, Iris. <u>Old Wives Tales: Life Stories of African Women</u>. New York: Schocken Books, 1970.

126. Awori, Thelma. "For African Women Equal Rights Are Not Enough; The Real Task Is to Rethink the Role of Men in Present Day Society." <u>UNESCO Courier</u>, v. 21-25, March 1975.

127. Bernard, J. "La Femme dans la société africaine." <u>Afrique Documents</u>, v. 90, 1967: 5-64.

128. Brom, Olga J. <u>A Woman in Africa</u>. Trans. by Helen Ramsbotham. Toronto: British Book Service, 1961.

129. Chaton, J. H. "La Femme africaine." <u>Table Ronde</u>, v. 203, December 1964: 59-71.

130. Crane, Louise. *Africa: Profiles of Modern African Women.* Philadelphia: Lippincott, 1973.

131. Crapuchet, Simonne. "Femmes agni en milieu urbain." *Cahiers d'Études Africaines*, v. 11, 2 (42), 1971: 298-307.

132. "Dossier sur la femme africaine." *Presence Africaine*, v. 68, October-December 1968: 17-90.

133. Edme, P. "Kunda Kalumbi, fille d'Afrique." *Jeune Afrique*, v. 19, 1953: 41-46; v. 20, 1953: 32-35.

134. "La Femme africaine." *Vivante Afrique*, v. 243, March-April 1966: 1-56.

135. "La Femme dans la nation." *Afrique Nouvelle*, v. 709, 8 March 1961: 8-9.

136. "La Femme dans la société africaine." *Documentation Internationale*, v. 1, 1 May 1969: 37-44.

137. "First United States Conference on the Role of Women in Africa. *African Women*, v. 3 (4), June 1960: 88-89.

138. Goure, Claude. *Les Inconnus d'Afrique.* Paris: Editions Sper, 1968.

139. Gugler, Joseph. "The Second Sex in Town." *Canadian Journal of African Studies*, v. 6 (2), 1972: 289-301.

140. Hill, Adelaide Cromwell. "The Position of Women in Africa South of the Sahara." *American Society of African Culture Newsletter*, Supplement 15, 30 September 1960: 3-6.

141. Hodgkin, T. "Some African Women." *Spectator*, v. 192, 23 April 1954: 483.

142. Holleman, J. F. "The African Woman in Town and Tribe." *The Listener*, v. 1 (436), 4 October 1956: 496-497, 509.

143. Hottell, Althea K. "Challenge and Responsibilities for the Women in Africa." *Association of American University Women's Journal*, October 1964: 28-30.

144. International Federation of University Women. *Africa Today: Challenge and Responsibility for the Women of Africa.* London: International Federation of University Women, 1964.

145. Jean Bernard, Sister. "La femme dans la société africaine." *Afrique Documents*, v. 90 (1), 1967 (special no.): 3-87.

146. Kelfa-Caulker O. "African Women in New Society." *Women Today*, v. 6 (5), December 1965: 103-104.

147. Kuoh, T. "Women's Place in the World, Not in the Home: Interview by M. B. Cissey...." *Atlas*, v. 20, February 1971: 39.

148. Leith-Ross, Sylvia. *African Conversation Piece*. London: Hutchinson, 1944.

149. Mackenzie, J. F. "Some African Women." *International Review of Missions*, v. 12, January 1923: 98-111.

150. Mercier, P. "La Femme et les sociétés africaines." *Tropiques*, v. 53 (379), 1955: 21-28.

151. Moore, J. Aduke. "The Sphere and Influence of Women in Africa." *Journal of Human Relations*, v. 8 (3/4), 1960: 709.

152. Murray, G. "Nugget of Gold." *Christian Century*, 26 July 1961.

153. Nwokocha, J. K. U. *African Women Today*. London: West Indies Observer, 1964.

154. Paulme, Denise, ed. *Women of Tropical Africa*. Berkeley: University of California Press, 1963.

155. Petty, I. "Women's Voices." *African Review*, v. 14, May-June 1969: 79-80.

156. Raphael, Sister. "Brief Bright Star (Women in Africa)." *Medical Missionary*, v. 38, January-February 1964: 17+.

157. Reyher, Rebecca. "Where Are the Women?" *Africa Report*, v. 13 (2), 1968:2.

158. Rosaldo, Michelle Zimbalist, and Louise Camphere. *Woman, Culture and Society*. Stanford: Stanford University Press, 1974.

159. Scharf, Traute. "The African Women's Position in Social, Economic and Political Life." *Afrika*, v. 9 (3), 1968: 61+.

160. Schuller, Mary Craig, and Elizabeth Huntington Wheeler. *The Role of Women in Africa*. New York: Women's Africa Committee of the African-American Institute, 1960.

161. Scobie, Alistair. *Women of Africa*. London: Cassell, 1960.

162. "Some Glimpses of an African Woman's Life." UNICEF News, v. 4 (4), 1974: 12-15.

163. Sunons, Harold. African Women. Evanston: Northwestern University Press, 1968.

164. Suret Canale, J. "La Femme dans la société africaine." Vie Africaine, v. 56, March 1965: 25-32.

165. Tévoedjré, Albert. "Femme noire, cette inconnue." Afrique Nouvelle, v. 438, 13 December 1955: 1-7.

166. Touré, Sékou. "The African Woman." The Black Scholar, v. 4 (6-7), March-April 1973: 32-36.

167. Vialle, J. "Femmes africaines." Civilisations, v. 1 (4), 1951: 55-58.

168. Vincent, Jeanne Françoise. Femmes africaines en milieu urbain. Paris: OSTROM, 1966.

169. Wheeler, Elizabeth H. "Sub-Saharan Africa." In R. Patai, ed., Women in the Modern World. New York: Free Press, 1967.

170. "The Woman in African Society." The African Clarion, March-April 1973: 1-8.

171. "Women." In Galbraith Welch, ed., Africa Before They Came. New York: William Morrow, 1965: 307-344.

172. Women in Africa and the 1960's: A Preliminary Survey. Washington, D.C.: African Bibliographic Center, 1965.

173. "Women of Africa." Sign, v. 41, March 1962: 56-63.

Rural Only

174. Castillo, Gelia T. The Changing Role of Women in Rural Societies: A Summary of Trends and Issues. Agricultural Development Council Seminar Report No. 12, February 1977.

175. Evans-Pritchard, E. E. The Position of Women in Primitive Societies and Other Essays in Social Anthropology. London: Faber and Faber, 1965.

176. Junod, H. "Life-Cycle of a Woman, from Birth to Death." In Moeurs et coutumes des Bantous. Paris: Payot, 1936: 162-205.

177. Le Maire, C. Africaines, contribution à l'histoire de la femme en Afrique. Brussels: C. Bulens, 1897.

178. Mauzi, Ezequiel P. G. "A mulher na sofia Bantu: Notas para uma antropologia Bantu." Portugal em Africa, v. 146, March-April 1968: 88-98.

179. Romero Moliner, R. "Notas sobre la situación social de la mujer indígena en Fernando Póo." Cuadernos de Estudios Africanos, v. 18, 1952: 21-38.

180. du Sacré-Coeur, Marie André, Sister, et al. La Femme noire dans la société africaine. Lectures given at the Institut Catholique de Paris, 1938-1939. Paris: Union Missionnaire du Clergé, 1940.

181. United Nations Economic Commission for Africa. Women in the Traditional African Societies. United Nations Document # E/CN.14 URB/13. Prepared by the Secretariat for the Workshop on Urban Problems. Lagos, September 1963.

182. Viard, R. "Position of Gere Women." In Les Guérés, peuple de la fôret. Paris: Ed. Geographiques, Maritimes et Coloniales, 1934: 128-139.

183. Welch, Galbraith. Africa Before They Came: The Continent North, South, East and West, Preceding the Colonial Powers. New York: William Morrow, 1965.

184. Wills, J. A Study of Time Allocation of Rural Women and Their Place in Decision Making. Kampala: Makerere University, 1967.

West Africa

185. Adetowun-Ogunsheye, F. "Les Femmes du Nigeria." Présence Africaine, v. 32-33, June-September, 1960: 121-138.

186. Assalé, D. "L'Homme et la femme en Côte d'Ivoire." Terre Entiere, v. 36, July-August 1969: 48-56.

187. Baker, Tanya. "(Women's Role in) Nigeria." Institut International des Civilisations Différentes, Comptes Rendus, v. 31, 1959: 73-83.

188. Basden, George Thomas. Edith Warner of the Niger: The Story of Thirty-Three Years of Zealous and Courageous Work Among Ibo Girls and Women. London: Seeley Service, 1927.

189. Christian, A. "The Place of Women in Ghana Society." African Women, v. 3 (3), December 1959: 57-59.

190. Clignet, Remi. "Quelques remarques sur le rôle des femmes africaines en milieu urbain: Le Cas du Cameroun." Canadian Journal of African Studies, v. 6 (2), 1972: 303-315.

191. Essuah, Joseph A. "Women in West Africa." Medical Missionary, v. 38, July-August 1964: 99-101.

192. "La Femme dans l'Union Français." Tropiques, v. 379, 1955: 2-9

193. Grehan, I. "Women of Nigeria." Spectator, v. 203, 27 November 1959: 761+.

194. Hares, B. "Men and Women in Africa Today: A Consultation (Ibadan, Nigeria, January 1958)." International Review of Missions, v. 47, July 1958: 306-311.

195. Klingshirn, A. "The Social Position of Women in Ghana." Verfassung Recht in Übersee, v. 6 (3), 1973: 289-297.

196. Laurentin, Anne. "Nzakara Women." In Denise Paulme, ed., Women of Tropical Africa. London: Routledge and Kegan Paul, 1963: 121-178.

197. Le Cour Grand Maison, Colette. Femmes Dakaroises. Paris: Librarie Klincksieck, 1973. Also cited as: Abidjan: Annales de l'Université d'Abidjan, 1972.

198. Leith-Ross, Sylvia. African Women: A Study of the Ibo of Nigeria. London: Faber and Faber, 1939. Also cited as: London: Routledge and Kegan Paul, 1965.

199. L'Union Mondiale des Organisations Féminines Catholiques. Femmes Africaines; Témoignages de femmes du Cameroun, du Congo Belge, du Congo Français, de la Côte d'Ivoire, du Dahomey, du Ghana, de la Guinée, de la Haute-Volta, du Nigéria, du Togo, Réunies à Lomé. Paris: Editions du Centurion, 1959.

200. Maunier, R. La Femme noire en Afrique française. Paris: Le Monde Colonial Illustré, 1939: 143-144.

201. M'Baye, Annette. "La Femme Sénégalaise." Jeune Afrique, v. 158, 18-24 November, 1963: 45-46.

202. Nicod, A. La Femme au Cameroun. Paris: Société des Missions Évangéliques, 1927

203. Ogunsheye, Felicia Adetowun. "Les Femmes du Nigeria." Présence Africaine, y. 32, June-September 1960: 121-138.

204. Oppong, Christine, ed. "Domestic Rights and Duties in Southern Ghana." Legon Family Research Paper No. 1. Legon: Institute of African Studies, University of Ghana, 1974.

205. Pellow, Deborah. "Women of Accra: A Study in Options." Ph.D. dissertation, Northwestern University, 1974.

206. Ross, S. V. B. "Women in the Guianese Society." African Women, v. 5, December 1962: 21-22.

207. du Sacré-Cœur, Marie André, Sister. La Femme noire en Afrique Occidentale. Paris: Payot, 1939.

208. Scarbrough, E. M. "Women of Liberia." African Women, v. 3 (2), July 1959: 35-37.

209. Stratton, F. "West Africa's Women." West African Review, v. 35 (410), February 1962: 10-13.

210. Tullar, L. E., and K. Akinsemoyin. "Women's Part in the New West Africa." West African Review, v. 21 (269), 1950: 136-138.

211. "Women in Gabon." In Charles F. and Alice B. Darlington, eds., African Betrayal. New York: McKay, 1968: 235-251.

Rural Only

212. Burness, H. M. "Women in Katsina Province, Northern Nigeria." Overseas Education, v. 29 (3), October 1957: 116-122.

213. Chapmann, Jeanne. "La Femme pendant les funérailles." Ebur, v. 1 (3), 1954: 8-18.

214. Chardey, F. "Deuil et veuvage au Togo sud." Anthropos, v. 45 (3-4), 1951: 622.

215. Eggars, Olga. "Women of the Liberian Hinterland." West African Review, v. 9, December 1938: 23-24.

216. Femmes des villages aujourd'hui. Abidjan: Service Feminin de l'INADES, 1969-1971. (19 pamphlets in 1 vol.)

217. Gessain, Monique. "Coniagui Women (Guinea)." In Denise Paulme, ed., Women of Tropical Africa. London: Routledge and Kegan Paul, 1963: 17-46.

218. Goody, J. R., and E. Goody. "The Circulation of Women and Children in Northern Ghana." Man, v. 2 (2), June 1967: 226-248.

219. Gourou, Pierre. "Problèmes de géographie humaine au Cameroun septentrional." Les Cahiers d'Outre-Mer, v. 11 (44), October-December 1958: 426-430.

220. Grandmaison, Colette le Cour. "Rôles traditionnels féminins et urbanization: Lebou et Wolof de Dakar." Ph.D. dissertation, University of Paris, 1970.

221. Hauferlin, C. "La Vie d'une femme dans un village de Dahomey." Le Courier de l'UNESCO, March 1957: 4-10; May 1957: 14-15, 32-33.

222. Henderson, Helen Kreider. "Ritual Roles of Women in Onitsha Ibo Society." Ph.D. dissertation, University of California (Berkeley), 1969.

223. Hill, Polly. Rural Hausa. Cambridge: Cambridge University Press, 1972.

224. Jeffreys, M. D. "Some Notes on the Igbo Female." Afrika und Übersee, v. 52 (1), 1969:37-44.

225. Just, Peter. "Men, Women and Mukanda: A Transformational Analysis of Circumcision among Two West Central African Tribes (Nbembur and Luvale)." African Social Research, v. 13, June 1972: 187-206.

226. Léger, J. "La Femme en pays dogon." Vivante Afrique, v. 195 (22), 1958: 10-12.

227. Malcolm, L. W. G. "Note on the Seclusion of Girls among the Efik of Old Calabar (Nigeria)." Man, v. 25, 1925: 113-114.

228. Meek, C. K. Tribal Studies in Northern Nigeria. London: Kegan Paul, Trench, and Trubner, 1931.

229. Ominde, Simeon H. The Luo Girl from Infancy to Marriage. London: Macmillan, 1952.

230. Opuku-Ampomah, J. K. "Introducing an Ashanti Girl into Womanhood." Ghana Notes and Queries, v. 2, May-August 1961: 7-9.

231. du Sacré-Coeur, Marie-André, Sister. "La Condition de la femme indigène dans la boucle du Niger." Revue d'Histoire des Missions, v. 14, 1937: 471-477.

232. _____. "Vers l'évolution de la femme indigène en A.O.F. (Afrique française)." Le Monde Colonial Illustré, v. 16 (178), 1938: 68-69.

233. _____. "La Condition de la femme indigène en A.O.F. (Afrique française)." Renseignements Coloniaux, v. 49, 1939: 121-126.

234. Sanon, Anselme. "La Jeune Fille sage et la jeune fille insensée (conte bobo)." Cahiers d'Études Africaines, v. 8, 2 (30), 1968: 270-283.

235. Skinner, Elliott P. "The Mossi Pogsioure." Man, v. 60, February 1960: 20-23.

236. Smith, Mary F. Baba of Karo, a Woman of the Muslim Hausa: With an Introduction and Notes by M. G. Smith. London: Faber, 1954. Also cited as: London: Faber, 1964; New York: Praeger, 1964.

237. Talbot, P. Amaury. Women's Mysteries of a Primitive People: The Ibibios of Southern Nigeria. London: Cassell, 1915. Also cited as: London: Frank Cass, 1968.

238. Temple, Olive. "Women in Northern Nigeria." Blackwood's Magazine, v. 197, August 1914: 257-267.

239. Yeld, E. R. "A Study of the Social Position of Women in Kebbi (Northern Nigeria)." M.A. thesis, London University, 1960-1961.

Central Africa

240. Canters, H. "Barundikazi: Women of Urundi." Community, v. 20, May 1961: 8-9.

241. Debra, A. "La Femme noire dans les centres extra-coutumières et les camps de travailleurs congolais." Bulletin du CEPSI, v. 9, 1949: 131-141.

242. Gnali, Mambou Aimée. "La Femme africaine, un cas: La Congolaise." Présence Africaine, v. 68, 1968: 17-31.

243. Kiba, Simon. "Les Femmes d'Afrique au Centre International du Mont Carmel en Israel. Report." Afrique Nouvelle, No. 1260, 29 September 1971.

244. Mulenzi, Janvier. "La Femme dans la société ruandaise." Perspectives de Catholicité, v. 14 (4), 1955: 51-59.

245. _____. "La Femme dans la société ruandaise." <u>Echanges</u>, v. 26, 1956: 30-34.

246. "Le Programme d'action sociale de la femme au Ruanda." <u>Servir</u>, v. 25 (1), 1964: 36-37.

247. Soares Fernandes, J. A. "A mulher african." <u>Estudos Políticos e Sociais</u>, v. 4 (2), 1966: 575-684; v. 4 (3), 1966: 1027-1095.

248. Vincent, Jeanne Françoise. "Women in Brazzaville-Congo." <u>Women Today</u>, v. 6 (5), December 1965: 116.

Rural Only

249. Calame-Griaule, Geneviève. "Le Rôle spirituel et social de la femme dans la société Soudanaise traditionnelle." <u>Diogène</u>, v. 37, January-March 1962: 81-92.

250. Catteen, D. P. "La Femme congolaise." <u>Grand Lacs</u>, v. 63 (2), 1947: 5-14.

251. Collard, J. "La Femme dans la sensibilité bantoue." <u>Synthèses</u>, v. 11 (121), 1956: 288-291.

252. Cunnison, Ian. "The Position of Women among the Humr." <u>Sudan Society</u>, No. 2, 1963: 24-34.

253. Doucy, A. "Réflexions sur le rôle de la femme indigène au Congo Belge." <u>Bulletin de l'Union des Femmes Coloniales</u>, v. 26 (4-5), 1955: 4-5.

254. Evans-Pritchard, E. E., ed. <u>Man and Woman among the Azande</u>. New York: Free Press, 1974.

255. Hulstaert, G. "Le Coutume nkundo (mongo) et le décret sur la fille indigène non pubère." <u>Congo</u>, October 1937: 269-276.

256. Ilonga, L. "La Femme et le ménage indigène." <u>Voix du Congolais</u>, v. 4 (30), September 1948: 373-375.

257. Kellersberger, J. C. <u>Congo Crosses: A Study of Congo Womanhood</u>. Boston: Central Committee of United States and Foreign Missions, 1936.

258. "L'Enfant dans la famille gabonaise." <u>Bulletin de la Société de Recherches Congolaises</u>, v. 2, 1923: 15-22.

259. Richards, A. I. Chisungu: A Girl's Initiation Ceremony among the Bemba of Northern Rhodesia. London: Faber, 1956.

260. Riehl, A. "A familia indigena no Congo." Portugal em Africa, v. 3 (14), 1946: 88-98.

261. Saleeb, H. "The Life of the Girl Student in Khartoum University College." al-Kulliya, v. 1, 1952: 47-48.

East Africa

262. Bernatzik, I. "Dark Africa's Lighter Side." Atlas, v. 9, February 1965: 93-96.

263. Carlebach, Julius. "The Position of Women in Kenya." United Nations Economic Commission for Africa, Workshop on Urban Problems, Addis Ababa, 1963. U.N. Document # E/CN.14/URB/9.

264. Dobson, Barbara. "Women's Place in East Africa." Corona, v. 6 (12), December 1954: 454-457.

265. Edgvist, Dagmar. Black Sister. Trans. from the Swedish by Joan Tate. Garden City, N. Y.: Doubleday, 1963.

266. "Ethiopian Women." Ethiopia Observer, v. 1 (3), February 1957: 74-76.

267. Forbes, R. "Women of Ethiopia." Great Britain and the East, v. 45, 7 November 1935: 584-586.

268. Karienye Yohanna, M. "The African Woman." Kenya Weekly News, no. 1787, 28 April 1961: 46.

269. Kisosonkole, P. E. "African Women in International Society." East African Journal, v. 4 (4), July 1967: 7-10.

270. Mboya, Pamela. "Sideview of a Women's Seminar." (Kabete Institute of Administration, April 1964). East African Journal, v. 1 (3), June 1964: 15-16.

271. "The Role of Women in Kenya." Voice of Women, v. 1 (8), June 1969.

272. UNICEF (United Nations Children's Fund). "The Women of Tanzania." UNICEF News, no. 51, c. 1975.

Rural Only

273. Curley, Richard T. Elders, Shades, and Women: Ceremonial Change in Lango, Uganda. Berkeley: University of California Press, 1973.

274. Dooley, C. T. "Child-Training among the Wanguru." Primitive Man, v. 8 (1), 1934: 27-30.

275. Earthy, Emil D. Valenge Women: The Social and Economic Life of the Valenge Women of Portuguese East Africa: An Ethnographic Study. London: Frank Cass, 1968.

276. Elam, Yitzchak. The Social ans Sexual Roles of Hima Women: A Study of Nomadic Cattle Breeders in Nyabushozi Country, Ankole, Uganda. Manchester: Manchester University Press, 1973.

277. Mallet, Marguerite. A White Woman Among the Masai. London: Unwin, 1923.

278. Von Bosse Casqueiro M. "A mulher indigena." Boletîm da Sociedade de Estudios Coloniais de Moçambique, v. 21, 1951: 5-25.

Southern Africa

279. Calkins, Thomas K. Kisimusi: The Study of a Zulu Girl. Milwaukee: Bruce Publishing Co., 1962.

280. Dahlschen, Edith. Women in Zambia. Lusaka: National Educational Company of Zambia, 1970.

281. Earthy, E. Dora. Valenge Women: An Ethnographic Study. London: Oxford University Press for the International African Institute, 1933.

282. Preston, H. A. "African Women of Southern Rhodesia." Women Today, v. 6 (1), December 1963: 1-4.

283. Sloan, Agnes. "The Black Woman." Nada, v. 1, 1923: 60-69.

284. Waters, Mary M. "The Need Today of Native Women and Girls." South African Outlook, v. 59, 1929: 97-99; 113-115.

Rural Only

285. Godliffe, W. M. "Social Work Among Native Women." In Wayfarer Proceedings of the Southern Rhodesia Missionary Conference, Salisbury, 1928: 45-46.

286. Magidi, Doea T. (pseud. of John Blacking). Black Background: The Childhood of a South African Girl. New York: Abelard, 1964.

287. Makanya, V. S. "The Problem of the Zulu Girl." Native Teachers' Journal, v. 10, 1931: 116-120.

288. Von Bosse Casqueiro, M. "The Native Woman." Boletím da Sociedade de Estudos da Colónia de Moçambique, v. 21 (68), January-March 1951: 5-25.

Latin America--General

289. Basset, Grace. "Report on Seminar of Latin American Women (on Role of Women), Santiago, Chile, 1972." Political Affairs, v. 52, March 1973: 30-40.

290. Boletín Bibliográfico Iberoamericano. Special Issue: "La Mujer en América Latina." Mimeo. Madrid: Comisión Episcopal de Misiones y Cooperación entre las Iglesias, n.d.

291. Delgado Capeáns, Ricardo. La mujer en la vida moderna. Lima: Ed. Bruno del Amo, n.d.

292. Lavrín, Asunción. "Historia y mujeres en América Latina." Boletín Documental sobre las Mujeres, v. 4 (4), 1974: 9-18.

293. Reiter, R., ed. Toward an Anthropology of Women. New York: Monthly Review Press, 1975.

294. Rincón de Gautier. "Role of Women in Latin America." Journal of Home Economics, v. 53, 1961: 523+.

295. "Seminario sobre la realidad de la mujer latinoamericana, Costa Rica, 1975." Boletín Documental sobre las Mujeres, v. 5 (2), 1975: 55-62.

296. Subercaseaux, Benjamín. Contribución a la realidad (sexo, raza, literatura). Santiago: Ed. Letras, 1939.

297. Veana y Guevara, Jesús. Homenaje a la mujer. Puebla: Talleres Gráficos EPIPSA, 1966.

298. Vidarreta de Tjarks, Alicia. "Participación de la mujer en el proceso histórico latinoamericano." Revista Universitaria Nacional de Córdoba, v. 10 (1/2), May-June 1969: 153-186.

299. Ware, Caroline F. "Mujeres ciudadanas." América, v. 20 (1), January 1968: 30-34.

300. Youssef, Nadia H. "Cultural Ideals, Feminine Behavior and Kinship Control." Comparative Studies in Society and History, v. 15 (3), June 1973.

Rural Only

301. Arizpe, Lourdes. "La mujer campesina, mujer indígena." Mimeo. Mexico City: Colegio de México, 1975.

302. Carre, Shirley Kiborn Desbon. "Women's Position on a Yucatecan Henequin Hacienda." Ph.D. dissertation, Yale University, 1976.

303. Dole, Gertrude E. "The Marriage of Pacho: A Woman's Life among the Amahuaca." In C. Matthiasson, ed., Many Sisters: Women in Cross-Cultural Perspective. New York: Macmillan, 1974.

304. Lombardo Otero de Soto, Rosa María. La mujer tzeltal. Mexico City: 1944.

305. Michaelson, Evalyn Jacobson, and Walter Goldschmidt. "Female Roles and Male Dominance among Peasants." Southwestern Journal of Anthropology, v. 27 (4), 1971: 330-352.

306. Oberg, Kalervo. "Types of Social Structure among Lowland Tribes of South and Central America." American Anthropologist, v. 57, 1955: 472-488.

307. Sánchez Morales, Aurelia. "La familia campesina...vista por el campesino." Boletín Documental sobre las Mujeres, v. 4 (4), 1974: 41-45.

308. "Seminario sobre la situación de la mujer indígena en América: Auspiciado por el gobierno de México, país sede, y por la Comisión Interamericana de Mujeres." Chiapas, Mexico, June 1972.

Mexico and Central America

309. Alegría, Juana Armanda. Psicología de las mexicanas. México City: Ed. Samo, 1974.

310. Batres, Lilia. "La mujer mexicana en la post-guerra." Mundo Libre, December 1944: 21-24.

311. Cancian, F. M. "Affection and Dominance in Zinacantan and Cambridge Families." Journal of Marriage and the Family, v. 33, February 1971: 207-213.

312. Castillo Ledón, Amalia C. "La mujer mexicana ante el mundo." Revista Internacional y Diplomática, v. 2 (7), 25 May 1951: 57-58.

313. Durand, Luz María. "La mujer mexicana en la vida social." Acción Social, October-November 1947: 18-19.

314. Escala, V. La mujer y la seguridad social. Panama City: Caja del Seguro Social, 1973.

315. Formoso de Obregón Santacilia, Adela. La mujer mexicana en la organización social del país. Mexico City: Talleres Gráficos de la Nación, 1939.

316. _____, "El papel de la mujer iberoamericana en la postguerra." Nueva Era, September 1944: 7-11.

317. González, Otto Raúl. "Mujeres guatemaltecas ante la cultura y la política." Revista del Maestro, v. 6 (19), 1951: 93-99.

318. González Vázquez, Eva. "La mujer como factor en el desenvolvimiento humano." Vanguardia, v. 12 (42), September 1944.

319. Palavichini, Laura. "La mujer en la historia de México." Combate, v. 13, 1960: 47-52.

320. Pogolotti, Marcelo. La clase media en México. Mexico City: Diógenes, 1972.

321. Solanilla de Paz, S. "La mujer panameña en la cultura." Thesis, Universidad de Panamá, 1955.

Rural Only

322. Ayala, D., and N. E. Massah. "Estudio de la mujer Chocoe." Thesis, Universidad de Panamá, 1968.

323. Brown, Judith K. "Sex Division of Labor Among the San Blas Cuna." Anthropological Quarterly, v. 43 (2), 1970: 57-63.

324. Díaz, May N. Tonalá: Conservatism, Responsibility, and Authority in a Mexican Town. Berkeley: University of California Press, 1970.

325. Elmendorf, Mary Lindsay. "The Dilemma of Peasant Women: A View from a Village in Yucatán." In Irene Tinker and Michele Bo Bramsen, eds., Women and World Development. Washington, D. C.: Overseas Development Council, 1976: 88-94.

326. Farber, Anne. "Language Choice and Sex Roles in Highland Guatemala." Paper presented at the Annual Meeting of the American Anthropological Association, Mexico City, November 1974.

327. Fernández, Martha. "La realización de la mujer indígena y sus problemas." América Indígena, v. 35 (1), 1975: 117-120.

328. Lombardo Otero de Sota, Rosa María. La mujer tzeltal. Mexico City: 1944.

329. Moore, G. Alexander. "Marriage, an Indian Woman Comes of Age." In G. Alexander Moore, ed., Life Cycles in Atchalán: The Diverse Careers of Certain Guatemalans. New York: Teachers College Press, 1973: 33-46.

330. Nash, June C. Social Relations in Amatenango del Valle: An Activity Analysis. Cuernavaca, Mexico: Centro Intercultural de Documentación, 1969.

331. _____. Bajo la mirada de los antepasados: Creencias y comportamiento en una comunidad maya. Mexico City: Instituto Indigenista Interamericano, 1975. (Also in English) In the Eyes of the Ancestors: Belief and Behavior in a Maya Community. New Haven: Yale University Press, 1970.

332. Paul, Lois. "The Mastery of Work and the Mystery of Sex in a Guatemalan Village." In M. Z. Rosaldo and L. Lamphere, eds., Woman, Culture and Society. Stanford: Stanford University Press, 1974: 281-299.

333. Pozas, Isabel H. de. "La posición de la mujer dentro de la estructura social tzotzil." Ciencias Políticas y Sociales, v. 5 (18), October-December 1959: 565-575.

334. Royce, Ana. "Comparative Roles of Zapotec and Mexican Women in Juchitán, Oaxaca." In A. Schlegel, ed., Emergent Women. Pittsburhg: University of Pittsburgh Press, 1976.

335. Saquic Calel, Rosalío. "La mujer indígena guatemalteca." Guatemala Indígena, v. 8 (1), January-March 1973: 81-110.

336. Smith, H. Allen. "The Aphrodites of Tehuatepec." Mexican Life, v. 39 (10), October 1963: 13-14, 63-66.

337. Torres de Ianello, Reina. "Posición social de la mujer dentro de la cultura kuna." Lotería, v. 32, 1958: 91-101.

338. Vázquez Fuller, Beatriz. "La mujer indígena." América Indígena, v. 34 (3), 1974: 663-675.

Caribbean

339. Carrera, Julieta. Sexo, femineidad y economía. Havana: Hechos Sociales, 1934.

340. Henry, Frances, and Pamela Wilson. "Status of Women in Caribbean Societies: An Overview of Their Social, Economic and Sexual Roles." Social and Economic Studies, v. 24 (2), June 1975: 165-198.

341. Lasaga, José I. "La mujer privilegiada." Havana: Agrupación Católica Universitaria, 1956.

342. Macaya, Margarita O. de. "Women--Their Role, Present and Potential, in the Caribbean." In A. C. Wilgus, ed., The Caribbean: Its Hemispheric Role. Gainesville: University of Florida Press, 1967.

343. Olesen, Virginia. "Context and Posture: Notes on Socio-Cultural Aspects of Women's Roles and Family Policy in Contemporary Cuba." Journal of Marriage and the Family, v. 33 (3), August 1971: 548-560.

344. Ortiz Lamadrid, Rubén. "La mujer en Cuba." El Mundo, 5 May 1955: 8.

345. Redondo, Susana. "La mujer en la vida y en la cultura americana." América, v. 37, November 1952: 73-82.

346. Salado, Minerva. "La mujer en el mundo actual." Cuba International, April 1972: 4-9.

347. Stycos, J. Mayone. Family and Fertility in Puerto Rico. Westport, Connecticut: Greenwood Press, 1955.

348. Tancer, Shoshana B. "La Quisqueyana: The Dominican Woman, 1940-1970." In Ann Pescatello, ed., Female and Male in Latin America: Essays. Pittsburgh: University of Pittsburgh Press, 1973: 209-230.

349. Torre, Silvio de la. Mujer y sociedad. Havana: Ed. Universitaria, 1965.

350. Vidaurreta, Antonio Julio. "La mujer campesina." In Un año de periodismo. Santa Clara: Ediciones Culturales, 1952.

Andean Region

351. Ahumada, Ernesto Cortés. "De la mujer a la antimujer." Boletín Cultural Bibliográfico, v. 5 (9), 1962: 1200-1203.

352. Bolivia. Biblioteca Municipal. "La mujer boliviana y las instituciones sociales." Revista de la Biblioteca Municipal, v. 1 (3), 1949: 65-70.

353. García y García, Elvira. La mujer moderna en su casa. Cuzco: 1919.

354. _____. Actividad femenina. Lima: Casa Editora "La Opinión Nacional," 1928.

355. Gutiérrez de Pineda, Virginia. "Roles e imágenes de hombre y de mujer en Colombia: Tradicionalismo y modernismo." Paper presented at the Conference on Feminine Perspectives in Social Science Research in Latin America, Buenos Aires, 1974.

356. Gutiérrez Mejía, Ricardo. "El valor de la mujer en la vida nacional." Revista Boliviana, v. 7 (57), December 1956: 68-70.

357. Martin, Richard R. "Women and the Mass Media in a Venezuelan City." Paper presented at the Annual Meeting of the International Communications Association, Portland, Oregon, 1976.

358. Osorno Cárdenas, Marta C. La mujer colombiana y latinoamericana Medellín: Tipografía Italiana, 1974.

359. Palma, Ricardo. La limeña. Paris: Franco-Ibero-Americana, 1922

360. Paredes de Martínez, Irene. "Responsabilidad de la mujer en el mundo actual." Quito: Taller Gráfico Minerva, 1970.

361. Peattie, Lisa Redfield. The View from the Barrio. Ann Arbor: University of Michigan Press, 1972, chapters 5 and 6.

362. Ramírez Romero, Ramiro. La mujer destinada por el sexo. Caracas: EDIME, 1966.

363. Rendón de Mosquera, Zoila. "La mujer en los diversos organismos humanos." Previsión Social, v. 22, September-December 1948: 150-162.

364. Salcedo Román, Elvira. "La mujer en la vida bogotana." Cromos, v. 8-9, 29 September 1945: 58-59.

365. Valdez Ducasting, Lucila. "La mujer ante los problemas sociales Conferencia sustentada en la Unión Patriótica del Perú el 4 de julio de 1941." Lima: Ed. Peruanas, 1941.

366. Vasconez Guvi, Victoria. Actividades domésticas y sociales de la mujer. Quito: Taller Tip. Nacionales, 1975.

Rural Only

367. Alvarez Morán, Yolanda. "Intervención de la mujer en la vida social y económica de los pueblos." Thesis, Universidad Nacional Mayor de San Marcos, Lima, 1954.

368. Carpio, Lourdes. "Las mujeres campesinas en el Perú." Boletín Documental sobre las Mujeres, v. 4 (2), 1974: 31-42.

369. _____. "The Rural Women in Peru: An Alarming Contradiction." Women: A Journal of Liberation, 1973.

370. _____. "La mujer campesina: Una alarmante postergación." Educación, v. 1 (3), 1976: 9-17.

371. De Grys, Mary Schweitzer. "Women's Role in a North Coast Fishing Village in Peru: A Study in Male Dominance and Female Subordination." Ph.D. dissertation, New School for Social Research, 1973.

372. Fals Borda, Orlando. Peasant Society in the Colombian Andes: A Sociological Study of Saucío. Gainesville: University of Florida Press, 1955.

373. Fortun, Julia Elena. "La mujer aymará en Bolivia." América Indígena, v. 32 (3), 1972: 935-947.

374. Isbell, Billie Jean. "La otra mitad esencial: Un estudio de complementaridad sexual en los Andes." Estudios Andinos, v. 5 (1), 1976: 37-56.

375. Llanaque Chana, Domingo. "La campesina en el altiplano aymará." Boletín Documental sobre las Mujeres, v. 4 (2), 1974: 43-52.

376. _____. "La mujer campesina aymará." Allpanchis Phuturinga, v. 4, 1972: 101-119.

377. Nuñez del Prado Béjar, Daisy Irene. "El rol de la mujer campesina quechua." América Indígena, v. 35 (2), 1975: 391-401.

378. Ramírez Canseco, Teresa. "La mujer campesina en Bolivia." América Indígena, v. 32 (3), 1972: 1025-1027.

379. Vásquez Fuller, Gladys. "Mujer indígena." Norte, no. 256, November-December 1973: 49-50.

380. Whitten, Norman E., Jr. "Ritual Enactment of Sex Roles in the Pacific Lowlands of Ecuador and Colombia." Ethnology, v. 13 (2), 1974: 129-143.

381. Zuna Rico, Enrique. Estudio socioeconómico de una comunidad rural boliviana. Tupiza: Ediciones Rico, n.d.

Chile and the Platine

382. Duarte, María Amalia. "La mujer en la historia argentina." Revista Universitaria Nacional de Córdoba, v. 10 (1-2), March-June 1969: 127-151.

383. Eriksson, N. "The Argentine Woman: Her Social, Political and Economic Role." Review of the River Plate, v. 52, December 1972: 959-961; 985-988.

384. Fabbri, Enrique E. "El mundo en la mujer." Criterio, v. 39 (1508), September 1966: 686-690.

385. _____. "La mujer en el mundo." Criterio, v. 39 (1512), November 1966: 851-855.

386. Godoy, Julia Toro. Presencia y destino de la mujer. Santiago: Ediciones Maipo, 1967.

387. Grez, Alonso. "Chilean Women Playing Their Part in National Life." South Pacific Mail, 4 January 1934: 14.

388. Imaz, José Luis de. La clase alta de Buenos Aires. Buenos Aires: Colección Estructura, 1965.

389. Iñigo Carrera, Héctor. La mujer argentina. Buenos Aires: Centro Editor de América Latina, 1972.

390. Lillo Catalán, Victoriano. "La influencia de la mujer." Revista Americana de Buenos Aires, August 1931: 1-48; September 1931: 49-79; November-December 1940: 1-110.

391. Navarro L., Eugenia. "La mujer argentina en la vida del país." Dinámica Social, v. 7 (81), July 1957: 44-45.

392. Romera Vera, Angela. "Ubicación de la mujer en la realidad argentina." Revista Universitaria Nacional de Córdoba, v. 10 (1/2), March-June 1969: 183-196.

393. Schultz Cazenueva de Mantovani, Fryda. La mujer en la vida nacional. Buenos Aires: 1960.

394. Urbieta Rojas, Pastor. La mujer en el proceso cultural del Paraguay. Buenos Aires: Ed. Ayacucho, 1944.

395. Vittone, Luis. La mujer paraguaya en la vida nacional. Asunción: 1968.

Rural Only

396. Taylor, Carl C. Rural Life in Argentina. Baton Rouge: Louisiana State University Press, 1948.

Brazil

397. Azevedo, Thales de. "As negras do namoro no Brasil: Um padrão tradicional." América Latina (Rio de Janeiro), v. 13 (2-3), April-September 1970: 128-149.

398. Azevedo Goldberg, María Amelia. "Concepções sobre o papel da mulher no trabalho, na política e na família." Cadernos de Pesquisa, no. 15, December 1975: 86-123.

399. Bettencourt Thome, Yolanda. A mulher no mundo de hoje. Petropolis: Ed. Vozes, 1968.

400. Bosco, Santa Helena. "Perfil socio-económico da mulher migrante nordestina." Sociologia (São Paulo), v. 27 (1), March 1965: 57-62.

401. da Silva, Odete Rosa. "Status e papel da mulher no bairro de Palmeirinhas." Cadernos de Estudos Rurais e Urbanos, v. 1 (1), 1968: 20-28.

402. da Silva, Valentim Berúcio. "A mulher na evolução do Brasil." Revista do Instituto Histórico e Geográfico Brasileiro, v. 212, 1953: 106-123.

403. Martínez Alier, Verena. "Qual é a mulher que merecemos?" Cadernos de Pesquisa, no. 15, December 1975: 132-134.

404. Pearse, Andrew. "Sexual Nature and Sex Roles: A Brazilian Sample." Unpublished paper, 1958.

405. Piersen, Donald. "Status e papel da mulher em Cruz das Almas." Sòciologia (São Paulo), v. 13 (2), May 1951: 148-162.

406. Pug, Amanda. La mujer chilena. Santiago: 1972.

407. Raphael, Alison. "Two Kinds of Women: The Middle Class." Department of State Newsletter, AR-3, February 1976.

408. Studart, Heloneida. A mulher, brinquedo do homen? Petropolis: Ed. Vozes, 1969.

409. Tappen, K. B. "The Status of Women in Brazil." Washington, D.C.: 1944.

Rural Only

410. Hamburger, Adelaide. "A familia numa pequena comunidade paulista." Sociologia (São Paulo), v. 16 (3), August 1954: 284-292.

C. SOCIAL ASPECTS (includes feminine culture and values, stereotypes, social conditions and alternative lifestyle).

Africa--General

411. "Les africaines des cités et ses problèmes." Afrique Nouvelle, v. 22 (1100), 5-11 September, 1968: 10; v. 22 (1101), 12-18 September 1968: 10.

412. Aguessy, Dominique. "La Personalité de la femme africaine." Afrique Nouvelle, v. 14 (759), 21 February 1962: 14-16.

413. Amzat, E. H. A. "Fonction de la femme africaine dans l'art nègre." Sentiers, June 1966: 14-18.

414. Anciaux, L., et al., "La Femme noire vue par les écrivans africainistes (Causeries de l'Association des Écrivans et Artistes Africainistes." Classe des Sciences Morales et Politiques Academie Royale des Sciences de Outre-Mer, v. 34 (3), 1967.

415. Ardener, Edwin. "Belief and the Problem of Women." In Shirley Ardener, ed., Perceiving Women. London: Malaby Press, 1975: 1-17.

416. Awori, Thelma. "For African Women Different Goals: Their Need Is for Responsible Males, Not More Rights." Atlas World Press Review, August 1975: 33-34.

417. Céline. "Image de la femme dans la société." Afrique Nouvelle, v. 914, 11-17 February 1965; v. 915, 18-24 February 1965: 12.

418. Chapman, J. "La Femme est une valeur." Revue de l'O.A.M.C.E., v. 5, March 1964: 29+.

419. Conde, M. "Blurred Image." Ceres, v. 8 (2), April 1975: 37-39.

420. Da Silva, Maria da Conçeição Tavares l'Ourenço. "Femininidade e cultura. 1. O problema. 2. O caso africano." Estudos Ultramarinos, v. 4, 1960: 73-90.

421. Fontaine, C. "De la Femme-ojet a la femme-sujet." Revue de Psychologie des Peuples, v. 18 (3), 1963: 273-282.

422. Ighudaro, Irene E. B. "Women: An African Viewpoint." Continuous Learning, v. 4, March-April 1965: 85-89.

423. Jocelyne. "Des problèmes du monde feminin." Afrique Nouvelle, v. 20 (992), 11-17 August 1966: 8-9

424. _____. "La Notion de 'féminité' dans la sociéte africaine." Afrique Nouvelle, v. 20 (996), 8-14 September 1966: 8; v. 20 (997), 15-21 September 1966: 8.

425. Marwick, Max G. Sorcery in its Social Setting. Manchester: Manchester University Press, 1965.

426. Mathieu, N. C. "Homme-Culture, Femme-Nature?" L'Homme, July-September 1973: 101-113.

427. Matinkus-Zemp, Ada. "Européocentrisme et exotisme: L'Homme blanc et la femme noire (dans la littérature francaise de l'entre-deux-guerres)." Cahiers d'Études Africaines, v. 13 (1), 1973: 60-81.

428. Mbilinyi, Marjorie J. "Traditional Attitudes towards Women: A Major Constraint on Rural Development." In Conference of the Provisional Council for the Social Sciences in East Africa, Dar es Salaam, 1970, Proceedings, v. 5, 1970: 510-561.

429. Mutiso, G. C. M. "Women in African Literature." East African Journal, v. 8 (3), March 1971: 4-13.

430. Padmore, Mai. "Some Misconceptions about Women in Africa." Africa Report, v. 6 (6), June 1961: 7-8.

431. Rubenstein, Roberta. "The Third World's Second Citizens: National Independence in Africa Has Not Brought Independence to Women." Progressive, v. 39, March 1975: 33-35.

432. Shelton, Austin J. "The 'Miss Ophelia Syndrome' in African Field Research." Practical Anthropology, v. 11, November 1964: 259-265.

433. Ware, Helen. "The Relevance of Changes in Women's Roles to Fertility Behavior: The African Evidence." Paper presented at the Annual Meeting of the Population Association of America, Seattle, Washington, April 1975.

434. Wipper, Audrey. "African Women, Fashion, and Scapegoating." Canadian Journal of African Studies, v. 6 (2), 1972: 329-349.

435. "Women in Africa Combine Economic Chores with Onerous Social Roles." U. N. Monthly Chronicle, v. 12, June 1975: 44-45.

436. World Union of Catholic Women's Organizations. Regional Seminar, Lomé, Togo. 1958. African Women Speak. (National Catholic Welfare Conference, Office for U. N. Affairs, ed.) Maryknoll, N.Y.: World Horizon Reports, no. 26, 1960.

West Africa

437. Agblemagnon, F. N'Sougan. "Research on Attitudes towards Togolese Women." International Social Science Journal, v. 14 (1), 1962: 148-156.

438. Clignet, Remi. "The Psychology of Women in the Ivory Coast." Bulletin of the Inter-African Labour Institute, v. 8 (1), February 1961: 64-91.

439. _____. "Les Attitudes de la société à l'égard des femmes en Côte d'Ivoire." Revue Internationale des Sciences Sociales, v. 14 (1), 1962: 137-148.

440. _____. "Social Change and Sexual Differentiation in the Camerouns and Ivory Coast." Paper presented at the Wellesley Conference on Women and Development, June 1976. Available from Wellesley Center for Research on Women, 828 Washington St., Wellesley, Massachusetts 02181.

441. Dyja Ruelland, Suzy. "Images de la femme dans les littératures orales ashanti et fon." Paris: Thèse-École Pratique des Hautes Études, 1971.

442. Eguchi, M. J. "Aspects of the Life Style and Culture of Women in the Fulbe Districts of Maroua." Kyoto University African Studies, v. 8, 1973: 17-92.

443. Gervais, Jeanne; M. L. Adebe; and A. Tesa. "Positions and Problems of the Women in French-Speaking Africa. I. Ivory Coast." Women Today, v. 6 (3), December 1964: 49-53.

444. Green, M. M. Igbo Village Affairs. London: Frank Cass, 1964.

445. Igu, Thomas. Why Men Never Trust Women. Onitsha (Nigeria): Appolos Brothers, 1960.

446. _____. "Images of Women in Society Covering France, Poland, Morocco, Canada, Ivory Coast, Togo, Austria, and Yugoslavia." International Social Science Journal, no. 1, 1962.

447. Jahoda, G. "Boys' Images of Marriage Partners and Girls' Self-Images in Ghana." Sociologus, v. 8 (2), 1958: 155-169.

448. Jane, S., Sister. "The Girl Problem in Ghana." World Mission, v. 12, Fall 1961: 72-79.

449. Joseph, G. "Condition de la femme en Cote d'Ivoire." Bulletins et Memories de la Société d'Anthropologie de Paris, v. 14 (5), 1913: 585-589.

450. Lafon, Suzanne. "La parure chez les femmes peul du Bas-Sénégal." Notes Africaines, v. 46, April 1950: 37-41.

451. Leech, William David. "Changing Attitudes towards Sex and Marriage among Urban Nigerians as Revealed in Two Lagos Newspapers, the 'West African Pilot' and the 'Daily Service.'" Master's Thesis, University of Pennsylvania, 1946.

452. Little, Kenneth. "Women in African Towns South of the Sahara: The Urbanization Dilemma." In Irene Tinker and Michele Bo Bramsen eds., Women and World Development. Washington, D.C.: Overseas Development Council, 1975: 78-87.

453. Maclatchy, A. "Condition of Women. L'Organization social de la région de Mimongo (Gabon)." Bulletin de l'Institut d'Études Centrafricaines, v. 1 (1), 1945: 68-69.

454. Marchal, R. P. La Condition de la femme indigène. Étude sur le problème de l'évolution des coutumes familiales dans quelques tribus de L'A.O.F. (Afrique Occidental Française) Observations sur le même sujet relatives à L'Algerie. Lyon: Chronique Sociale de France. 1930.

455. Palme (Schaeffner), Denise. "The Social Conditions of Women in Two West African Societies (Kissi and Dogon)." Man, v. 48 (45), April 1948: 44. Also cited in: Africa, v. 18 (4), October 1948: 302-303.

456. N'Sougan Agblemanon, F. "Recherche sur les attitudes vis-à-vis de la femme Togolaise." Revue Internationale des Sciences Sociales, v. 14 (1), 1962: 151-159.

457. Rein-Wuhrmann, Anna. Au Cameroun. Portraits de femmes. Trans. by E. Lack. Paris: Société des Missions Evangélique, 1931.

458. Remy, Dorothy. "Underdevelopment and the Experience of Women: A Zaria Case Study." In Rayna Reiter, ed., Towards an Anthropology of Women. New York: Monthly Review Press, 1976.

459. du Sacré-Coeur, Marie-André, Sister. "La Condition de la femme au Mossi." Grand Lacs, v. 54, 1937-1938: 177-181. Summarized in Bibliographie Ethnographique du Congo Belge, Tervuren, Belgium, 1938.

460. Stephen, Felix N. How to Get a Lady in Love. Onitoha (Nigeria): Survival Bookshop, n.d.

461. Udo Ema, A. J. "Fattening Girls in Oron." Nigeria Magazine, v. 21, 1940: 386, 388-389.

462. Wane, Yaya. "La Condition Sociale de la femme toucouleur (Fouta Toro)." Bulletin de l'IFAN, v. 28 B(3/4), July-October 1966: 771-825.

Central Africa

463. Albert, Ethel M. "Women of Burundi: A Study of Social Values." In Denise Paulme, ed., Women of Tropical Africa. London: Routledge and Kegan Paul, 1963: 179-216.

464. Dartevelle, A. "La Femme: Étude de sa condition et de sa situation sociale chez les Ba-Vili (Congo français)." Bulletin de la Société Royale Belge d'Anthropologie et de Préhistoire, v. 54, 1939: 99-100.

465. Ennis, E. L. "Women's Names among the Ovimbundu of Angola." African Studies, v. 4 (1), 1945: 1-8.

466. Gillard, M. L. "La Condition de la femme noire." Centre d'Études et de Documentation Sociales de la Province de Liège, v. 8 (10), 1954: 549-559.

467. Godeliva-Mariya, Sister. "La Personalité de la femme rwandaise." Trait d'Union, v. 70 (6), July-August 1961: 5-9.

468. Hout, L. "L'Âme noire: La Femme chez les primitifs centre-africains." Mercure de France, v. 151, October 1921: 20-47.

469. Le Blanc, Maria. "Acculturation of Attitude and Personality among Katangese Women." Journal of Social Psychology, v. 47, 1958: 257-264.

470. _____. Personalité de la femme katangaise: Contribution à l'etude de son acculturation. Louvain: Publications Universitaires, 1960.

471. Le Gal, J. R. "La Parure de la femme en Afrique Équatoriale." Science et Voyage, v. 29 (22), September 1947: 283-284.

472. Maistriaux, Robert. La Femme et la destin de l'Afrique: Les Sources psychologiques de la mentalité dite "primitive." Elisabethville: Editions CEPSI, 1964. Also cited as: Brussels: Editest, 1964.

473. Mikanda-Vundowe, S. "Féminisme congolais aujourd'hui." Congo-Afrique, v. 6 (2), February 1966: 71-78.

474. Monod, Théodore. "Une simple impression (ressemblance de femmes belles avec les femmes du groupe Khoisan)." Notes Africaines, v. 21, January 1944: 18.

475. Siret, M. "La Situation des femmes abandonnées et des femmes seules dans les centres extra-coutumiers d'Usumbura." Bulletin du CEPSI, v. 32, 1956: 250-268.

476. Smith, M. "Sudanese Woman and Her Outlook on Life." Moslem World, v. 14, April 1924: 143-147.

East Africa

477. Berger, Iris. "Women, Religion and Social Change: East and Central African Perspectives." Paper presented at the Wellesley Conference on Women and Development, June 1976. Available from Wellesley Center for Research on Women, 828 Washington St., Wellesley, Massachusetts 02181.

478. Conant, Francis P. "Frustration, Marriage Alternatives and Subsistence Risk among the Pokot of East Africa." Anthropological Quarterly, v. 47, July 1974: 314-327.

479. "La Condition de la femme en Afrique oriental anglaise." Revue Missionnaire des Jesuites Belges, v. 8, 1932: 368+.

480. Culwick, A. M. "New Ways for Old Treatment of Adolescent African Girls." Africa, v. 12 (4), 1939: 425-432.

481. Mbilinyi, Marjorie. "Education, Stratification and Sexism in Tanzania: Policy Implications." African Review, v. 3 (2), 1973: 327-340.

482. Stamp, Patricia. "Perceptions of Social Change among the Kikuyu Women of Mitero." Unpublished paper presented at the Annual Meeting of the Canadian Association of African Studies, York University, 1975.

483. Thurnwald, Richard. Black and White in East Africa: The Fabric of a New Civilization; A Study in Social Contact and Adaptation of Life in East Africa (with a chapter on women by Hilde Thurnwald). London: Routledge, 1935.

484. United Nations Economic Commission for Africa Human Resources Development Division. "The Changing Roles of Women in East Africa: Implications for Planning Family-Oriented Programs." Paper prepared for FAO/SIDA Workshop for Intermediate Level Instructors in Home Economics and Rural Family-Oriented Programs in East and Southern Africa, Njore, Kenya, 1-15 May 1974.

485. Wipper, Audrey. "The Politics of Sex: Some Strategies Employed by the Kenyan Power Elite to Handle a Normative-Existential Discrepancy." African Studies Review, v. 14 (3), December 1971: 463-482.

Southern Africa

486. Iyala, B. S. "Womanhood in the Kalabari." Nigeria Magazine, v. 98, 1968: 216-224.

487. Junod, H. A. The Fate of Widows Among the Ba-Ronga. Capetown and Johannesburg: Report of the South African Association for the Advancement of Science, 1909.

488. Keirn, Susan Middleton. "Spirit Mediumship and Status Ambiguity: Apartheid and the Urban African Woman." Paper presented at the American Anthropological Association Annual Meetings, Mexico City, 1974.

489. Kunene, D. P. "Notes on Hlonepha (Respect) among the Southern Sotho." African Studies, v. 17 (3), 1958: 159-182.

490. Maxeke, C. M. "Social Conditions among Bantu Women and Girls." Christian Studies and Modern South Africa, 1930: 111-117.

491. Mueller, Martha. "Women and Men, Power and Powerlessness in Lesotho." Paper presented at the Wellesley Conference on Women and Development, June 1976. Available from Wellesley Center for Research on Women, 828 Washington St., Wellesley, Massachusetts 02181.

492. Ntantala, Phyllis. An African Tragedy: The Black Woman under Apartheid. Detroit: Agascha Productions, 1976.

493. Pye, F. "Aspects of the Psychology of South African Women." Race, v. 7 (2), October 1965: 123-130.

494. Willoughby, W. C. Race Problems in the New Africa. Oxford: Clarendon Press, 1923, Part II, 46-138.

Latin America--General

495. Adolph, José B. "The South American Macho: Mythos and Mystique." Impact of Science on Society, v. 21 (1), 1971: 83-92.

496. Ander Egg, Ezequiel, et al. Opresión y marginalidad de la mujer en el orden social machista. Colección Desarrollo Social, No. 14. Buenos Aires: Ed. Humanitas, 1972.

497. Ávila, Julio Enrique. "Nuestra mujer, prodigio de hispanoamerica." Revista Conservadora del Pensamiento Centroamericano, v. 15 (75), December 1966: 41-44.

498. Blasi Brambilla, Alberto. "Las tres Marías." Américas, v. 21 (8), August 1969: 35-39.

499. Brown, G. M. L. "The Women of Spanish America." Canadian Magazine, v. 27, 1906: 321-328.

500. Buitrón, Aníbal. "La mujer latinoamericana." Revista Conservadora del Pensamiento Centroamericano, v. 15 (75), December 1966: 27-29.

501. Cerni, Horst Max. "Setting New Sights for Latin America's Women." UNICEF News, v. 4 (4), 1974: 36+.

502. Chaney, Elsa M. "What Choices for Rosa?" UNICEF News, v. 78, December 1973-January 1974.

503. Cortada de Kohan, Nuría. "Un estudio experimental sobre el machismo." Revista Latinoamericana de Psicología, v. 2 (1), 1970: 31-54.

504. Covarrubias, Paz and Mónica Muñoz. Algunos factores que inciden en la participación laboral de las mujeres de estratos bajos. Santiago: Instituto de Sociología, Universidad Católica de Chile, 1972.

505. "Declaración de las Naciones Unidas sobre la eliminacíon de la discriminación contra la mujer." Ciencia Interamericana, v. 16 (3-4), July-December 1975: 10-11.

506. de la Torre Mulhare, Mirta. "The Cult of Virginity and the Double Standard: Latin American Models." Paper presented at the 70th Annual Meeting of the American Anthropological Association, New York, 1971.

507. Farcía Gradilla, Natividad. "La condición de la mujer en las sociedades indígenas latinoamericanas." Boletín Nosotras, v. 1 (11), 1974.

508. García, Margarita and Juanita A. Dongman. "Sex-Role Stereotypes among Latinos." Paper presented at the Annual Meeting of the American Psychological Association, Chicago, September 1975.

509. Kinzer, Nora Scott. "Myths and Misinterpretations of the Latin American Female." International Congress of Americanists, Rome-Geneva, 1972. III, 453-458.

510. Koch-Grunberg, Theodor. "South America." In T. A. Joyce, ed., Woman of All Nations, II. New York: Funk and Wagnalls, 1915.

511. "La Comisión Interamericana de Mujeres y la problematica común femenina en América Latina." Ciencia Interamericana, v. 16 (3-4) July-December 1975: 12-13.

512. Marti, Rosa Signorelli de. "Spanish America." In Raphael Pat, ed., Women in the Modern World. New York: Free Press, 1967.

513. Nash, June C. "Perspectiva de la mujer latinoamericana y en las ciencias sociales." La Mujer en América Latina, Mexico City: Sepsetentas, 1975. II, 9-34.

514. Nicassio, Perry M. "Machismo, Feminine Identity and Fertility in Latin America: Some Empirical Insights." Paper presented at the American Psychological Association Annual Meetings, New Orleans, 1974.

515. Robles de Mendoza, Margarita. "Mujeres de América." Nueva Democracia, August 1944: 14.

516. Patai, Raphael, ed. Women in the Modern World. New York: Free Press, 1967.

517. Pescatello, Ann, ed. Female and Male in Latin America: Essays Pittsburgh: University of Pittsburgh Press, 1973.

518. Philippon, Odette. "El feminismo católico y la misconcepción de la mujer latinoamericana." Latinoamerica, v. 4 (45), 1 September 1952: 399-401.

519. Sassone, Felipe. "Las mujeres de nuestra América." Mundo Hispánico, v. 3 (26), May 1950: 57-58.

520. Schultz Casenueva de Mantovani, Fryda. "La mujer lationamericana." Cuadernos, v. 70, March 1963: 47-52.

521. Soiza Reilly, Juan José de. Mujeres de América. Buenos Aires: Librerías Anaconda, 1930.

522. Steinmann, Anne, and David J. Fox. "Specific Areas of Agreement and Conflict in Women's Self-Perception and their Perception of Men's Ideal Woman in South American Urban Communities and Urban Communities in the United States." Journal of Marriage and Family, v. 31, May 1969: 281-289.

523. Stevens, Evelyn P. "Marianismo: The Other Face of Machismo in Latin America." In Ann Pescatello, ed., Female and Male in Latin America. Essays. Pittsburgh: University of Pittsburgh Press, 1973: 89-102.

524. Torricelli, Graciela. "Engulfed in Myths." Ceres, March-April 1975.

525. "Women in Latin America." Special section in Journal of Marriage and the Family, v. 35 (2), 1973.

Mexico and Central America

526. Acosta, Mariclaire. "Los estereotipos de la mujer mexicana." Diálogos, v. 9 (53), 1973: 29-31.

527. Alessio Robles, Miguel. La mujer mexicana. Mexico CIty: 1931.

528. Arnaíz Amigo, Aurora. Feminismo y femineidad. Mexico City: 1965.

529. Arnold, Marigene. "Mexican Women: The Anatomy of a Stereotype in a Mestizo Village." Ph.D. dissertation, University of Florida, 1973.

530. Arosemena de Tejeira, Otilia. "La mujer moderna." Lotería, v. 137, 1967: 11-14.

531. Bermúdez, María Elvira. La vida familiar del mexicano. Mexico City: Antigua Librería Robredo, 1955.

532. Biesanz, John, and Mavis Biesanz. The People of Panama. New York: Columbia University Press, 1955.

533. Borah, Woodrow, and S. F. Cook. "Race and Class in Mexico." Pacific Historical Review, v. 23, 1954.

534. Brito de Martí, E. "La mujer ocupa su sitio." Siempre, no. 1057, September 1973: 31-41.

535. Campodónico, E. Crespo de. "La delincuencia de la mujer en Panamá." Thesis, Universidad de Panamá, 1935.

536. Castro Pozo, Hildebrando. "La mujer mexicana." Hatun Xaura, January-March 1945: 30-31.

537. Chazaro, Gabriel. De la mujer: Ensayo. Mexico City: Ed. Citlaltépetl, 1964.

538. Collante de Tapia, Lola. "Vivimos en el ciclo radiante de la mujer." Lotería, v. 9 (109), December 1964: 22-33.

539. Colón Ramírez, Consuela. Mujeres de México. Mexico City: Imp. Gallarcta, 1944.

540. Comisión Interamericana de Mujeres, OEA. "Informe final del seminario nacional sobre problemas de la mujer joven." Panama City: Comisión Interamericana de Mujeres, OEA, 1972.

541. Encuentro de Mujeres. "La mujer en Mexico." Punto Crítico, v. 8 1972: 25-33.

542. "Les Femmes de Mexico." L'Express, no. 1252, July 1975: 44-45

543. Gamio de Alba, Ana Margarita. La mujer indígena de Centroamérica. Mexico City: Ediciones Especiales del Instituto Indigenista Inter-Americano, 1957.

544. _____. "La mujer indígena de Centroamérica, sumaria recopilación acera de sus condiciones de vida." Edición especial No. 31. Mexico City: Instituto Indigenista Interamericano, 1967. Also cited as: Nicaragua Indígena, v. 2 (19-20), March-June 1958: 31-50.

545. _____. "La mujer indígena en México y Centroamérica." América Indígena, v. 20 (4), October 1974.

546. Garvey, M. "La mujer panameña en el mundo actual." Thesis, Universidad de Panamá, 1959.

547. Gruening, Ernest. Mexico and Its Heritage. New York: Greenwood Press, 1968. Chapter entitled "Women."

548. Hernández Michel, Susan. "Algunas características de la mujer mexicana de clase media." Revista Mexicana de Ciencia Política, v. 17 (65), 1971: 99-105.

549. Jiménez, Liliam. "La mujer salvadoreña." Casa de las América v. 1 (5), March-April 1961: 68-73.

550. Karlson, Karl. The Unknown Woman of Mexico." *Mexican Life*, April 1934: 19-20.

551. Lewis, Oscar. "Husbands and Wives in a Mexican Village: A Study of Role Conflict." In Olen Leonard and Charles Loomis, eds., *Readings*. East Lansing: Michigan State University, 1953: 23-28.

552. Lomnitz, Larissa. "La mujer marginada de México." *Diálogos*, v. 9 (54), 1973: 29-31.

553. Luros, Pablo. *La educación de las jóvenes*. San José, Costa Rica: Imprenta Borrase Hnos., 1938.

554. Mendieta, Edmundo. "La mujer nicaragüense." *Revista Conservadora del Pensamiento Centroamericana*, v. 15 (75), December 1966: 24-26.

555. Miller, Max. "The Women of Tehuantepec." *Mexican Life*, October 1938: 15-16.

556. Ocampo, María Luisa. "Mujer mexicana." *La República*, v. 27, 1 April 1950: 35; and v. 28, 15 April 1950: 35.

557. Pasos, Joaquín. "Origen e interpretación de la mujer nicaragüense." *Revista Conservadora del Pensamiento Centroamericana*, v. 18 (90), March 1968: 54-57.

558. Paz, Octavio. *The Labyrinth of Solitude: Life and Thought in Mexico*. Trans. by Lysander Kemp. New York: Grove Press, 1961.

559. Racasens Siches, Luis. "Algunas notas sociológicas sobre la familia." *Criminalia*, v. 32 (5), May 1966: 242-257.

560. Rodríguez, R., et al. *Virginidad y machismo en México*. Mexico City: Ed. Posada, 1973.

561. Sáenz Elizondo, Carlos Luis. *Costarriqueñas del '56*. San José, Costa Rica: Imprenta Las Américas, 1956.

562. Saquic Calel, Rosalío. "La mujer indígena guatemalteca." *Guatemala Indígena*, v. 8 (1), 1973: 81-110.

563. Sanders, T. G. "Mexican Women." *Fieldstaff Reports*, 3 (6), 1975.

564. Stevens, Evelyn P. "Mexican Machismo: Politics and Value Orientation." *Western Political Quarterly*, v. 18 (4), December 1965: 848-857.

565. Torres de Ianello, Reina. "La mujer Cuna." *América Indígena*, v. 16 (4), October 1956; v. 17 (1), 1957: 9-38.

566. _____. *La mujer Cuna de Panamá*. Mexico City: Instituto Indigenista Interamericano, 1957.

Caribbean

567. Angelis, María Luisa A. *Mujeres puertorriqueñas*. San Juan: Tipografía Real Hermanos, 1910.

568. Brown, Susan E. "Lower Economic Sector Female Mating Patterns in the Dominican Republic: A Comparative Analysis." Ph.D. dissertation, University of Michigan, 1972.

569. _____. "Lower Economic Sector Female Mating Patterns in the Dominican Republic: A Comparative Analysis." Paper presented at the International Congress of Anthropological and Ethnological Sciences, 1972. Also cited in R. R. Leavitt, ed., *Cross Cultural Perspectives on the Women's Movement and Women's Status*. The Hague: Mouton, 1976.

570. _____. "Poor Women in Santo Domingo." In R. Reiter, ed., *Toward an Anthropology of Women*. New York: Monthly Review Press, 1975.

571. _____. *Women and Their Mates: Coping with Poverty in the Dominican Republic*. New York: MSS Information Corporation, 1976.

572. Camarano, Chris. "On Cuban Women." *Science and Society*, v. 35, Spring 1971: 48-58.

573. Choca, Santiago. "A nadie (después de Dios) debe amar más la mujer que a su marido." Havana: Agrupación Católica Universitaria 1956.

574. Fernández Cintrón, Celia, and Marcia Rivera Quintero. "Bases de la sociedad sexista en Puerto Rico." *Revista Interamericana*, v. 4 (2), Summer 1974: 239+.

575. Fox, Geoffrey E. "Honor, Shame and Women's Liberation in Cuba: Views of Working Class Emigré Men." In Ann Pescatello, ed., *Female and Male in Latin America: Essays*. Pittsburgh: University of Pittsburgh Press, 1973: 273-291.

576. Herrera, Aída T. de. "¡Un vítor a las mujeres cubanas!" *Spanish Bulletin*, v. 79, March 1944: 136-140.

577. Longres, John F. "Social Conditions Related to the Acceptance of Modern Medicine among Puerto Rican Women." Ph.D. dissertation, University of Michigan, 1970.

578. Ribes Tovar, Federico. The Puerto Rican Woman. New York: Plus Ultra Educational Publishers, 1972.

Andean Region

579. Andrade Coello, A. "Cultura femenina: Floración intelectual de la mujer ecuatoriana en el siglo XX." El Libertador, July-September 1942: 316-337.

580. _____. Cultura femenina: Floración intelectual de la mujer ecuatoriana en el siglo XX. Quito: Talleres Gráficos del Ministerio de Educación, 1942.

581. Barreto Fernández, María Isabel. "La mujer peruana." Thesis, Universidad Nacional Mayor de San Marcos, 1945.

582. Bono, Agostine. "Juana Washes Clothes...and Hopes." UNICEF News, v. 4 (4), 1974: 29-31.

583. Bensusan, M. D. "Women in Venezuela." Brazilian American, v. 24, June 1939: 7-10.

584. Buitnago, Jaime. "La mujer bogotana." Cromos, 8 December 1945: 1-3, 53.

585. _____. "Situación económica, social y cultural de la mujer en los países andinos." América Indígena, v. 16 (2), April 1956: 83-92.

586. Certad, Aquiles. "Valores femeninos venezolanos." Repertorio Americano, 13 October 1945: 71.

587. Clason, Carla. "La Campesina." World Education Reports, no. 10, December 1975.

588. Clemente Travieso, Carmen. Mujeres venezolanas y otros reportajes. Caracas: Ávila Gráfica, 1951.

589. Cortés Ahumada, Ernesto. "De la mujer a la antimujer." Boletín Cultural y Bibliográfico, v. 5 (19), 1962: 1200-1203.

590. Estrada E., Alcides. Características socio-demográficas de las mujeres colombianas. Bogotá: Encuesta Nacional de Fecundidad, 1973.

591. García y García, Elvira. "Peruvian Women of Today." New West Coast Leader, 14 November 1933; 21 November 1933; 28 November 1933; 12 December 1933.

592. Glicerio Manrique, Mario. "Crisis de la educación femenina." Nueva Educación, v. 1 (4), 1946: 37-39.

593. Hammel, Eugene A. "Some Characteristics of Rural Village and Urban Slum Populations on the Coast of Peru." Southwestern Journal of Anthropology, v. 20 (4), Winter 1964: 346-358.

594. Harkess, Shirley J. "The Pursuit of an Ideal: Migration, Social Class and Women's Roles in Bogotá, Colombia." In Ann Pescatello, ed., Female and Male in Latin America: Essays. Pittsburgh: University of Pittsburgh Press, 1973: 231-254.

595. Jiménez Sarmiento, Arturo. "Problemas de la familia rural." Educación Boliviana, v. 8 (23), March 1960: 23-30.

596. Marin, Barbara. "Estereotipos em ralação a papéis sexuais na Colombia." Cadernos de Pesquisa, no. 15, December 1975: 3-7.

597. Melo Lancheros, L. S. Valores femeninos en Colombia. Bogotá: Ed. Andes, 1967.

598. Otero, Gustavo Adolfo. "Los ideales de la mujer boliviana." América (Quito), January-December 1946: 314-327.

599. Peláez Echeverrí, Gabriela. La condición social de la mujer en Colombia. Bogotá: Editorial Cromos, 1944.

600. Puga, Mario A. "La mujer en el Perú." Cuadernos Americanos, v. 62 (2), March-April 1952: 152-174.

601. Rico, Heidi K. de. Páginas íntimas de la mujer boliviana. Tupiza: Ed. Rico, 1970.

602. Romero de Nohra, Flor, and Gloria Pachón Castro. Mujeres en Colombia. Bogotá: Ed. Andes, 1961.

603. Torre Revello, José. "Las mujeres limeñas." Revista de Historia de América, v. 52, December 1961: 521-526.

604. UNICEF (United Nations Children's Fund.) "Sheep Girl of the Andes." UNICEF News, no. 43, n.d.

605. Valdez, Blanca. "La mujer peruana." María Aestus, Organo de la Biblioteca del Ministerio de Relaciones Exteriores, December 1963: 68-69.

606. "Women of Peru." Peruvian Times, 12 January 1935: 11-12.

Chile and the Platine

607. Abeijón, Carlos. La mujer argentina antes y después de Eva Perón. Buenos Aires: Ed. Cuarto Mundo, 1975.

608. Amadeo, Tomás. "Cultura femenina uruguaya." El Libertador, January-March 1943: 101-122.

609. Andrade Coello, A. Cultura femenina uruguaya. Quito: Taller Gráfico del Ministerio de Educación, 1943.

610. Argentine Republic. Oficina Nacional de la Mujer. "Realidad económica social de la mujer trabajadora." Buenos Aires: Oficina Nacional de la Mujer, 1969.

611. Bachem D'Aragon de Ruiz Moreno, Liliane. "La mujer, antítesis del comunismo." Boletín del Museo Social Argentino, v. 44 (330), January-March 1967: 43-56.

612. Bals, Eulalia Cantwell de. "Mujeres del Uruguay." Antigas, March 1947: 36-39; June 1947: 55+; September 1947: 86-93; October 1947: 129-136.

613. Bambirr, Vania. "The Chilean Woman." In New Chile. New York: NACLA, 1973: 34-36.

614. Barra, Olga de la. "Women of Chile." Latin American World, May 1931: 303-304.

615. Barroso, H. M. "La mujer argentina." Mundo Nuevo, no. 46, 1970: 43-50.

616. Fingermann, Gregorio. "Sexo y profesión." Boletín del Museo Social Argentino, v. 43 (328), July-September 1966: 90-96.

617. Gallardo, Sara. "La mujer porteña: Un retrato visto desde lo más lejos y desde lo más cerca posible." Visión, v. 3 (4), July 1966: 26-27.

618. García, Marta M. de. "Women in Free Argentina." Americas, v. 9 (4), April 1957: 32-33.

619. Gregorio Lavie, Lucila de. Trayectoria de la condición social de las mujeres argentinas. Santa Fe, Argentina: Universidad Nacional del Litoral, 1947.

620. Íñigo Carrera, Héctor. La mujer argentina. Buenos Aires: Centro Editor de América Latina, 1972.

621. Lungo, Teresita D. C. "Situación social de la mujer en el norte de Córdoba." Revista Universitaria Nacional de Córdoba, v. 10 (1-2), March-June 1969: 467-473.

622. Machado Bonet, Ofelia. "Women in Uruguay." In R. R. Leavitt, ed., Cross Cultural Perspectives on the Women's Movement and Women's Status. The Hague: Mouton, 1976.

623. Mafud, Julio. "El machismo en la argentina." Mundo Nuevo, v. 16, October 1967: 72-78.

624. Ocampo, Victoria. "La condición inhumana." Sur, v. 318, March-June 1969: 10-16.

625. Pichel, Vera. Mi país y sus mujeres. Buenos Aires: Ed. Sudestade, 1968.

626. Rovillon, Josefina M. "Mujeres patagónicas." Argentina Austral, v. 32 (355), May 1961: 9+; v. 32 (356), June 1961: 14-15; v. 34 (375), January 1963: 14+.

627. Schultz Cazenueva de Mantovani, Fryda. "Bocetos de la Argentina: Mujeres." Nueva Revista Urbana, v. 1 (2), July-September 1959: 42-49.

628. Toro Godoy, Julia. Presencia y destino de la mujer en nuestro pueblo. Santiago: Ediciones Maipo, 1967.

629. Zegers Samaniego, Julio. Estudios económicos. Santiago: Imprenta Nacional, 1908.

Brazil

630. Amora, Paulo. Rebelião das mulheres em Minas Gerais. Rio de Janeiro: Ed. GRD, 1968.

631. Barroso, Carmen Lucia de Melo. "Estereotipos sexuais: Possíveis contribuições de psicologia para sua mudança." Cadernos de Pesquisa, no. 15, December 1975: 135-137.

632. Bittencourt, Adalzira. A mulher paulista na historia. Rio de Janeiro: Livros de Portugal, 1954.

633. Cannon, Mary Minerva. "Women in Brazil." Zontian, October 1946: 7-9.

634. Cruz, Levy. "Brazil." In Raphael Patai, ed., Women in the Modern World. New York: Free Press, 1967.

635. Giner, P. Mujeres de América. Barcelona: La Vita Literaria, n.d.

636. Hohenthal, William P. "Sex, Class and Status in Racial Relations, Northeast Brazil." Anthropological Society Papers, v. 21, Fall 1959: 17-24.

637. Jesus, Carolina María de. Child of the Dark. New York: New American Library, 1962.

638. Landes, Ruth. A cidade das mulheres. Rio de Janeiro: n.d. Also cited as The City of Women. New York: Macmillan, 1947.

639. Lima, Lauro de Oliveira. "A imaturidade psicossociologica da mulher." Vozes, v. 63 (5), May 1969: 416-426.

640. MacLachlan, Colin M. "The Feminine Mystique in Brazil: A Middle-Class Image." In Pacific Coast Council in Latin American Studies, Proceedings II. Monterrey, California: 1972.

641. Martínez-Alier, Verena. "The Women of Rio das Pedras." Paper presented at the Conference on Feminine Perspectives in Social Science Research in Latin America, Buenos Aires, March 1974.

642. Parker, Ann. "Brazilian Women Today." Brazil, January 1945: 18-19.

643. Pearse, Andrew. "Integração social das familias dos favelados." Educaçao e Ciencias Sociales, v. 2 (6), November 1957: 245-278.

644. Pereira, Armando. Mulheres deitadas. Rio de Janeiro: Gráfica Record, 1969.

645. Ribeiro, Carolina. "A mulher paulista en 32." Revista do Instituto Histórico e Geográfico de São Paulo, v. 59, 1961: 247-262.

646. Saffioti, Heleith Iara B. "A mulher: No Brazil e no mundo." Banas, no. 1055, 1974: 46-50.

647. Studart, Heloneida. "Da mulher brasileira." Comentario, v. 13 (51), 1972: 52-53.

648. Teixeira, María de Lourdes. "As mulheres machadianas." Revista Brasiliense, v. 4, March-April 1956: 65-75.

649. Thome, Yolanda Bettencourt. <u>A mulher no mundo de hoje</u>.
Petropolis: Ed. Vozes, 1967.

650. Werneck, Olga. "O subdesenvolvimento e a situação da
mulher." <u>Revista Civilização Brasileira</u>, v. 1, September
1965: 331-341.

Chapter II

WOMEN AND THE LAW

Chapter 2, section A, deals with the civil and legal status of women. The African entries cover such areas as women's property rights, changes in women's status during the pre- and post-colonial periods, and comparisons of women's rights with those of men. The Latin American entries deal with female status in general, social treatment of women, and women's rights. Labor and contractual references are included under section B for both areas. There is much more information available for Latin American than for Africa on labor and contractual legislation in the sources consulted.

We did not include references on suffrage in this bibliography unless they deal with the implications of suffrage for the integration of women into public (e.g., economic) activity.

A. CIVIL AND LEGAL STATUS

Africa--General

651. Atangana, N. "La Femme africaine dans la société." Presénce Africain, v. 13, April-May 1957: 133-142.

652. Costa, J. "La Nouvelle Famille africaine dans les droits de l'indépendance, essai de sociologie normative." Année Sociologique, v. 22,

653. Landes, R. "Negro Slavery and Female Status." African Affairs, v. 52 (206), 1953: 54-57.

654. Lewin, Julius, et al. "The Legal Status of African Women." *Race Relations Journal*, v. 26 (4), October-December 1959: 152-159.

655. Mendy, Justin. "La Femme est-elle l'egale de l'homme? 1. Situation de la femme dans le monde. 2. Egalité et distinction." *Afrique Nouvelle*, v. 21 (1036), 15-21 June 1967:8; v. 21 (1037), 22-28 June 1967: 11.

656. Morris, H. F. "Report of the Commission on Marriage, Divorce and the Status of Women." *Journal of African Law*, v. 10 (1), 1966: 1-7.

657. N'Dour, Birane. "De l'egalité de l'homme et de la femme." *Afrique Nouvelle*, v. 23 (1182), 2-8 April 1970: 11; v. 23 (1184), 16-22 April 1970: 11.

658. du Sacré-Coeur, Marie André, Sister. *La Condition humaine en Afrique noire*. Paris: Grasset, 1953.

659. Schmidt, W. "The Position of Women With Regard to Property in Primitive Society." *American Anthropologist*, v. 37 (2), 1935: 224-256.

660. Tillett, Gladys A. "A Family Law and the Women of Africa: U.N. Seminar on the Status of Women in Family Law." *U.S. Department of State Bulletin*, v. 52, 15 February 1965: 229-233.

661. Vives, Franç oise R. "Votre femme, est-elle une esclave?" *Jeune Afrique*, v. 449, 12-18 August 1969: 47-54; v. 45, 19-25 August 1969: 48-54; v. 463, 12-18 November, 1969: 16-18.

662. Wentzer, David. "The Legal Plight of the African Women." *Race Relations*, v. 11 (3-4), 1944: 66-69.

West Africa

663. Akande, Jadesola O. "Woman's Rights in Property in Nigeria." Master's thesis, Lagos University, 1968.

664. Angela, Chr. "Situation et statut juridique de la femme ghanéenne." *Vivante Afrique*, v. 243, March-April 1966: 19-21.

665. Djasgaral, L. "Grosses différences dans les droits accordés aux hommes et aux femmes." *Revue de L'O.A.M.C.E.*, v. 5, March 1964: 56-59.

666. Dobkin, M. "Colonialism and the Legal Status of Women in Francophonic Africa." *Cahiers d'Etudes Africaines*, v. 8 (3), 1968: 390-405.

667. Emane, J. "Les Droits patrimoniaux de la femme mariée ivoirienne." Annales Africaines, 1967: 85-126.

668. George, Aguin O'Connor. "The Status of Women in Selected Societies of West Africa: A Study in the Concept in Law and Practice." Ph.D. dissertation, New York University, 1960.

669. Gilles de Pelichy, Dom. Condition de la femme d'après le droit coutumier de l'Ouest Africain. Rapports et Comptes rendus de la XXe Semaine de Missiologie de Louvain, 1950. Brussels: Edition Universelle, 1951: 155-177.

670. Hazoume, G. P. "Accra: Les Femmes d'Afrique se concertant au sujet de leurs droits." Bingo, v. 194, March 1969: 23-25.

671. Hecker, Monique. "UNESCO and Women's Rights: An Experimental Project in Upper Volta." UNESCO Chronicle, v. 16 (6), June 1970: 257-265.

672. Kane, Elimane. "Le Disposition des cases des fammes dans le carré du mari commun (Sénégal)." Notes Africaines, v. 26, April 1945: 11-12.

673. Kane, Malmouna. "The Status of Married Women under Customary Law in Senegal." American Journal of Comparative Law, v. 20 (4), Fall 1972: 716-723.

674. Labouret, H. "Situation matérielle, morale et coutumière de la femme dans l'Ouest Africain." Africa, v. 13, 1940: 97-124.

675. Muhammad, Yahaya. "The Legal Status of Muslim Women in the Northern States of Nigeria." Journal of the Centre for Islamic Legal Studies, v. 1 (2), 1967: 1-38.

676. Obi, S. N. Chinwuba. On the Ibo Law of Property. London: Butterworth, 1963.

677. _____. "Women's Property and Succession Thereto in Modern Ibo Law (Eastern Nigeria). Journal of African Law, v. 6 (1), Spring 1969: 6-18.

678. Rattray, R. S. "The Family: The Wife." In Ashanti Law and Constitution. Oxford: Clarendon Press, 1929: 22-32.

679. du Sacré-Coeur, Marie André, Sister. "La Femme mossi, sa situation juridique." L'Ethnographie, v. 33-34, 1937: 15-33.

680. _____. "La Situation juridique de la femme indigène dans la boucle du Niger." In: Reports et Comptes Rendus du

Congrès Internationale de l'Evolution Culturelle des Peuples Coloniaux. Paris: 1938: 96-102.

681. Talbot, P. Amaury. "Woman, Marriage, etc." In Life in Southern Nigeria. London: Macmillan, 1923: 203-214.

682. Vincent, Jeanne-Françoise. "Données sur le mariage et la situation de la femme Mofu (Massifs de Duvanger et de Wasan, Cameroun du Nord)." Cahiers O.R.S.T.O.M., Série Sciences Humaines, v. 9 (3), 1972: 309-324.

683. Ward, Edward. "The Yoruba Husband-Wife Code." Ph.D. dissertation, Catholic University of America, 1938.

Central Africa

684. Cyfer-Diderich, G. Le Statut juridique de la femme indigène au Congo Belge. Brussels: Conseil National des Femmes Belges, 1950.

685. _____. "La Condition juridique de la femme au Congo Belge." Civilisations, v. 1 (4), 1951: 59-67.

686. Françoise-Marie, Sister. "La Femme indigène dans la legislation coutumière au Nepoko." In Rapports et Comptes Rendus de la XXe Semaine de Missiologie de Louvain, 1950. Brussels: Edition Universelle, 1951: 210-223.

687. Makonga, B. "La Position sociale de la mère." Bulletin du CEPSI, v. 17, 1951: 243-259.

688. Mangwaya-Bukuku, Claver. "Travail et syndicat: La Protection du contrat de la femme en cas de maternité." Congo Afrique, v. 10 (46), June-July 1970: 329-336.

689. Missia. "L'Éducation de la femme en pays Kivu. Afrique Ardente, v. 82, 1954: 14-18.

690. Nyirasafari, Gaudentia. "L'Évolution du statut de la femme au Ruanda." Les Carnets de l'Enfance, v. 27, July-September 1974: 84-106.

691. Roberts, A. "La Condition juridique et sociale de la femme en Afrique Equatoriale." Revue Juridique et Politique d'Outre Mer, No. 4, October-December 1962: 520-540.

692. Sendanyoye, Gratien. "Jugement annoté: Veuvage. Droits de la veuve sur les biens de son mari. Droit du tuteur sur les orphelins." Bulletin de Jurisprudence du Ruanda-Urundi, v. 1,

1926: 36-37.

693. _____. "Du bail à femme en droit coutumier ruandais." Bulletin de Jurisprudence de Ruanda-Urundi, v. 11, 1953: 559-572.

694. Sheik el Din, Dina. "How Sudanese Fare with Customary and State Law." Paper presented at the Wellesley Conference on Women and Development, June 1976. Available from Wellesley Center for Research on Women, 828 Washington St., Wellesley, Massachusetts 02181.

695. Siquet, M. "Legal and Customary Status of Women." In La Promotion de la femme au Congo et en Ruanda-Urundi. Brussels: Congrès Nationel Colonial, 12th Session, 1956: 197-251.

696. Sohier, A. "Évolution de la condition juridique de la femme indigène au Congo Belge. Contribution to the 24th session of l'Institut Colonial International, Rome, 1939. Brussels, 1939: 149-217.

697. _____. "L'Évolution de la condition juridique de la femme indigène aux colonies." Bulletin de l'Union des Femmes Coloniales, no. 105, 1939: 156-158; no. 106, 1939: 178-180; no. 107, 1939: 203-204; no. 108, 1939: 230-231; no. 109, 1939: 255-256; no. 110, 1939: 282-283.

698. _____. "La Reforme de la dot et la liberté de la femme indigène." Bulletin des Juridictions Indigènes et du Droit Coutumier Congolais, v. 18 (7), January-February 1950: 217-221.

699. Van Caeneghem, R. "Étude sur les dispositions pénales coutumières contre l'adultère chez les Baluba et les Bena Lulua du Kasai." Bulletin du CEPSI, v. 8, 1949: 5-46.

East Africa

700. Brown, Winifred. "Status of Uganda Women in Relation to Marriage Laws." African Women, v. 4 (1), 1960: 1-4.

701. Castelnuovo, Shirley. "Legal Status of Women in Tanzania, Uganda and Kenya and an Assessment of Some Reception Problems of the Tanzanian Marriage Law of 1971." Paper presented at the Annual Meeting of the African Studies Association, San Francisco, October-November 1975.

702. Perlman, M. L. "Law and the Status of Women in Uganda: A Systematic Comparison Between the Ganda and the Toro." Tropical Magazine, v. 2, 1969: 60-106.

703. Tadesse, Mary. "Rights of Women." Ethiopia Observer, v. 1 (3), February 1957: 104-105.

704. Van Den Bergh, Leonard John. "The Legal Status of Women in Uganda." Ph.D. dissertation, University of California at Berkeley, 1919.

Southern Africa

705. Horrell, Muriel. The Rights of African Women: Some Suggested Reforms. Johannesberg: South African Institute of Race Relations, 1968.

706. Landis, Elizabeth S. "Apartheid and the Disabilities of African Women in South Africa." Objective Justice, v. 7, January-March 1975: 5-10. Also cited as: Freedomways, v. 15 (4), 1975: 272-276.

707. Mindolo Ecumenical Foundation. Conferences and Consultation Programme. Women's Rights in Zambia: Report of a Consultation, November 20-24th, 1970. Kitwe, Zambia: Mindolo Ecumenical Foundation, 1970.

708. Morojele, Lindiwe C. "Legal Status of Women in Basutoland." Women Today, v. 6 (3), December 1964: 54-55.

709. Shropshire, D. W. T. The Bantu Women Under the Natal Code of Native Law. Lovedale: Lovedale Press, 1941.

710. Simmons, H. J. "African Women and the Law in South Africa." The Listener, v. 55 (1416), 1956: 626-627, 644.

711. _____. African Women: Their Legal Status in South Africa. Evanston: Northwestern University Press, 1968.

712. Suttner, R. S. "The Legal Status of African Women in South Africa: A Review Article." African Social Research, v. 8, December 1969: 620-627.

Latin American--General

713. Álvarez Vignoli de Demicheli, Sofía. "Condición jurídica de la mujer en Latinoamérica." Revista Universitaria Nacional de Córdoba, v. 10 (1-2), March-June 1969: 105-120.

714. _____. Igualdad Jurídica de la mujer. Buenos Aires: Ediciones Depalma, 1973.

715. Crawford, Harry Paine. "Civil Rights of the Latin American

Woman." Bulletin of the Pan American Union, v. 70, July 1936: 541-548.

716. Duff, E. A. "Marital Regime in Latin America." Inter-American Law Review, v. 8, 1966: 137-157.

717. García Garza, I. A. de. "Derechos de la mujer en América Latina." Justicia, v. 28, August 1968: 51+.

718. Leret de Matheus, María Gabriela. La mujer: Una incapaz como el demente y el niño (según las leyes latinoamericanas). Mexico City: B. Costa-Amic Ed., 1975.

719. Lleras Camargo, Alberto. "La inferioridad jurídica de la mujer." La Nueva Democracia, v. 33 (4), October 1953: 116.

720. Miller-Freienfels, W. "Modernas tendencias del desarrollo del derecho de familia." Revista de la Facultad de Derecho, v. 29, June 1964: 9+.

721. Muller, Gesche, and J. Arellano Alarcón. "Exposición comparativa de algunos aspectos del derecho de familia en Argentina, Brasil y Chile, en la legislación y en la práctica." Revista de Derecho y Ciencias Sociales, v. 38, July-December 1970: 17+.

722. Ochoa Restrepo, Guillermo. "Licencia marital." Estudios de Derecho, v. 22 (64), 1963: 223-231.

723. Wells, W. C. "Women's Property Rights in Latin America." Bulletin of the Pan American Union, v. 59 (232), 1925.

Mexico and Central America

724. Alianza de Mujeres de México. "La situación jurídica de la mujer mexicana." Thesis, Universidad Nacional Autónoma de México, 1953.

725. Baqueiro Rojas, E. "Derecho de familia en el código civil de 1970." Revista de la Facultad de Derecho de México, v. 21, July-December 1971: 379-394.

726. Barret, Ofelia Mendoza de. "Posición jurídica de la mujer hondureña." Norte, v. 9 (8), May 1949: 43.

727. Barroso Figueroa, J. "Autonomía del derecho de familia." Revista de la Facultad de Derecho de México, v. 17, October-December 1967: 809+.

728. Bialostosky de Chazán, Sara. Condición jurídica de la mujer

en México. Mexico City: Universidad Nacional Autónoma de México, Facultad de Derecho, 1975.

729. Blanco, Francisco J. La mujer ante la legislación hondureña. Tegucigalpa: Taller Tipo-Litográficos Aristón, 1955.

730. Buen Lozano, N. de. "Tendencias modernas en el derecho de la familia." Anuario de Derecho, v. 6, 1963-65: 81+.

731. Cabrera Muñoz, Rosalinda. "El derecho de familia y la legislación guatemalteca." Thesis, Universidad de San Carlos, 1964.

732. Carrillo, Alfonso. "La mujer guatemalteca y su situación jurídica." Speech presented at the Pan American Round Table, San José, Costa Rica, November 1940. Guatemala: Imprenta Lehmann, 1940.

733. Fernández Clérigo, Luis. "El Derecho de familia en la legislación comparada." Thesis, Universidad Nacional Autónoma de México, 1947.

734. González de Behringer, C. La mujer ante el derecho panameño. Panama City: Imprenta Nacional, 1922.

735. Guerra de Villalez, A. E. "La mujer y sus derechos." Boletín Informativo de la Sociedad de Esposas de Abogados, v. 4, 1968.

736. Gutiérrez, C. J. "Proyecto de código de familia." Revista de Ciencias Jurídicas, v. 21, November 1971.

737. Maldonado Cámara, María Eugenia. "La situación de la mujer en el derecho internacional." Thesis, Universidad Nacional Autónoma de México, 1964.

738. Ortega Arenas, Joaquín. "La familia." Mimeo. Mexico City: Universidad Nacional Autónoma de México, 1948.

739. Pacheco Garduño, Olga. "Estudio histórico-comparado sobre la potestad marital." Thesis, Universidad Nacional Autónoma de México, 1963.

740. Pan American Union. "Additional Rights for Women in Costa Rica." Bulletin of the Pan American Union, v. 75, March 1941: 194.

741. Pérez Gabriel, Ana María. "La capacidad jurídica de la mujer en el derecho civil mexicano." Thesis, Universidad Nacional Autónoma de México, 1962.

742. Sánchez Carrillo, Rosa M. "Ensayos sobre el nivel social y jurídico de la mujer a traves de los tiempos." Thesis, Universidad Nacional Autónoma de México, 1939.

743. Spota Valencia, Alma L. La igualdad jurídica y social de los sexos: Filosofía, sociología e historia. Mexico City: Ed. Porrúa, 1967.

744. Valdelamar, Emilia. Condición jurídica y social de la mujer y la planificación de la familia. Panama City: APLAFA, 1973.

745. Vanegas, J. "La personalidad jurídica de la mujer nicaragüense." Ateneo, May-August 1942: 70-74.

746. Williams, W. "Evolución social de los derechos de la mujer." Justicia, v. 31, October 1972: 55-60.

Caribbean

747. Abreu de Mota, Christiana. "La hipoteca legal de la mujer casada, del menor y del interdicto." Revista Jurídica Dominicana, v. 20, January-December 1958: 22-53.

748. Azcuy, Aracelio. El derecho de la mujer. Havana: Editorial Lex, 1951.

749. Comisión de Derechos Civiles. La igualdad de los derechos y oportunidades de la mujer puertorriqueña. San Juan, P.R.: 1973.

750. "Cuban Family Code." Center for Cuban Studies, v. 2 (4), 1975.

751. Gorrín Padilla, José E. "La capacidad de la mujer casada conforme a la constitución." Revista del Colegio de Abogados de La Habana. October-December 1946: 700-719.

752. "Maternity Law." Cuban Review, v. 4, September 1974: 15.

753. Quintana, Oscar. La ley de equiparación de la mujer y el derecho de familia. Matanzas: Pedro P. Soles y Cía., 1952.

754. Randall, Margaret. "Introducing the Family Code." Cuban Review, v. 4, September 1974: 31.

755. Rego, Oscar F. "La ley de los derechos civiles de la mujer ¿Producirá esta ley serios conflictos conyugales?" Carteles, v. 32 (6), n.d.: 74-76.

756. Rodríguez Esquivel, Leoncio A. Capacidad civil de la mujer.

Havana: Ed. Lex, 1955.

757. Zaldívar, Aurelio. "Los derechos de la mujer." <u>Carteles</u>, v. 32 (2), 14 January 1951: 72.

Andean Region

758. Abad, Aída. "De la condición civil de la mujer casada." Thesis, Universidad Nacional Mayor de San Marcos, Lima, 1950.

759. Acosta Najarro, Hugo D. "La sociología del derecho y familia." Thesis, Universidad Nacional Mayor de San Marcos, Lima, 1972.

760. Alzamora Valdez, Mario. "La mujer peruana ante el derecho." <u>Revista del Foro</u>, v. 42, August 1955: 285-296.

761. Amézquita de Almeyda, Josefina. "La ley y el status de las mujeres colombianas. Compliación y análisis de las leyes que discriminan a la mujer." Mimeo. Medford, Mass.: Tufts University, The Fletcher School of Law and Diplomacy, Law and Population Program, 1975.

762. Bolivia. Dirección General de Protección Social a la Mujer. "Ley de 20 de Noviembre de 1957." <u>Anales de Legislación Boliviana</u>, v. 9 (35), October-December 1957: 38.

763. Bustamante, María. "La mujer casada y la legislación peruana." Thesis, Universidad Nacional Mayor de San Marcos, Lima, 1960.

764. Chavarriaga, José Luis. "Derechos y reivindicaciones de la mujer colombiana." Ph.D. thesis, Universidad Nacional, Bogotá, 1940.

765. Coello García, Enrique. "La familia y la propiedad en la constitución de 1967." <u>Anales de la Universidad Central</u>, v. 95 (350), 1967: 123-141.

766. Conde Barrozzi, Juan. <u>Matrimonio y responsabilidad civil</u>. Caracas: Editorial Arte, 1968.

767. Cuadros E., Raúl. <u>Los derechos de la mujer: Divulgación de la ley</u>. Lima: Escuela Tipográfica Salesiana, 1951.

768. Echecopar H., Carlos. "The Civil and Political Status of Women in Peru." <u>Bulletin of the Pan American Union</u>, v. 72 (8), 1938: 462-464.

769. Fernández Márquez, César. "Proyecto de reforma al código civil (mujer casada para administrar sus bienes)." <u>Anales de</u>

la Universidad de Cuenca, v. 18 (3), July-September 1962: 239-253.

770. Gallardo, Benjamín H. Reintegración de los derechos civiles de la mujer. La Paz: Talleres "La República," 1925.

771. Gómez Garzón, Soledad. "Reformas legales que la mujer debe pedir ante las cámaras legislativas." Univérsitas, v. 11, June 1958: 123-134.

772. Hinostrosa, F. "Panorama del derecho de familia en Colombia." Interamerican Law Review, v. 8, 1966: 183-243.

773. Jaramillo Arbeláez, Delio. "La mujer diferenciada es una realidad en pugna con la ley." Universidad de Antioquía, May-June 1944: 489-499.

774. López J., Emilio. "Capacidad de la mujer para el ejercicio de la tutela y curatela." Estudios de Derecho, v. 23 (65), March 1964: 79-82.

775. Patrón Faura, Pedro. Legislación de la mujer peruana: Prontuario. Lima: Imprenta Colegio Militar Leoncio Prado, 1972.

776. Pinzón, Gabino. "Capacidad de la mujer casada para el comercio. Univérsitas, v. 3, 1952: 173-182.

777. Rendón de Mosquera, Zoila. "La mujer en los diversos organismos humanos." Previsión Social, v. 22, 1949: 150-162.

778. Rodríguez de Muñoz, Carmen, and Elsa Roca de Salonén. "Compilation and Analysis of Laws Discriminating against the Woman in Peru." Mimeo. Medford, Mass.: Tufts University, The Fletcher School of Law and Diplomacy, 1975.

779. Salazar, Mario E. "La mujer en la legislación boliviana." Revista de Estudios Jurídicos, Políticos y Sociales, v. 3 (213), November 1951: 208-211.

780. Sallent Casas, Ignacio. "La ley del matrimonio ¿hay igualdad de derechos y deberes entre los cónyuges?" Arco, Revista de las Areas Culturales Bolivarianas, v. 5 (38), October 1963: 736-741; v. 5 (39), November 1963: 839-843.

781. Segura, J. M. Derechos civiles y responsabilidad de la mujer. Bogotá: Ed. Presencia, 1957.

782. Solarte Hurtado, Daniel. "La mujer colombiana ante la ley civil." Revista de la Universidad de Cauca, January-February 1961: 7-60.

783. Terrazas Torres, Carlos. "La capacidad jurídica de la mujer." Revista de Derecho, v. 7/8 (25/26), December 1955-March 1956: 15-2

784. Torres-Rivero, Arturo Luis. Derecho de familia: Parte general 3 vols. Caracas: 1967-1970.

785. Tovar Langa, Silvestre. El cuasicontrato de comunidad en el concubinato (Venezuela). Caracas: Ed. Edime, 1951.

786. Urquidi, José Macedonio. "La condición jurídica de la mujer en Bolivia." Revista de Derecho Internacional, 30 September 1938: 44-134, 31 December 1933: 244-285.

787. Villegas D., Rodrigo. "La situación de la mujer casada en la legislación ecuatoriana." Estudios de Derecho, v. 21 (61), 1962: 11-19.

788. Zárate Plasencia, Fidel A. Los derechos políticos de la mujer peruana. Lima: Colegio de Abogados de Lima, 1954.

Chile and the Platine

789. Alvarez Vignoli de Demicheli, Sofía. Igualdad jurídica de la mujer. Alberdi, su precursor en América. Textos legales vigentes Buenos Aires: Ed. Depalma, 1973.

790. Aratz, Roberto Mario. "La mujer en el derecho civil argentino. Ibero América, June 1946: 2-3.

791. Arteaga Infante, Claudio. La mujer chilena, esclava de la ley. Santiago: Ed. Minerva, 1922.

792. Belluscio, Augusto Lesar. Manual de derecho de familia. Bueno Aires: Ediciones Depalma, 1974.

793. Borda, Guillermo A. Tratado de derecho civil argentino: familia. 2 vols. Buenos Aires: Ed. Perrot, 1955.

794. Caffarena de Jiles, Elena. Capacidad de la mujer casada con relación de sus bienes. Santiago: Imprenta Universitaria, 1944.

795. Gallo Chinchilla, Margarita. La mujer ante la legislación chilena. Santiago: Memoria de Prueba, 1945.

796. Gómez Sánchez, Enriqueta. "Derechos integrales de la mujer paraguaya." El Paraguayo, 2 October 1945: 2.

797. Guastavino, Elías P. "La mujer en el derecho civil argentino. Revista Universitaria Nacional de Córdoba, v. 10 (1/2), March-

June 1969: 43-70

798. Irala Burgos, Jerónimo. "El status jurídico de la mujer en el Paraguay. Compilación y análisis de leyes sobre el particular." Mimeo. Asunción: Centro Paraguayo de Estudios de Población, 1975.

799. Klein Reidel, Federico. Peculio profesional de la mujer casada. Santiago: Imprenta Nascimiento, 1934.

800. Migliorini, Inés Candelaria. "Los derechos civiles de la mujer en la República Argentina." Mimeo. Buenos Aires: Centro Nacional de Documentación e Información Educativa, 1972.

801. Montano, Pedro A. "Derechos civiles de la mujer." Revista del Notariado, March 1948: 123-133.

802. Orgaz, Alfredo. "La ley uruguaya de derechos civiles de la mujer." Revista de Derecho, Jurisprudencia y Administración, January 1949: 7-13.

803. Pan American Union. "Changes in the Civil Code of Chile Affecting Women." Bulletin of the Pan American Union, v. 69, May 1935: 433-434.

804. Rivarola, Domingo M. "Apuntes para el estudio de la familia en el Paraguay." Asunción: Centro Paraguayo de Estudios Socioeconómicos, 1971. Also cited as: Revista Paraguaya de Sociología, v. 8 (21), May-August 1971: 84-106.

805. Rossel Saavedra, Enrique. Manual del derecho de la familia. Santiago: Ed. Jurídica de Chile, 1968.

806. Spota, Alberto. "La familia y el derecho." Revista del Colegio de Abogados, v. 7, 1961.

807. Vasconcellos, Amílcar. La mujer ante el derecho positivo uruguayo. Montevideo: Organización Taquigráfica Medina, 1947.

Brazil

808. Bueno, Ruth. Regime jurídico da mulher casada. Rio de Janeiro: Forense, 1970.

809. Cardone, Marley A. "A mulher nas constituções brasileiras." Revista dos Tribunais, v. 360, October 1965.

810. "Condição da mulher no direito brasileiro." Jus Documentação, v. 7 (3), March 1954: 35-51.

811. Dolinger, Jacob. A capacidad civil da mulher casada e as relações conjuga-s de ordem pessoal, no código civil e na reforma da lei 4.121. Brazil: Edições Biblos Ltda., 1966.

812. Farhat, Alfredo. A mulher perante o direito: Doutrina, Legislação, jurisprudencia e formulario. São Paulo: Edição Universidade de Direito, 1971.

813. Gomes Chiarelli, Carlos Alberto. "Proteção a mulher na legislação social do Brazil." Revista Iberoamericana de Seguridad Social, v. 14 (3), May-June 1965: 391-410.

814. Lagos Valenzuela, Tulio. "Implicações sociológicas no reconhecimento da capacidade da mulher casada no direito civil brasileiro." In Estudios de Sociología, No. 8. Buenos Aires: Biblio. Omeba, n.d. (circa 1967).

815. Rezende, Zeia Pinho. Situação jurídica da mulher. Rio de Janeiro: Instituto do Açúcar e do Alcool, 1966.

816. Rodrigues, João Batista Cascudo. A mulher brasileira: Direitos políticos e civis. Fortaleza: Imprensa Universitaria do Ceará, 1962.

817. Sabino Junior, Vicente. A emancipação socio-jurídica da mulher. São Paulo: Editora Juriscredi, 1972.

818. Tabak, Fanny. "A declaração universal e os direitos da mulher." Revista de Ciencia Política, v. 2 (4), October-December 1968: 115-143.

Note: For additional references to legislation on women see: Pan American Union, Index to Latin American Periodical Literature 1921-1960 (8 vols.) and supplements 1961-1965 (2 vols.).

B. LABOR AND CONTRACTUAL LEGISLATION

Africa-General

819. "Les Droits de la femme, un probleme préoccupant." Afrique Nouvelle, v. 17 (926), 6-12 May 1965: 12.

820. "Legislation Concerning Female Wage-Earners in Africa South of the Sahara." Bulletin of the Inter-African Labour Institute, v. 2 (2), March 1955: 29-50.

West Africa

821. "Reglements concernant le travail des femmes et des enfants

dans la République du Togo." Informations Sociales, v. 22 (12), 15 December 1959: 445-447.

Latin America - General

822. Anderson, Mary. "What the Americans are doing for the Woman Worker." Bulletin of the Pan American Union, v. 69 (7), 1935: 521-535.

823. Cannon, Mary Minerva. "La mujer que trabaja y la legislación social." Noticias de la Oficina de Información Obrera y Social, April 1946: 3-5.

824. Inter-American Commission of Women. "Legal Conditions Governing Women's Work in Industrial, Commercial and Agricultural Pursuits in 1938 (in its Report to the Eighth International Conference, Lima, 1938)." Washington, D.C.: 163rd Pan American Union Proceedings, 1938.

825. International Labour Organization. "Protection of Women Home Workers in Latin America." Industrial and Labour Information, v. 72 (6), 1939: 159-161.

826. _____. "Protection of Maternity in Latin America." Industrial and Labour Information, v. 69 (1), 1939: 3-4.

827. "Laws for Latin American Wage-Earning Women." The Woman Worker, v. 20 (6), 1940: 5-6.

828. U. S. Department of Labor. "Labor Legislation for Women in Latin American Countries." Monthly Labor Review, May 1939: 1071-1072.

829. _____. Women in the World Today: Protective Labor Legislation for Women in 91 Countries. Washington, D.C.: 1963.

830. Zimmerman, Mary H. "The Contractual Capacity of Married Women in the Americas." Michigan State Bar Journal, v. 33, 1954: 27-36.

Mexico and Central America

831. Avila Osorio, Lidia. "La capacidad jurídica de la mujer en el derecho agrario." Thesis, Universidad Nacional Autónoma de México, 1963.

832. Gómez R., Gudelia. "Atribuciones y funcionamiento del Departamento de Protección al Trabajo de Mujeres y Menores." Revista Mexicana de Trabajo, v. 12 (1), 1965: 31-34.

833. González Pineda, Héctor. "El trabajo de la mujer en la legislación laboral guatemalteca." Thesis, Universidad de San Carlos, Guatemala, 1964.

834. "Honduras, Decreto No. 15, sobre trabajo de menores y de mujeres." La Gaceta, 17 January 1953.

835. International Labour Organization. "Employment of Women and Young Persons (Honduras). Decreto No. 15 to Amend the Law on the Employment of Young Persons and Women, 13 January 1953." Legislative Series, September-October 1954.

836. _____. "Equal Remuneration in Costa Rica." Industry and Labour, v. 5 (9), 1951: 344.

837. López González, Isabel. "La mujer en la relación jurídica contractual en materia de trabajo." Thesis, Universidad National Autónoma de México, 1962.

838. Matilla López, Graciela. "Los derechos agrarios de la mujer campesina." Thesis, Universidad Nacional Autónoma de México, 1965.

839. Mazadiego López, Xochitli. "Estudio sobre el trabajo de la mujer y su reglamentación." Thesis, Universidad Nacional Autónoma de México, 1966.

840. Quiñónez Castillo, Zoila. "El trabajo industrial a domicilio y el trabajo doméstico de la mujer." Revista del Ministerio de Trabajo y Bienestar Social, v. 1 (2), 1958: 20-32.

841. "Reglamento de labores peligrosas e insalubres para mujeres y menores." Revista Mexicana de Trabajo, v. 7 (7-8), 1960: 63-69.

842. Romo Chávez Mejía, Enriqueta. "Reformas al código agrario en beneficio de la mujer campesina." Thesis, Universidad Nacional Autónoma de México, 1963.

Caribbean

843. Arocena, Berta. "La mujer cubana y el retiro tabacalero." Ellas, 9 May 1954.

844. Córdova y Cordovés, Efrén. "Trabajo de la mujer." In Efrén Córdova y Cordovés, Derecho Laboral Cubano. Havana: Ed. Lex., 1957: v. 1, 343-350.

845. González del Valle, Ambrosio. "La mujer casada comerciante:

Problemas jurídicos que plantea esta situación." Revista de Derecho Puertorriqueño, v. 7 (27), 1968: 219-224.

846. Lens y Díaz, Eduardo C. La mujer ante el contrato de trabajo. Havana: Ed. Lex., 1948.

Andean Region

847. Alcántara Chávez, César. "El ejercicio del comercio por el menor de edad y la mujer casada." Thesis, Universidad Nacional Mayor de San Marcos, Lima, 1962.

848. Castañeda Durand, Carmen. "La legislación del trabajo de la mujer peruana." Thesis, Universidad Nacional Mayor de San Marcos, Lima 1955.

849. Colombia. Ministerio de Trabajo. El trabajo de la mujer: Disposiciones legales. Bogotá: Imprenta Nacional, 1953.

850. Duque de Carbonell, Martha and Isabel Monsalve Cuellar. "La capacidad de la mujer casada mayor de edad para ejercer el comercio." Univérsitas: Ciencias Jurídicas y Socioeconómicas, v. 26, June 1964: 100-104.

851. Gil Napan, Rosa. "Derecho laboral de la mujer casada." Thesis, Universidad Nacional Mayor de San Marcos, Lima, 1961.

852. Lafosse de Vega-Centeno, Violeta. "La ley de reforma agraria #17716 y sus implicaciones en la estructura familiar." Documento de Trabajo No. 3. Lima: Publicaciones CISEPA, 1971.

853. León de Izaguirre, Virginia. "Legislación del trabajo: Mujer Trabajadora." Lima: EETSA, 1960.

854. "La independencia económica de la mujer casada. Ley No. 28 de 1932 (Colombia)." Negocios Colombo-Americano, April 1933: 800-801.

855. International Labour Organization. "Maternity Protection in Colombia." International Labour Review, v. 49 (6), 1944: 678.

856. Patrón Faura, Pedro. Legislación de la mujer peruana: Prontuario. Lima: Imprenta Colegio Militar Leoncio Prado, 1972.

857. Pérez Guevara, Ada. "Situación de la mujer casada en la legislación de comercio." Progreso y Cultura, June-July 1947.

858. Portocarrero Mori, Jorge L. "Comentarios sobre el regimen

legal del trabajo de mujeres y menores en el Perú." Thesis, Pontificia Universidad Católica, Lima 1971.

859. Urquidi, Arturo. "La reforma agraria en Bolivia." América Indígena, v. 32 (3): 865-880.

Chile and the Platine

860. "Argentina: Beneficios, obligaciones y derechos para el personal que presta servicios en casas de familia, Buenos Aires, 14-1-56, Decreto No. 326." Revista Iberoamericana de Seguros Sociales, v. 5 (2), March-April 1956: 468-475.

861. Argentine Republic. "Decreto No. 1.652/45 reglamentando el trabajo del personal femenino mayor de 18 años en todos los establecimientos del país (Buenos Aires, 24 de enero de 1945)." Boletín Oficial, 2 February 1945: 14+.

862. Del Campo, Guillermina. "Oportunidad y protección en el trabajo." Revista Universitaria Nacional de Córdoba, v. 10 (1-2), 1969: 93-104.

863. Delpino Albornoz, Gioconda. Los empleados del servicio doméstico en la legislación chilena. Santiago: Universidad de Chile, 1948.

864. Guevara, Rafael Eduardo. La mujer y la seguridad social en la legislación argentina. Buenos Aires: Centro Nacional de Documentación e Información Educativa, 1972.

865. International Labour Organization. "New Maternity Protection Act in Chile." Industry and Labour, v. 11 (1), 1954: 493-495.

866. _____. "Night Work of Women in Chile." Industrial and Labour Information, 31 October 1938: 147.

867. Jubilación de la mujer. Santiago: Ed. Gutenberg, 1962 and 1969 (updated).

868. Martínez Vivot, Julio José. Trabajo de menores y mujeres. Estudios de Derecho Social, No. 3. Buenos Aires: Ed. Depalma, 1964.

869. Sciarra de Arico, María Antonieta. "Realidad social y jurídica de la mujer que trabaja." Revista Universitaria Nacional de Córdoba, v. 10 (1/2), March-June 1969: 71-92.

870. Stratia, Osvaldo J. "Capacidad de la mujer casada para formar parte de sociedades comerciales." Revista de Ciencias Jurídicas y Sociales, v. 7 (47), 1946: 95-114.

Brazil

871. Brandao Reis, Daniel Luiz, et al. Trabalho da mulher e do menor. Rio de Janeiro: Ministerio de Trabalho e Previdencia Social, 1965.

872. "Brazilian Regulations on Work of Women in Industry." Monthly Labor Review, October 1932: 833.

873. Callage, Fernando. "O trabalho da mulher em face de legislaçao social brasileira." Cultura política, September 1942: 30-38.

874. Cardone, Marly A. "Influencia da gravidez no contrato de trabalho da mulher." Mimeo. São Paulo: 1965.

875. _____. "Trabalho noturno da mulher." Revista Latino-americana de Trabajo, v. 34 (787), 1970.

876. Catharino, José Martins. "Contrato de trabalho entre marido e esposa." Revista do Trabalho, November-December 1947: 5-8.

877. Kiehl, María. "O trabalho da mulher fora do lar." Boletín do Ministerio do Trabalho, Industria e Comercio, v. 9 (97), September 1942: 97-129.

878. Leite, J. C. P. "Proteção ao trabalho da mulher--Revisão de conceitos." Revista Legislação do Trabalho, v. 39 (32), 1975.

879. Malta, Christovão Piragibe Tostes. "Proteção ao trabalho da mulher." Industria e Produtividade, March 1970.

880. "Regulation of the Employment of Women and Children in Brazil." International Labour Review, April 1943: 515.

881. Rezende, Zeia Pinho. O trabalho e a mulher. Rio de Janeiro: Separata de Jurisdica, Instituto do Açúcar e do Alcool, 1970.

Chapter III

WOMEN AND THE FAMILY

This chapter presents entries dealing with specific roles of women in the familial unity. Section A, "Familial Roles and Statuses," includes references on wifely and maternal duties and privileges, on status in the family setting, and on brideprice and dowry. The latter is cited only in the African section and is valuable for linking women's social and economic positions.

The types of data available differ, and for this reason, the entries for Africa and Latin America diverge slightly. For Africa, entries refer specifically to woman's role or status as wife, mother, daughter, daughter-in-law, etc., and do not include references on the family in general unless part of the work cited deals with or includes a section on women as separate entities. For Latin America, however, a wealth of research on the family unit exists but much less on women's individual roles. This research orientation results from the widespread interest in the phenomenon of machismo, with the descriptions of women's roles and statuses being placed in the context of the family, where her position would be analyzed with respect to that of the male. Consequently, the Latin American entries are less specific than those for Africa.

Under section A, enough entries are identifiable as specific to the rural woman to warrant separating these from general references in the sub-areas of each region. Also, many references for Latin America discuss the phenomenon of the abandoned or unmarried mother. These entries have been compiled separately under section B, "The Single Mother."

A. FAMILIAL ROLES AND STATUSES (Includes wife and maternal roles, status in family structures, bride-price literature).

Africa-General

882. Béart, C. "Intimité: Les Lettres de la fiancée." Présence Africaine, v. 8-9, 1950: 271-288.

883. Briffault, R. The Mothers. A Study of the Origins of Sentiments and Institutions. London: Allen and Unwin, 1927.

884. Brown, E. F. "Hehe Grandmothers." Journal of the Royal Anthropological Institute, v. 65, January-June, 1935: 83-96.

885. Cordier, M. Fabiola. "La Mère et l'enfant africains." Dialogue et Culture, v. 8 (7-8), July-August 1970: 14-17.

886. Gourlay, Rae. "Here Comes the Bride--In Africa." His, v. 26, May 1966: 12-14.

887. Gutkind, Peter C. W. "African Urban Family Life and the Urban System." Journal of Asian and African Studies, v. 1 (1), 1966: 35-46.

888. _____. "African Urban Family Life: Comment on and Analysis of Some Rural-Urban Differences." Cahiers d'Études Africaines, v. 3 (10), 1962-1963: 149-217.

889. Lambo, T. Adeoye. "The Child and the Mother-Child Relationship in Major Cultures of Africa." 1975 reprint from Carnets de l'Enfance, v. 10. Available through UNICEF.

890. Le Beuf, J. P. "Foyers Kotoko." Journal de la Société des Africanistes, 1942: 260-263.

891. "Price is Right." Time, 2 May 1960.

892. du Sacré-Couer, Marie André, Sister. "La Femme dans la famille Africaine." L'Afrique Contemporaine, v. 4 (22), November-December 1965: 15-18.

893. Sinclair, Adelaide. "UNICEF and the African Mother." Journal of the American Association of University Women, v. 54, March 1961: 143-146.

894. Southall, A. "The Position of Women and the Stability of Marriage." In Aiden W. Southall, ed., Social Change in Modern Africa. London: Oxford University Press, 1961.

895. Werner, A., and W. Hichens. The Advice of Mwana Kupoua upon the Wifely Duty. Medstead: The Azanian Press, 1934.

Rural Only

896. Andreski, Iris. Old Wives Tales. London: Routledge and Kegan Paul, 1970.

897. Bloomhill, Greya. "Africa en Famille: Women and Children in a Primitive (Matabele) Society." African World, March 1961: 12-14.

898. Brain, Robert. Bangwa Kinship and Marriage. Cambridge: Cambridge University Press, 1972.

899. Child, H. F. "Family and Tribal Structure: Status of Women." Nada, v. 35, 1958: 65-70.

900. Durtal, J. "Ou en est la femme noire?" Hommes et Mondes, v. 28 (111), 1955: 366-376.

901. Engwall, Martin S. "The Status of Women in a Matrilineal Society." Ph.D. dissertation, Hartford Seminary Foundation, 1941.

902. Goody, Jack. Tradition, Technology and the State in Africa. London: Oxford University Press, 1971.

903. _____. "Bridewealth and Dowry in Africa and Eurasia." In John R. Goody and S. J. Tambiah, eds. Bridewealth and Dowry. Cambridge: Cambridge University Press, 1973: 1-58.

904. Mercier, P. "Le Consentement au mariage et son évolution chez les Betamúradibe." Africa, v. 20 (3), 1950: 219-227.

905. Netting, Robert M. "Household Organization and Intensive Agriculture: The Kofyar Case." Africa, v. 35 (4), 1965: 422-429.

906. Shapera, I. Married Life in an African Tribe. London: Faber, 1940. Also cited as New York: Sheridan House, 1940.

907. Uwemedimo, Rosemary. Mammy-Wagon Marriage. Toronto: Nelson, Foster and Scott, 1961. Also cited as London: Hurst and Blackett, 1961. Autobiography.

West Africa

908. Allen, N. "Ghana: Susa, Mother of Three." Africa Report, v. 18, November 1973: 16-18.

09. Aluko, Timothy Mofolorunso. "Polygamy and the Surplus of Women." West African Review, v. 21 (270), 1950: 259-260.

10. Ariwoola, O. The African Wife (Yoruba). London: O. Ariwoola, 1965.

11. Brandel, M. "Urban Lobolo Attitude: A Preliminary Report." African Studies, v. 17 (1), 1958: 34-50.

12. Clignet, Remi. Many Wives, Many Powers: Authority and Power in Polygynous Families (Abure and Bete, Ivory Coast). Evanston: Northwestern University Press, 1970.

13. Comhaire-Sylvain, Suzanne. "Le Probléme du mariage à Lagos, Nigeria." Revue de l'Institut de Sociologie, v. 4, 1956: 449-521.

14. Cridel, B. "La Jeune fille, l'épouse et la mère dans la societé Kabrè." Documents du Centre d'Études et de Recherches de Kara, 1967: 78-93.

15. Kroch, A., and M. Gessain. "Mari et femme: Analyse des trois contes coniaqui." Bulletin et Mémoires Social Anthropologie, v.2 (1/2), 1967: 97-114.

16. Lloyd, Peter Cutt. "The Status of the Yoruba Wife." Sudan Society, v. 2, 1963: 35-42.

17. Newkirk, G. "Ghanian Women's Perception of the Ideal Child." Journal of Home Economics, v. 59, April 1967: 271-274.

18. Omari, T. P. Marriage Guidance for Young Ghanians. London: Nelson, 1962.

19. _____. "Role Expectation in the Courtship Situation in Ghana." Social Forces, v. 42 (2), December 1963: 147-156.

20. Oppong, Christine. "Nursing Mothers: Aspects of the Conjugal and Maternal Roles of Nurses in Accra." Paper presented at the Canadian African Studies Association Conference, Toronto, February 1975.

21. _____. "Ghanian Women Teachers as Workers, Kin, Wives, and Mothers: A Study of Conjugal Family Solidarity-Norms, Reality, and Stress." Paper presented at the Wellesley Conference on Women and Development, June 1976. Available from Wellesley Center for Research on Women, 828 Washington St., Wellesley, Massachusetts 02181.

922. Pool, Janet F. "A Cross-Comparative Study of Aspects of Conjugal Behavior among Women of Three West African Countries." Canadian Journal of African Studies, v. 6 (2), 1972: 233-259.

923. "Quelques coutumes particulières du mariage au Cameroun." Togo-Cameroun, 1929: 58-64.

Rural Only

924. Bekombo, Manga. "La Femme, le mariage et la compensation matrimoniale en pays Dwala." Ethnographie, v. 62-63, 1968-69: 179-188.

925. Birahim, B. "Les Bobos, la famille, les coutumes." Education Africaine, v. 23, 1954: 61-75.

926. Bledsoe, Caroline Hazel. "Women and Marriage in Kpelle Society" Ph.D. dissertation, Stanford University, 1976.

927. Brygoo, J. "Le Nouveau-né et la femme enceinte aux environs d'ayos." Bulletin de la Société d'Études Camerounaises, v. 21-22 June-September 1948: 49-68.

928. Fegan, Ethel S. "Some Notes on the Bachama Tribe, Adamawa Province, Northern Provinces, Nigeria." Journal of the African Society, v. 29 (115), April 1930: 269-279; v. 29 (116), July 1930 376-400.

929. Fonsica, Claudia. "I Didn't Choose My Husband; My Father Gave Me to Him. An Inquiri on the Situation of Woman Villagers in Upper Volta." UNESCO Courier, v. 28, August 1975: 5-12.

930. Gomila, J. "Note sur le polygamie et la fécondité respective des hommes et des femmes chez les Bedik (Sénégal Oriental)." Bulletins et Mémoires de la Société d'Anthropologie de Paris, v. 5 (1-4), 1969: 5-16.

931. Goody, Esther N. Contexts of Kinship: An Essay in the Family Sociology of the Gonja of North Ghana. Cambridge: Cambridge University Press, 1973.

932. Grandmaison, Collette le Cour. "Stratégies matrimonales des femmes dakaroises." Cahiers OSTROM, v. 8 (2), 1971: 201-220.

933. Herskovits, M. J. "A Note on 'Woman Marriage' in Dahomey." Africa, v. 10, 1937: 335-341.

934. Konan, M. A. "Occupations and Family Patterns among the Hausa in North Nigeria." Samaru Misc. Paper, no. 52. Zaria, Nigeria: Institute for Agricultural Research, 1975.

935. Mirchaulum, P. T. "The Survival of the Matrilineal System among the Longuda of Nigeria." Paper presented at the annual meeting of the African Studies Association, San Francisco, October-November 1975.

936. Ortoli, Henri. "Le Déces d'une femme enceinte chez les Dogon de Bandiagara." Bulletin de L'IFAN, v. 3 (1/4), January-October 1941: 64-73.

937. Prost, R. P. "Marriage and the Condition of Women, in 'Notes sur les Sonhay'." Bulletin de L'IFAN, 1954: 193-213.

938. du Sacré-Coeur, Marie André, Sister. La Condition humaine en Afrique noire. Paris: Grasset, 1953.

939. Taraore, Dominique. "Yaru hã ou mariages entre femmes chez les Boho Niéniégué." Journal de la Société des Africanistes, v. 11 (1/2), 1941: 197-200.

940. Uchendu, Victor Chikezie. "Concubinage among Ngwa Igbo of Southern Nigeria." Africa, v. 35 (2), April 1965: 187-197.

Central Africa

941. Bernard, Guy. "Conjugalité et rôle de la femme à Kinshasa." Canadian Journal of African Studies, v. 6 (2), 1972: 261-274.

942. Charles, V. "L'Équilibre des sexes parmi les adultes dans les milieux extra-coutumiers." Zaire, v. 3 (1), January 1949: 47-51.

943. Dutilleux, G. "L'Opinion des femmes du centre extra-coutumier d'Élisabethville sur le mariage, la famille, l'éducation des enfants." Bulletin du CEPSI, v. 17, 1951: 219-223.

944. Estermann, Carlos. "A mulher e dois filhos: Conto com diversos elementos aculturados." Boletim do Instituto de Angola, v. 17, January-December 1963: 59-72.

945. Frazão, Francisco Serra. "A mulher na fàmilia gentflica." Mensário Administrativo, v. 55/56, March-April 1952: 9.

946. Makonga, Bonaventure. La Mère africaine. Brussels: Editions Remarques Congolaises, 1964.

947. Pauwels, Marcel. "Finacée et jeune mariée au Ruanda." Zaire, v. 5 (2), February 1951: 115-135.

948. Sendanyoye, Gratien. "De la situation des veuves et de leur déplacement en dehors de la résidence maritale." Bulletin de Jurisprudence de Ruanda-Urindi, v. 10, 1952: 515-517.

949. Sohier, A. "Le Rôle de la femme dans la famille congolaise." Etapes, v. 21, 1947: 93-97.

Rural Only

950. Bradley, K. "My Cow, My Wife and my Old Clay Pipe." African Observer, v. 7 (3), 1937: 33-37.

951. Colson, Elizabeth. Marriage and the Family among the Plateau Tonga of Northern Rhodesia. Manchester: Manchester University Press, 1958.

952. Decapmaker. "Sanctions coutumières contre l'adultère chez les Bakongo de la région de Kasi." Congo, 1939: 134-148.

953. Dick-Read, Grantley. No Time for Fear. London: Heinemann, 1955.

954. Frazão, Francisco Serra. "A mulher e o casamento." Mensário Administrativo, v. 51-52, 1951: 47-58.

955. Kagame, A. "Les Organisations socio-familiales de l'ancien Ruanda." Memoires de L'Academie Royale des Sciences Coloniales, Classe des Sciences Morales et Politique, v. 38 (3), 1954: 71-94.

956. Lancaster, Chet S. "The Economics of Social Organization in an Ethnic Border Zone: The Goba (Northern Shona) of the Zambezi Valley." Ethnology, v. 10, 1971: 445-465.

957. Pailloux, René. "La Place de la femme chez les Babemba." Pères Blancs, v. 98, 1952: 10-15; v. 99: 9-14. Also cited as: Grands Lacs, v. 164, 1953: 9-16; v. 165: 37-40.

958. Richards, Audrey I. "Some Types of Family Structure amongst the Central Bantu." In A. R. Radcliffe-Brown and C. Daryll Forde, eds., African Systems of Kinship and Marriage. London: Oxford University Press, 1950: 207-251.

959. Van Caeneghen, R. "La Femme du Lupangu." Zaire, v. 6 (5), May 1952: 463-486; v. 6 (6), June 1952: 569-595.

East Africa

960. Were, Miriam Khamadi. The Eighth Wife. Nairobi: East Africa Pub. House, 1972.

Rural Only

961. Alberto, Manuel Simões. "A mulher indígena moçambicana perante a estrutura familiar da tribo." Boletim da Sociedade de Estudos Moçambique, v. 24 (83), January-February 1954: 93-104.

962. Bauer, Dan F. "The Tigray Household: A Decision Analysis of Ethiopian Social Organization." Lansing: Michigan State University, Committee on Ethiopian Studies of the African Studies Center, April 1976.

963. Culwick, Arthur T., and G. M. Culwick. "The Functions of Bride-Wealth in Ubena of the Rivers." Africa, v. 7, 1934: 140-159.

964. _____. "Fostermothers in Ulanga." Tanganyika Notes and Records, no. 1, March 1936: 19-24.

965. Dalton, George. "Bride-Wealth vs. Bride-Price (among the Sonjo People)." American Anthropologist, v. 68, June 1966: 732-738.

966. Gray, Robert F. "Sonjo Bride-Price and the Question of African 'Wife Purchase.'" American Anthropologist, v. 62 (1), February 1960: 34-57.

967. Gulliver, P. H. "Reply (to Sonjo Bride-Price and the Question of African Wife Purchase. R. F. Gray, v. 62, February 1960: 34-57)." American Anthropologist, v. 63, October 1961: 1098-1100.

968. Huber, Hugo. "Woman-Marriage in Some East African Societies." Anthropos, v. 63-64 (5-6), 1968-1969: 745-752.

Southern Africa

969. Lessing, Doris. A Man and Two Women. New York: Simon and Schuster, 1963.

970. Pierard, Richard V. "The Transportation of White Women to German Southwest Africa, 1898-1914." Race, v. 12 (3), January 1971: 317-322.

Latin America-General

971. Aguilar Alvarez, Ernesto. "Sociedad y familia." Istmo, v. 68, May-June 1970: 7-16.

972. Buompadre, Anna María. "El mito de la madre universal." Comunidad, v. 4 (2), October 1969: 633-639.

973. Carlos, Manuel L., and Lois Sellers. "Family, Kinship Structure, and Modernization in Latin America." Latin American Research Review, v. 7 (2), 1972: 95-124.

974. Godoy Urzua, Hernán. "Bosquejo sociológico de la familia en América Latina." Ciencias Sociales, v. 4 (30-31), January-February 1967: 55-64.

975. Pezet, Magdalena H. de. "La autoridad paterna en la vida familiar." Tierra y Dos Mares, v. 7 (37), December 1967: 16.

Mexico and Central America

976. Altmann Smythe, Julio. "La familia como realidad social." Criminalia, v. 33, February 1967: 80-90.

977. Anitua, Santiago de. "¿Hacia dónde va la institución familiar contemporánea?" Estudios Centroamericanos, v. 2 (245), February 1969: 9-15.

978. de Hoyos, A., and G. de Hoyos. "The Amigo System and Alienation of the Wife in the Conjugal Mexican Family." In B. Farber, ed., Kinship and Family Organization. London: Wiley, 1966.

979. Esteva Fabregat, Claudio. "Familia y matrimonio en México: El patrón Cultural." Revista de Indias, v. 29 (115-118), 1969: 173-278.

980. Hayner, Norman S. "The Family in Mexico." Journal of Marriage and Family Living, v. 14 (4), November 1954: 369-373.

981. _____. "Notes on the Changing Mexican Family." Journal of Marriage and Family Living, v. 7 (4), 1942: 489-497.

982. Hubbell, Linda J. "The Network of Kinship, Friendship, and Compadrazgo among Middle Class Mexican Women." Paper presented at the 7th Annual Meeting of the American Anthropological Association, New York, 1971.

983. Hutchinson, M. "Un estudio sobre la institución del matrimonio con examen especial de sus impedimentos." Thesis, Universidad de Panamá, 1966.

984. Leñero Otero, Luis. Investigación de la familia en México; presentación y avance de resultados de una encuesta nacional. Mexico: IMES, 1968.

985. Lewis, Oscar. The Children of Sánchez. New York: Random House, 1961.

986. _____, Five Families. Mexican Case Studies in the Culture of Poverty. New York: The New American Library, 1959.

987. McGinn, Noel F. "Marriage and Family in Middle-Class Mexico." Journal of Marriage and the Family, v. 28 (3), August 1966: 305-313.

988. Murdock, George Peter. "La familia nuclear." La Palabra y el Hombre, v. 31, July-September 1964: 343-363.

989. Nolan, Mary Lee. Aspects of Middle Class Family Organization in Monterrey, Mexico. Master's Thesis, University of Texas, 1967.

990. Paredes, Querubina de, and Armando Mendoza Suría. "Consideración sobre la familia en El Salvador." Revista Salvadoreña de Ciencias Sociales, v. 1, January-March 1965: 165-186.

991. Peñalosa, F. "Mexican Family Roles." Journal of Marriage and the Family, v. 30, November 1968: 680-689.

992. Ramírez, Santiago, and Ramón Parres. "Some Dynamic Patterns in the Organization of the Mexican Family." International Journal of Social Psychiatry, v. 3, Summer 1957: 18-21.

993. Villaseñor Martínez, Irene. "El Mexicano: La familia." Thesis, University of Guadalajara, 1964.

994. Williamson, Robert C. "Some Variables of Middle and Lower Class in the Central American Cities." Social Forces, v. 42, December 1962: 195-207.

995. Zetina Lozano, Guadalupe. "El trabajo de la mujer y su vida familiar." In María del Carmen Elu de Leñero, ed. Mujeres que hablan. Mexico City: Instituto Mexicano de Estudios Sociales, 1971: 164-183.

996. _____. "El trabajo de la mujer casada y su vida familiar ante el cambio social." Thesis, Ibero-American University, Mexico City, 1972.

Rural Only

997. Bushnell, J. H., and D. D. Bushnell. "Sociocultural and Psychodynamic Correlates of Polygyny in a Highland Mexican Village." Ethnology, v. 10, January 1971: 44-55.

998. Gross, Joseph J. "Domestic Group Structure in a Mayan Community of Guatemala." Ph.D. dissertation, University of Rochester, 1974.

999. Humphrey, Norman Daymont. "Family Patterns in a Mexican Middletown." Social Service Review, v. 26 (2), June 1952: 195-201.

1000. Lewis, Oscar. Life in a Mexican Village. Tepoztlán Restudied. Urbana, Ill.: University of Illinois Press, 1951.

1001. Monteil, Marie Noelle. "Campesinas en el norte de México." Boletín Documental sobre las Mujeres, v. 4 (3), 1974: 32-34.

1002. Moore, G. Alexander. Life Cycles in Atchalán. The Diverse Careers of Certain Guatemalans. New York: Teachers College Press, 1973. Chapters 3 and 4.

1003. Moreno, Antonio de P. "Grupos y cuasi-grupos sociales de la comunidad rural." Estudios Sociales, v. 1, 1955: 249-281.

1004. Nutini, Hugo G. San Bernadino Contla: Marriage and Family Structure in a Tlaxcalan Municipio. Pittsburgh: University of Pittsburgh Press, 1968.

1005. Plattner, S. "Occupation and Marriage in a Mexican Trading Community." Southwestern Journal of Anthropology, v. 28, Summer 1972: 193-206.

1006. Slegel, Morris. "Effects of Culture Contacts on the Form of the Family in a Guatemalan Village." Journal of the Royal Anthropological Institute of Great Britain and Ireland, v. 72, 1942: 55-68.

1007. Young, F. W., and R. C. Young. "Differentiation of Family Structure in Rural Mexico." Journal of Marriage and the Family v. 30, February 1968: 154-161.

Caribbean

1008. Fernández Méndez, Eugenio. "Algunos cambios culturales, económicos, y sociales que afectan la familia en Puerto Rico." Revista de Ciencias Sociales, v. 8 (2), June 1964: 167-173.

1009. Lewis, Oscar. La Vida: A Puerto Rican Family in a Culture of Poverty in San Juan and New York. New York: Random House, 1966.

1010. Rodríguez, Aníbal C. "Sobre la familia cubana." Universidad de la Habana, v. 26 (156), May-June 1962: 7-29.

1011. Safa, Helen I. "From Shantytown to Public Housing: A Comparison of Family Structure in Two Urban Neighborhoods." Caribbean Studies, v. 4 (1), 1964.

Rural Only

1012. Buitrago Ortíz, Carlos. Esperanza: An Ethnographic Study of a Peasant Community in Puerto Rico. Viking Fund Publications in Anthropology, no. 50. Tucson: University of Arizona Press, 1973.

Andean Region

1013. Abouhamad, Jeannette. Los hombres de Venezuela. Caracas: Universidad Central de Venezuela, 1969.

1014. Alcántara de Samaniego, Elsa. "Estructura de la autoridad en la familia peruana." Thesis, Pontífica Universidad Católica, Lima, 1970.

1015. Anderson, Jeanine. "Estudio de la clase media peruana, Residencial San Felipe." Ph.D. dissertation, Cornell University, 1973.

1016. Angulo, Alejandro. "La familia colombiana." Revista Javeriana, v. 72 (359), October 1969: 364-367.

1017. Arriaga, Eduardo E. "Some Aspects of Family Composition in Venezuela." Eugenics Quarterly, v. 15 (3), 1968: 177-190.

1018. Castro de la Mata, Renato, et al. "Dinámica de la familia peruana." Revista de Ciencias Psicológicas y Neurológicas, v. 4, 1964.

1019. _____. "Un intento de clasificación de la familia peruana." Thesis, Universidad Cayetano Heredia, Lima, 1972.

1020. Centro de Estudios Sociales con AITEC. Efectos del empleo sobre el status de la mujer. Estudios de caso con una muestra de mujeres del barrio las Minas de Baustra, July 1975. Available from CES, Apartado 14.385, Caracas, Venezuela.

1021. Corredor, Berta. La familia en América Latina. Bogotá: Oficina Internacional de Investigaciones Sociales de FERES, 1962.

1022. Gallagher, Mary Liam, Sister. "Social Class and Social Change in the Colombian Family." Ph.D. dissertation, St. Louis University, 1964.

1023. Gamboa Villarroel, Miryam, and E. Javier Alonso Hernández. La familia en Lima. Lima: Collección Santo Toribio de Mogrovejo, 1968.

1024. García de Mejía, Martha Olga. Mujer, participación y planificación familiar. Bogotá: Population Reference Bureau, 1973.

1025. Gutiérrez de Pineda, Virginia. Estructura, función, y cambio en la familia en Colombia. Bogotá: Asociación Colombiana de la Facultad de Medicina, 1975.

1026. _____. "La familia en Colombia: Estudio antropológico." Paper. Bogotá: Oficina Internacional de Investigaciones Sociales de FERES, 1963.

1027. _____. Familia y cultura en Colombia. Bogotá: Tercer Mundo, 1968. Reissued by Instituto Colombiano de Cultura, 1975.

1028. Jaramillo J., Alfredo. "Estructura familiar: Estudio sobre los sectores populares de Quito, Ecuador." Revista Paraguaya de Sociología, v. 10 (28), September-December 1973: 59-152.

1029. Rosenthal, Celia Stopnicka. "Lower Class Family Organization on the Caribbean Coast of Colombia." Pacific Sociology Review, v. 3 (1), Spring 1960: 12-17.

1030. Schrimshaw, Susan C. "A Description of Non-Coresidential Polygyny in Spanish Ecuador." Paper presented at the 70th Annual Meeting of the American Anthropological Association, New York, 1971.

1031. Veliz Lizarraga, Jesús. "Cambio social en familias del Perú." Revista de Sociología (Lima), v. 4 (6), January-June 1967: 114-144.

Rural Only

1032. James, William Russell. "Household Composition and Domestic Groups in a Highland Colombian Village." Ph.D. dissertation, University of Wisconsin, 1972.

1033. Moxley, R. L. "Family Solidarity and Quality of Life in an Agricultural Peruvian Community." Journal of Marriage and the Family, v. 35, August 1973: 497-504.

1034. Ruiz Zamalloa. "Participación de la familia y de la comunidad en el proceso de cambio." Documento no. 02-2. Lima: UNIPM Ministerio de Educación, 1972.

1035. Yepes del Pozo, Juan. "Grupos y cuasi-grupos sociales de la comunidad rural." Estudios Sociales, v. 1, 1955: 299-320.

Chile and the Platine

1036. Alvarez Andrews, Oscar. "El problema de la familia en Chile." Revista Mexicana de Sociología, v. 20 (2), May-August 1958: 413-428.

1037. Calderón Beltrão P. Familia y política social: Con un apéndice sobre la familia en Argentina. Buenos Aires: Ed. Sudamericana, 1963.

1038. Chamorro Greca, Eva. "La mujer en la estructura familiar." Revista Universitaria Nacional de Córdova, v. 10 (1-2), March-June 1969: 221-240.

1039. Cuevillas, Fernando. "La familia argentina ante el cambio social." América Latina, v. 7 (3), July-September 1964: 73-87.

1040. Economía Humana y Unión Nacional Católica de Acción Social. La familia en Montevideo. Montevideo: 1956.

1041. "Editorial: La familia en esta hora argentina." Estudios, no. 543, May 1963: 163-168.

1042. Fabbri, Enrique E. "Del sentido de la mujer en la pareja humana." Boletín Documental sobre las Mujeres, v. 4 (4), 1974: 25-40.

1043. Ganon, Isaac. "Sobre la familia uruguaya." Boletín Uruguayo de Sociología, v. 3 (4-5), August 1963: 7-24.

1044. Heintz, Peter. "La familia de clase baja en transición." Santiago: FLACSO, 1965. Also cited as Revista Latinoamericana de Sociología, v. 3 (3), November 1967: 433-447.

1045. Solari, Aldo E., and Rolando Franco. "La familia en el Uruguay." América Latina, v. 14 (3-4), July-December 1971: 3-33.

1046. Storni, Fernando. "Reformas sociales en torno de la familia." Estudios, v. 546, August 1963: 411-414.

Rural Only

1047. Forni, Floreal Homero. "Familia y sociedad rural en la Argentina." Cuadernos Latinoamericanos de Economía Humana, v. 5 (13), 1962: 59-69.

1048. Nuñez Carballo, Gabriel. "La familia en el Paraguay: Organización y función." Boletín de la Facultad de Derecho y Ciencias Sociales, v. 26 (4), 1962: 161-175.

1049. Sosa, Sonia, et al. Paso de las flores: Vida de la familia en el Uruguay rural. Montevideo: Ed. Signo, 1968.

Brazil

1050. Aguiar, Neuma. "Brazilian Families and Households in Different Systems of Production." Paper presented at the Wellesley Conference on Women and Development, June 1976. Available from Wellesley Center for Research on Women, 828 Washington St., Wellesley, Massachusetts 02181.

1051. Araujo, Alceu Maynard. "A familia numa comunidade alagoana." Sociologia (São Paulo), v. 17 (2), May 1955: 113-131.

1052. Azevedo, Thales de. "Family, Marriage, and Divorce in Brazil." In R. Adams, ed., Contemporary Cultures and Societies of Latin America. New York: Random House, 1965. Also cited (in Portuguese as Journal of Interamerican Studies, v. 3 (2), April 1961: 213-237

1053. Berlinck, Manoel Tosta. "The Structure of the Brazilian Family in the City of São Paulo." Ph.D. dissertation, Cornell University 1969.

1054. Brazil. Novos direitos e deveres da mulher casada e da companheira. Rio de Janeiro: Grafica Auriverde, 1975.

1055. Candido, A. "The Brazilian Family." In T. Lynn Smith and A. Marchant, eds., Brazil: Portrait of Half a Continent. New York: 1951.

1056. Candido, Antonio. "A vida familial do Caipira." Sociologia v. 16 (4), October 1954: 341-367.

1057. Frazier, E. Franklin. "The Negro Family in Bahía, Brazil." In Olen Leonard and Charles Loomis, eds., Readings. Lansing: Michigan State University Press, 1953.

1058. Freitas, Eurídice. "Aspectos e tendencias da familia em transição." Arquivos Brasileiros de Psicotecnia, v. 20 (1), March 1968: 79-90.

1059. Freyre, Gilberto. Casa-grande y senzala: Formaçao da familia brasileira sob o regimen de economia patriarchal. Rio de Janeiro: Schmidt, 1938.

1060. Gonçalves, Maria Aparecida A. Mulher você. Petropolis: Ed. Vozes, 1967.

1061. Guerrero, Sylvia H. "Marital and Family Satisfaction among Women Migrants in Brasilia." Thesis, University of Wisconsin, 1972.

1062. Harblin, Thomas Devaney. "Urbanization, Industrialization, and Low-Income Family Organization in São Paulo, Brazil." Ph.D. dissertation, Cornell University, 1971.

1063. Hutchinson, Carmelita J. A. "Notas preliminares ao estudo de familia no Brasil." In Anais da II Reunião Brasileira de Antropología, Bahia: 1957.

1064. Landes, Ruth. "A Cult Matriarchate and Male Homosexuality." Journal of Abnormal and Social Psychology, v. 35, 1940: 386-397.

1065. Martine, George. Formación de la familia y marginalidad urbana en Rio de Janeiro. Santiago: Celade, 1975.

1066. Medina, Carlos Alberto de. Familia e mudança. Petrópolis: Ed. Vozes, 1974.

1067. _____. et al. "Condições socioculturais do relacionamento familiar na transformação de sociedade brasileira." America Latina, v. 16, 1973: 3-37.

1068. Mendonça, Lycia de. "Nupcialidade no Rio de Janeiro." America Latina (Rio de Janeiro), v. 9 (2), April-June 1966: 103-137.

1069. Moreira, Aldemar. "A familia Paulista." In J. V. Marcondes, et al., eds., São Paulo: Espirito, povo e institucões. São Paulo: Liv. Pioneira, 1968: 299-307.

1070. Riveiro, René. "The Amaziado Relationship and Other Aspects of the Family in Recife (Brazil)." American Sociological Review, v. 10 (1), 1945.

1071. Rios, José Arthur. "Clase e familia no Brasil." Digesto Econômico, v. 6 (66), May 1950: 27-134.

1072. Rodríguez de Almeida, Maria Leda. "Familia e desenvolvimento: Uma análise bibliográfica." America Latina (Rio de Janeiro), v. 15, 1972: 123-156.

1073. Trombetta, Bruno. "Evolução sociocultural da familia." Ed. Vozes, v. 63 (6), June 1969: 572-575.

1074. Wilkening, E. A. "The Role of the Extended Family in Migration and Adaptation in Brazil." University of Wisconsin Land Tenure Center Reprint, no. 23. Madison: Land Tenure Center, 1967.

1075. Willems, Emilio. "A estrutura da família brasileira." Sociologia, (São Paulo) v. 16 (4), 1954: 327-340.

1076. _____. "The Structure of the Brazilian Family." Social Forces, v. 31 (4), May 1953: 339-345.

1077. Yahn, Mario. Preparación para el matrimonio: Cursos para novias. Buenos Aires: Ed. Humanitas, 1963.

Rural Only

1078. Costa, Esdras Borges. "Relações de família em Cerrado e Retiro." Sociologia, (São Paulo), v. 17 (2), May 1955: 132-146.

1079. Ferrari, Alfonso Trujillo. "A família em Potengi." Sociologia, (São Paulo) v. 17 (2), May 1955: 147-162.

1080. Hutchinson, Harry W. Village and Plantation Life in Northeastern Brazil. Seattle: University of Washington Press, 1957: 127-155.

1081. Pierson, Donald. "Familia e compadrio numa comunidade rural paulista." Sociologia (São Paulo), v. 15 (4), October 1954.

1082. Ribeiro, René. "Urbanizacão e familismo no Nordeste do Brasil." Boletim do Instituto Joaquim Nabuco de Pesquisas Sociais, v. 10, 1961: 63-79.

B. THE SINGLE MOTHER

Latin America--General

1083. Torres, Kay Sutherland. "Woman Focality in a Latin American Slum." Master's thesis, University of Texas, 1968.

Mexico and Central America

1084. Balli, Antonio. "No hay salvación para los hombres." Revista de Filosofía de la Universidad de Costa Rica, v. 7 (24), January-June 1969: 3-16.

1085. Campos, N. Moreno de. "Algunos factores que han influído en la condición social de las 100 madres solteras embarazadas atendidas en la Clínica Prenatal del área sanitaria de Colón." Thesis,

Universidad de Panamá, 1969.

1086. Folan, William J., and Phil C. Weigand. "Fictive Widowhood in Rural and Urban Mexico." Anthropologica, v. 10 (1), 1968: 119-127.

1087. González, Nancy L. Solien. Black Carib Household Structure: A Study of Migration and Modernization. Seattle: University of Washington Press, 1969.

1088. Martínez Domínguez, Alfonso. "No podemos hablar de justicia plena mientras hay muchos miles de mujeres y niños abandonados." Discurso. Mexico: Congreso Nacional Femenil Cetemista, 1969.

1089. Sanford, Margaret Sellars. "Disruption of the Mother-Child Relationship in Conjunction with Matrifocality: A Study of Child-Keeping among the Carib and Creole of British Honduras." Ph.D dissertation, Catholic University of America, 1971.

1090. Suárez, Luis. "El lastre humano de las mujeres abandonadas." Mañana, v. 64 (646), 14 January 1958: 38-42.

1091. Vega, Juan Ramón, and Greer Taylor. El concubinato en América Central. Cuernavaca: CIDOC, 1966.

1092. Wiest, Raymond E. "Wage-Labor Migration and Household Maintenance in a Central Mexican Town." Ph.D. dissertation, University of Oregon, 1970.

1093. _____. "Wage-Labor Migration and the Female-Headed Household: Cases from Central Mexico." Paper presented at the 69th Annual Meeting of the American Anthropological Association, November 1970.

Caribbean

1094. Safa, Helen I. "Female-Based Households in Public Housing." Human Organization, v. 24, 1965.

Andean Region

1095. Arias Cuneo, Martha. "El concepto cristiano de la familia y el problema de la madre soltera." Thesis, Universidad Nacional Mayor de San Marcos, Lima, 1970.

1096. Betancur, Cayetano. "La madre soltera." Arco, no. 171, 1975: 9-12.

1097. Chu Rubio, Rosa. "El problema de las madres solteras en el pueblo joven 'El Obrero' de Sullana." Thesis, Instituto Nacional de Investigación y Desarrollo de la Educación, 1973.

1098. Gonzáles Montalvo, Vicente. "Los derechos de la concubina." Thesis, Universidad Nacional Mayor de San Marcos, Lima, 1954.

1099. Samanez Concha, Elsa E. "Protección a la madre abandonada." Thesis, Universidad Nacional Mayor de San Marcos, Lima, 1972.

Chile and the Platine

1100. Bauzá, Julio A. "Informe sobre lo que ha podido realizar el Uruguay acerca de las recomendaciones expuestas en los diferentes capítulos del Acta Final del VIII Congreso Panamericano del Niño." Boletín del Instituto Internacional Americano de Protección a la Infancia, v. 23 (1), March 1949: 55-64.

1101. Forni, Floreal Homero. "Familia y sociedad rural en la Argentina." Cuadernos Latinoamericanos de Economía, Humana, v. 5 (13), 1962: 59-69.

Brazil

1102. Bock, E. Wilbur and Sugiyama Intaka. "Social Status, Mobility, and Premarital Pregnancy: A Case of Brazil." Journal of Marriage and the Family, v. 32 (2), May 1976: 284-192.

1103. Gonzaga, João Bernardino. "Do crime de abandono de familia." Revista da Universidade Católica de São Paulo, v. 30 (55-57), July 1965-March 1966: 18-30.

1104. Mortara, Giorgio. "As mães solteiras no Brasil." Revista Brasileira de Estatistica, v. 22 (85-86), January-June 1961: 1-32.

Chapter IV

WOMEN AND RELIGION

Chapter 4 consists of a sample of works dealing with the interaction between women's roles and religion. African references cover such topics as religious participation and the implication of Christianity and Islam for change in women's roles and statuses. The Latin American references deal principally with the influence of the Roman Catholic Church over women and its importance in defining women's roles, past and present.

Works included in this chapter are selective for the effect of religion on women or on participation in the development process. Not included are descriptions of religious ritual participation nor biographies and autobiographies of religious leaders or missionaries (with the exception of 1109).

Africa--General

1105. Berger, Iris. "Women, Religion, and Social Change: East and Central African Perspectives." Paper presented at the Wellesley Conference on Women and Development, June 1976. Available from Wellesley Center for research on Women, 828 Washington St., Wellesley, Massachusetts 02181.

1106. "Christian Conference on African Women." Shield, v. 45, December 1965-January 1966: 18.

1107. Cooke, E. M. "Reintegration of the Social Life of Native Women and Girls." In The Relignment of Native Life on a Christian Basis. Lovedale: Institution Press, 1928: 71-76.

1108. Gantin, Bernardine. "Christianity and the African Woman." World Mission, v. 13, Summer 1962: 13-22.

1109. Graham, J. R. "Moral Impact of the Gospel: A Record of Thirty Years' Work amongst African Women." International Review of Missions, v. 9, January 1920: 95-105.

1110. Holas, Bohumil. "L'Évolution du schéma initiatique chez les femmes Oubi." Africa, v. 27 (3), 1957: 241-250.

1111. Kilson, Marion. "Women in African Traditional Religions." Paper presented at the Wellesley Conference on Women and Development, June 1976. Available from Wellesley Center for research on Women, 828 Washington St., Wellesley, Massachusetts 02181. Forthcoming in Journal of Religion in Africa.

1112. National Catholic Welfare Conference, Office for United Nations Affairs. "African Women Speak." In Charles W. Forman, ed., Christianity in the Non-Western World. Englewood Cliffs, N.J.: Prentice-Hall, Inc., 1967: 131-136.

1113. Reyburn, William D. "The Church, Male and Female." Practical Anthropology, v. 4 (4), July-August 1957: 140-145.

1114. Reynolds, R. "Women in Africa: Notes on Religious and Social Trends." Antioch Review, v. 14, 1954: 312-322.

1115. Senior, M. M. "Women in the African Village Church." International Review of Missions, v. 37, October 1948: 403-409.

1116. Tanganyika Rapid Social Change Study Commission "E". The Church and the Role and Place of Women in a Changing Society. Dodoms: Central Tanganyika Press, 1968.

West Africa

1117. Adekogbe, E. "La Femme au Nigeria." Perspectives de Catholicité, v. 19 (3), 1960: 16-23.

1118. Barkow, Jerome H. "Hausa Women and Islam." Canadian Journal of African Studies, v. 6 (2), 1972: 317-388.

1119. Holas, Bohumil. "Décès d'une femme guerzé (circle de Nzérékoré)." Africa, v. 23 (2), April 1953: 145-155.

1120. Michson, E. K. Woman is Poison. Accra: State Publishing Corp., 1968(?).

1121. Rattray, R. S. "Widows and 'In-Laws' at Funerals." In

Religion and Art in Ashanti. Oxford: Clarendon Press, 1927: 171-174.

1122. Wilbois, J. L'Action sociale en pays de missions. Paris: Payot, 1939.

1123. Yeld, E. R. "Educational Problems among Women and Girls in Sokoto Province of Northern Nigeria." Sociologus, v. 11 (2), v. 11 (2), 1961: 160-173.

Central Africa

1124. Stefaniszyn, Bronislaw. Social and Ritual Life of the Ambo of Northern Rhodesia. London: International African Institute, 1964.

East Africa

1125. Earthy, E. D. "The Customs of Gazaland Women in Relation to the African Church." International Review of Missions, v. 15, 1926: 662-674.

1126. Harris, G. "Possession Hysteria in a Kenya Tribe." American Anthropologist, v. 59, December 1957: 1046-1066.

1127. Levine, Robert A. "Witchcraft and Co-Wife Proximity in Southwestern Kenya (Gusil, Kipsigis, Luo)." Ethnology, v. 1 (1), January 1962: 39-45.

Southern Africa

1128. Brandel-Syrier, Mia. Black Women in Search of God. London: Lutterworth, 1962.

Latin America--General

1129. Bandeira, Marina. "Diagnóstico acerca de la libertad de la mujer." Boletín Documental sobre las mujeres, v. 1 (1), 1971: 43-51.

1130. Borges Costa, Leticia, et al. "El rol de la mujer en la iglesia y en la sociedad." In Ponencias de las Jornadas Ecuménicas Latinoamericanas. Piriapolis, Uruguay: 1967.

1131. Crespo Toral, Remigio. La mujer en el plan divino. Quito: Imp. de Santo Domingo, 1932.

1132. Kinzer, Nora Scott. "Priests, Machos, and Babies: Or, Latin American Women and the Manichaean Heresy." Journal of Marriage and the Family, v. 35 (2), 1973: 300-312.

1133. Sánchez Morales, Aurelia Guadalupe. "Arquetipos y estereotipos religiosos. Su impacto en las relaciones hombre-mujer." Boletín Documental sobre las Mujeres, v. 4 (1), 1974: 4-22.

1134. Vallier, I. Catholicism, Social Control and Modernization in Latin America. Englewood Cliffs, N. J.: Prentice-Hall, Inc., 1970.

Andean Region

1135. Beaton, Catherine. "La mujer en la iglesia, objeto de discriminación." SIC: Revista Venezolana de Orientación, v. 31 (302), February 1968: 57-64.

1136. Flora, Cornelia Butler. "Pentecostal Women in Colombia: Religious Change and the Status of Working Class Women." Journal of Interamerican Studies and World Affairs, v. 17 (4), November 1975: 411-425.

Chile and the Platine

1137. Gilfeather, Katharine. "Women and Ministry." America, October 1976.

1138. _____. "Women--Changing Role Models in the Catholic Church in Chile." Paper presented at the Wellesley Conference on Women and Development, June 1976. Available from Wellesley Center for Research on Women, 828 Washington St., Wellesley, Massachusetts 02181. Forthcoming in Journal for the Scientific Study of Religion.

Brazil

1139. Albuquerque, João Batista da Mota. "A igreja e a familia brasileira." Sintese política, Econômica e Social, v. 7 July-September 1960: 6-14.

1140. Pessar, Patricia. "Religious Models and Roles for Brazilian Women." Paper presented at the Wellesley Conference on Women and Development, June 1976. Available from Wellesley Center for Research on Women, 828 Washington St., Wellesley, Massachusetts 02181.

Chapter V

WOMEN AND EDUCATION

Included in chapter 5 are materials dealing with women's participation in educational programs, both formal and non-formal, and the impact of education on women's roles and statuses. The entries in section A, General Topics, focus on the relationship between formal education and labor force participation, the incidence of education for females, and comparisons of male and female participation in educational programs. Section B, Specialized Training, contains references ranging from literacy, community education, vocational training and other non-formal instruction to specialized training in the professions. Leadership training and political education are also included, although they are limited to Latin America.

The preponderance of entries for Africa is attributable to the long range and widespread interest in female education from a variety of sources. These include early colonial governments and missionaries and the recent concern by international agencies and local governments over the effects of nontraditional education. Entries dealing specifically with the education of young girls in Africa have been identified under a subcategory entitled, "Education of Girls," and follow those entries dealing with all females or with adults only, which are listed under "Education of Women."

For additional references that contain information on the interaction between education and labor force participation, see chapter 8.

A. GENERAL TOPICS
Africa--General

Education of Women

1141. Appel, Patricia. "The Door is Always Open." New York United Nations, 1975. UNICEF Document #FS #68/2.

1142. Carley, Verna. African Women Educators Project Report. Washington: U.S. Agency for International Development, Bureau for Africa and Europe, 1962.

1143. Conference on African Women and Adult Education. Dakar: United Nations Educational, Scientific and Cultural Organization, 1962.

1144. De Carvalho, A. "Instrução e educação da mulher africana." Portugal em Africa, v. 13 (74), 1956: 65-75.

1145. Duperoux, A. "Quelques propos sur l'éducation de la femme noire." Bulletin de L'Union des Femmes Coloniales, v. 22 (136), 1951: 6-8.

1146. Eliou, Marie. "Scolaristion et promotion féminines en Afrique." International Review of Education, v. 19 (1), 1973: 30-46.

1147. _____. "Les Femmes africaines et l'éducation des adults." Revue Internationale de L'Éducation des Adultes et la Jeunesse, v. 15 (2), 1963: 90-98.

1148. Fortes, M. Social and Psychological Aspects of Education in Taleland. Oxford: Oxford University Press, 1938.

1149. Jiagge, J. A. "The Role of Non-Governmental Organizations in the Education of Women in African States." Convergence, v. 2 (2), 1969: 73-78.

1150. J. M. D. "Vers la réhabilitation de la femme en Afrique Occidental Francaise." Bulletin des Missions, v. 18 (3): 223-225.

1151. Krystall, Abigail, and Achola Pala. "Women in Education." Kenya Education Review, December 1975: 1-6.

1152. Le Ber, A; E. Demba, and J. Ki. "Éducation de la femme." Servir Outre-Mer, v. 9, 1952: 27-54.

1153. Leblanc, María. "Problèmes de l'éducation de la femme africaîne." La Revue Nouvelle, v. 25 (3), 15 March 1957: 257-275.

1154. MacNamara, C. T. "Women Are Going to School in Africa." World Mission, v. 10 (1), 1959: 18-28.

1155. Mogitz, Elizabeth. "The Education of the African Woman." University Woman, v. 1 (1), 1962: 25-26.

1156. Plummer, G. "Women's Part in African Education." Times British Colonies Review, v. 16, 1950: 12+.

1157. "La Promotion de la femme par 'accès a l'éducation." Afrique Nouvelle, v. 23 (1191), 4-10 June 1970: 11.

1158. Rivers-Smith, S. "Education of the African Woman." Bulletin of Educational Matters, v. 2 (3), 1928: 13-23.

1159. Robertson, Claire. "Some Socio-Economic Effects on G. A. of Differential Access to Education by Sex." Paper presented at the annual meeting of the African Studies Association, San Francisco, October-November 1975.

1160. du Sacré Coeur, Marie-André, Sister. "Education and the African Woman." In Rapports et Comptes Rendus de la 24 Semaine de Missiologie de Louvain. Brussels: Desclée de Brouwer, 1954: 44-62.

1161. Seye, Youssoupha. "La Femme africaine, problème d'éducation." Afrique Nouvelle, v. 634, 2 October 1959: 1-2.

1162. Smal, G. A., and J. W. Mbuyi. Femme africaine réveille-toi! Paris: Pensée Universelle, 1973.

1163. "Sweden Helps to Education African Women." New Africa, v. 6 (3), 1964: 15.

1164. United Nations Economic Commission for Africa and German Foundation for Developing Countries. "Report of the Regional Conference on Education, Vocational Training, and Work Opportunities for Girls and Women in African Countries." Rabat, Morocco, 20-29 May 1971.

1165. Welsh, Janet. "The Goal of Women's Education in Africa." Overseas Education, v. 9 (2), 1940.

1166. Wrong, M. "Education of African Women in Changing World." In Yearbook of Education. London: Evans, 1940: 497-520.

1167. You, and Allainmat. "L'Enseignement féminin." L'Éducation Africaine, v. 107, 1942: 37-82.

Education of Girls

1168. "African Girls Must be Well Educated." Shield, v. 43, April-

May 1964: 4-6+.

1169. Doo Kingue, Mme. "La scolaristion des filles." Connaissance de L'Afrique, v. 13, April 1965: 9+. Numero special.

1170. Douglas, Ruth L. "Education for African Girls." West African Review, v. 26 (335), 1955: 743-748.

1171. Dumont, R. "If Your Sister Goes to School, Your Next Meal Will Be Your Fountain Pen." In L. G. Gowan, J. O'Connell, and D. G. Scanlin, eds., Education and National Building in Africa. London: Pall Mall Press, 1965.

1172. "L'Éducation Féminine reste la parente pauvre de L'Énseignement Africain." Afrique, April 1965: 8-9.

1173. Jeanmart, Pierre. "Loisirs de jeunes etudiantes." Documents Pour L'Action, v. 21, May-June 1964: 153-160.

1174. Lynch, Jr. "Christian Education of Girls in Africa." Sacred Heart Messenger, May 1964: 42-45.

1175. "Meeting of Experts on Educational Opportunities for Girls at the Primary and Secondary Level in Tropical Africa." In The Education of Girls in Tropical Africa, Some General Information. Paris: UNESCO, 1960.

1176. Ngonyama, S. "The Education of the African Girl." Nada, v. 31, 1954: 57-58.

1177. Petit, M. "Les filles noires devant l'école familiale." La Nouvelle Revue Pédagogique, v. 12 (1), 1957: 35-38.

1178. Ross, MacGregor. "Some Aspects of Girls' Education in Africa." In Education in a Changing Commonwealth. London: New Education Fellowship, 1931.

West Africa

Education of Women

1179. "African Women and Education: The Dakar Colloquium." Journal of Adult and Youth Education, v. 5 (2), 1963: 81-88.

1180. Comhaire, Jean. "Énseignement féminin et mariages a Lagos, Nigeria." Zaire, v. 9 (3), March 1955: 261-277.

1181. Davis, H. O. "Emancipation of Women in West Africa." West

African Review, February 1938: 13-15.

1182. Fletcher, Catherine. "Preliminary Enquiry into Female Education in the Gold Coast with Special Reference to After School Life and Occupations." Mimeo, 1947.

1183. Fougeyrollas, Pierre. "Television and the Social Education of Women. A First Report on the UNESCO-Senegal Pilot Project at Dakar." Paris: UNESCO, 1967.

1184. Galadanci, S. A. "Education of Women in Islam with Reference to Nigeria." Nigerian Journal of Islam, v. 1 (1), January-June 1971: 5-10.

1185. Hazeley, Lottie. "Female Education in Sierra Leone." Africana, v. 1 (1), December 1948: 10-11.

1186. International Co-operative Alliance. "Report on Proceedings of the I.C.A. Regional Women Co-operators' Seminar, 14-18 January 1974." Mimeo. Moshi, Tanzania: ICA Regional Office for East and Central Africa, 1974.

1187. MacMath, A. M. "Developments in Female Education in Sierra Leone." Overseas Education, October 1939: 30-34; April 1943: 108-112.

1188. Masemann, Vandra L. "Motivation and Aspirations in a West African Girls' Secondary School." Ph.D. dissertation, University of Toronto, 1972.

1189. Mikolasek, Marguerite. "Some Attempts at Feminine Education in the Cameroons." International Review of Missions, v. 41 (164), v. 41 (164), October 1952: 493-495.

1190. Rhodes, Kathleen. "Home Responsibilities and Education." West African Journal of Education, June 1966: 68-70.

Education of Girls

1191. Bergeret, Ivette. Banganté (un internat de jeunes filles au Cameroun). Paris: Société des Missions Evangéliques, 1953.

1192. Bulifaut, J. C. "Education Plan for Girls." West African Review, v. 9, June 1938: 21-22.

1193. Comhaire-Sylvain, Suzanne. "L'Instruction des filles a Lomé." Problèmes Sociaux Congolais, v. 82, September 1968: 93-122.

1194. Congleton, F. I. "Some Problems of Girls' Education in

Northern Nigeria." Overseas Education, v. 30 (2), 1958: 73-79.

1195. Gueye, Falk Papa. "L'Enseignement des filles au Sénégal et dans la circonscription de Dakar." Bulletin de L'Enseignement de L'A.O.F., July-December 1934.

1196. Hauser, J. "Notes sur quelques attitudes de la collégienne dakaroise." Bulletin de L'IFAN, v. 17, B (1-2), 1955: 203-209.

1197. Ladurantie, G. "L'Éducation des filles au Dahomey." Encyclopédie Mensuelle d'Outre-Mer, v. 3, 1953: 310-312.

1198. _____. "Quelques aspects actuels de L'Enseignement des filles au Cameroun." Encyclopédie Mensuelle d'Outre-Mer, v. 3, 1953: 310-312.

1199. _____. Quelques aspects actuels de l'éducation des filles au Cameroun. Yaoundé: Union Féminine Civique et Sociale, 1956.

1200. LeGoff, G. "L'Education des filles en Afrique Occidentale Francaise: L'Education d'une fillette indigene par su famille." Overseas Education, v. 18 (4), July 1947: 547-563.

1201. _____. "L'Enseignement des filles en Afrique Occidentale Francaise." L'Education Africaine, v. 97, 1937: 189-199.

1202. Magdalen, M. C., Sister. "Education of Girls in Southern Nigeria." International Review of Missions, v. 17, 1928: 505-514.

1203. Manea, Lucien. "Éducation des filles, dot et société féminine chez les Beti." Revue de L'Action Populaire, v. 180, July-August 1964: 822-832.

1204. Muckenhirn, Erma Florence. "Secondary Education and Girls in Western Nigeria." Ph.D. dissertation, University of Michigan, 1966.

1205. Nasemann, Vandra. "The Hidden Curriculum of a West African Girls' Boarding School." Canadian Journal of African Studies, v. 8 (3), 1974: 479-494.

1206. Park, Eirlys. Careers for Nigerian Boys and Girls. Cambridge: Cambridge University Press, 1965.

1207. Tardits, Claude. "Réflexions sur le probleme de la scolarisation des filles au Dahomey." Cahiers D'Études Africaines, v. 3 (10), 1962: 266-281.

Central Africa

Education of Women

1208. Balde, S. "La Femme foulah et l'évolution." L'Éducation Africaine, v. 98, 1937: 214-219.

1209. Beasley, I. "Girls' Education in the Anglo-Egyptian Sudan." National Froebel Foundation Bulletin, v. 69, April 1951. Also cited as Colonial Review, 1951: 52.

1210. Deheyn, J. J. "The Education of Women in the Belgian Congo." African Women, v. 3 (2), June 1959: 33-35.

1211. Demba, E.; J. Ki; and A. LeBer. "La Femme africaine et son éducation." Informations Sociales, v. 6 (17), 1 October 1952: 934-938.

1212. Devaux, V. "La Femme congolaise et la civilisation européenne." Grands Lacs, v. 7, 1949-1950: 5.

1213. "Educational Needs of Women in Rhodesia." Women Today, v. 6 (5), December 1965: 104-105.

1214. El-Tayib, Griselda. "Women's Education in the Sudan." Kano Studies, v. 1, September 1965: 43-46.

1215. Gwilliam, Freda H. and Margaret Read. Report on the Education of Women and Girls. Lusaka: Government Printer, 1948.

1216. Renoirte, Therese. "Femmes de demain; l'énseignement féminin au Congo." Mimeo. Kinshasa: Bibliothéque de L'Étoile, 1964.

1217. Silva, María Luisa Cardoso E. "Aspectos da reeducação da mulher nativa angolana." Ultramar, v. 22, 1965: 37-49.

1218. Soyer, Poskin D. "Means of Education: Schools." In La Promotion de la femme au Congo et au Ruanda-Urundi. Brussels: Congrès Colonial National, 12th Session, 1956: 360-430.

1219. Swana, A. "L'Instruction et l'éducation début de la promotion de la femme congolaise." Bulletin Mensuel de Statistique, v. 5 (5-6), May-June 1965: 3-5.

1220. Verhaegen, P., et al. "L'Éducation de la population africaine féminine dan un milieu industriel du Haut-Katanga." Bulletin du CEPSI, v. 44, March 1959: 5-163.

Education of Girls

1221. Balde, S. "L'Éducation de la fille dans l'anciene famille foulah." Outre-Mer, v. 4, 1937: 322-330.

1222. Bongongo, L. "De l'éducation de nos filles." La Voix du Congolais, v. 45, 1959: 465-471.

1223. Brasley, Ina. "Girls' Education in Anglo-Egyptian Sudan." National Froebel Foundation Bulletin, no. 69, April 1951. Also cited in Colonial Review, v. 7 (3), June 1951: 52.

1224. "L'Education des filles á travers les siècles." Revue Pedagogique de la Republique Centrafricaine, v. 50, February 1967: 50-55.

1225. Evans, J. D. "Education of the Sudanese Girl." Overseas Education, v. 2, 1930: 25-32.

1226. Hulstaert, G. "L'Instruction des filles." Aequatoria, v. 4, 1951: 128-129.

1227. King, Eveline R. G. "On Educating African Girls in Northern Rhodesia." The Rhodes-Livingstone Journal, v. 10, 1950: 65-74.

1228. Lobet, E. "Quelques aperçus sour l'énseignement des filles au Ruanda." La Femme et le Congo, v. 29 (166), July 1959: 6-10.

1229. Sanderson, Lilian. "Some Aspects of the Development of Girls' Education in the Northern Sudan." Sudan Notes, v. 42, 1961.

1230. Van Hove, Rev. Mére. "L'Éducation de la jeune fille noire évoluée au Congo." Bulletin du CEPSI, v. 16, 1951: 151-161.

1231. Verhaegen, P. "Les Problèmes d'éducation de la femme et de l'enfance africaines." Bulletin du CEPSI, v. 44, March 1959: 7-15.

1232. Vincent, Jeanne-Françoise. "Les Citadins africains et le problème de la scolarisation des filles a BaCongo-Brazzaville." L'Enfant en Milieu Tropical, v. 23, May 1965: 24-36.

1233. Williams, K. O. "A Brief Summary of Girls' Education in the Anglo-Egyptian Sudan Based on the Sudan Education Reports 1928-1938." Mimeographed pamphlet, 1941.

East Africa

Education of Women

1234. "African Education in Kenya." East African Standard, 15 July 1933: 14.

1235. Awori, Wycliffe W., and James S. Gichuru. "A Memorandum on the Economical, Educational, and Social Aspects of the African in Kenya Colony." Mimeograph typescript. Nairobi (?): Kenya African Union, 1947.

1236. Bell, Jane. "Further Education for the Women of Uganda." African Women, v. 4 (4), June 1962: 73-77.

1237. Broomfield, G. W. "Education of African Women and Girls in Tanganyika." Bulletin of Educational Matters, v. 3 (2), 1929: 2-8.

1238. "The Education of Women and Girls in Uganda." Women Today, v. 6 (2), June 1964: 42-44.

1239. "Education of Woman-hood in East Africa." Convergence, v. 2 (2), 1969: 32-36.

1240. "Education of Women in Kenya." Kenya Weekly News, v. 18 (24), 16 June 1944: 25.

1241. Evans, D. R. "Image and Reality: Career Goals of Educated Ugandan Women." Canadian Journal of African Affairs, v. 6 (2), 1972: 213-232.

1242. Janish, Miriam. "Education of Women in Kenya." East African Standard, 21 March 1944: 3.

1243. Kinyanjui, Kabiru. "Education and Formal Employment Opportunities for Women in Kenya: Some Preliminary Data." Kenya Education Review, December 1975: 6-25.

1244. Maleche, A. J. "Sociological and Psychological Factors Favoring or Hindering the Education of African Women in Uganda." East African Institute of Social Research Conference paper, June 1961.

1245. Mbilinyi, Marjorie J. "Education, Stratification, and Sexism in Tanzania: Policy Implications." African Review, v. 3 (2), 1973: 327-340.

1246. Whitcombe, Fiona. "Women Students Reflect the New Africa." East Africa Standard, 28 June 1963: 15.

1247. "Women's Education in East Africa." African Women, v. 1 (3), December 1955: 55-56.

Education of Girls

1248. "African Schoolgirls in Tanganyika." African Women, v. 2 (2), June 1957: 31-34.

1249. "Africans and Europeans at School in East Africa." Times Educational Supplement, no. 2241, 2 May 1958: 692-693.

1250. "Asian Girls Must Go to Boys' Schools." East African Standard, 14 February 1953: 5.

1251. Bowen, Joan. "The Education of Girls in Zanzibar." Overseas Education, v. 32 (2), July 1960: 74-82.

1252. Douglass, Ruth L. "The Education of Girls in East Africa." East and West Review, v. 19 (1), January 1953: 28-32.

1253. "Education by Nuns Proposed for Kikuyu Girls." East African Standard, 5 February 1954: 11.

1254. Evans, David R., and Gordon Schimmel. The Impact of a Diversified Educational Programme on Career Girls: Tororo Girls in the Context of Girls' Education in Uganda. Amherst: University of Massachusetts, 1970.

1255. "Girls' Education in Kenya." Times Educational Supplement, no. 775, 8 March 1930: 109.

1256. Janisch, Miriam. "Views on the Education of African Girls." East African Standard, 21 November 1950: 5.

1257. _____. "Reinforcement for African Girls' Education in Kenya." Overseas Education, v. 26 (4), January 1955: 152-155.

1258. Kenya. Conference of Women Educationists to Consider the Beecher Report in Relation to the Education of African Girls. Nairobi: Government Printer, 1950.

1259. "Kikuyu Desire for Education of Girls." East African Standard, 2 February 1929: 17.

1260. "Landmark for African Girls' School." East African Standard, 17 March 1954: 4.

1261. Matheson, Alastair. "Overcoming Tribal Prejudices Against Educating Girls in Kenya." Journal of Negro Education, v. 23 (4), Fall 1954: 481-482.

1262. Mbilinyi, Marjorie J. The Education of Girls in Tanzania: A Study of Attitudes of Tanzanian Girls and Their Fathers Towards Education. Dar es Salaam: Institute of Education, University College, 1969.

1263. Naomi, Gebrat. "Girl Students." Ethiopia Observer, v. 1 (3), February 1957: 102+.

1264. Nichols, Zoe. Physical Education for Girls in the Tropics. Dar es Salaam: Evans Brothers, 1967.

1265. Odaga, James C. "Kenyan African Girls' Education." Ethiopia Observer, v. 3 (3), April 1959: 95+.

1266. "One in Three Schoolchildren is a Girl." East African Standard, 19 August 1953: 4.

1267. Shariff, E. "Girls' Education in Zanzibar." Makerere, v. 1 (3), September 1947: 112-116.

1268. Smith, M. M. "Notes on Visits Paid to Centres of Women and Girls' Education in Sudan, Uganda, and Kenya during the Period 6th October to 23rd November, 1945." Mimeographed pamphlet.

1269. "Training for Kenya Girls." East African Standard, 14 January 1938: 7-8.

Southern Africa

1270. "Girls' Education in Nyasaland." African Women, v. 1 (3), December 1955: 61-63.

1271. Gwilliam, Freda H., and Margaret Read. Report on the Education of Women and Girls in Nyasaland, August and September 1947. Zomba: Government Printer, 1948.

Latin America--General

1272. Arosemena de Tejeira, Otilia. "La educación de la mujer." Lotería, v. 12 (140), 1967: 45-48.

1273. Cowper, H. "Education of Women in Latin America." South Atlantic Quarterly, v. 19, 1920: 350-359.

1274. Inter-American Specialized Conference on the Integral Education of Women, Buenos Aires, 1972. Document # OEA/Ser. K/XIX. Washington, D.C.: Secretaría General, OAS, 1972. Also Document # OEA/Ser. C/ VI.20.1, "Final Report, August 1972, Buenos Aires." Washington, D.C.: General Secretariat, OAS, 1972.

1275. Ortíz de Macaya, Margarita. "Mujer, desarrollo social y educacional en América Latina." Boletín Documental sobre la Mujer, v. 0 (1), 1970: 59-62. Excerpts from a speech made at the International Seminar on La Participación de la Mujer en el Desarrollo Social y Educacional, Haifa, 1968.

1276. United Nations Educational, Scientific, and Cultural Organization. "La promoción de la mujer por el acceso a la educación." Paris: 1970.

1277. United Nations Economic Commission for Latin America. "Education for Females in the Americas: Policy-Related Aspects." Staff Paper no. 4. Caracas: 1975. Available from U.N. Center for Social and Humanitarian Affairs, U.N. Development Programme, New York.

1278. _____. "Socio-Cultural Determinants of Educational Opportunities of Women." Mimeo. Staff Paper no. 3. Caracas: 1970.

Mexico and Central America

1279. Castellanos, Rosario. Mujer que sabe Latín. Mexico: Secretaría de Educación Pública, 1973.

1280. _____. La participación de la mujer en la educación formal. Mexico City: Ed. Mundo Gráfico, Centro Nacional de la Productividad, 1970.

1281. _____. "La participación de la mujer en la educación formal." Diálogos, v. 44, 1972: 4-10.

1282. Duque, C. de. "Lo moderno y lo antiguo en la educación de la mujer." Lotería, v. 136, 1952: 6-9.

1283. Elu de Leñero, María del Carmen. "Education and Labor Force Participation of Women in Mexico: Some Significant Relationships Paper presented at the Wellesley Conference on Women and Development, June 1976. Available from Wellesley Center for Research on Women, 828 Washington St., Wellesley, Massachusetts 02181.

1284. Franco, Zoila. "Women in the Transformation of Cuban Education." Prospects. Quarterly Review of Education, v. 5 (3), 1975: 387-390.

1285. González Salazar, Gloria. "La mujer: Condiciones estructurales y educación." In Fernando Carmona, et al., eds., Reforma educativa y "apertura democrática." Mexico City: Ed. Nuestro Tiempo, 1972: 106-124.

1286. _____. "Participación laboral y educación de la mujer en México." Boletín Documental sobre las Mujeres, v. 4 (3), 1974: 14-22.

1287. Jerez Alvarez, Rafael. La educación de la mujer en Honduras. Tegucigalpa: Ministerio de Educación Pública, 1975.

1288. Perez-Venero, Mirna M. "Education of Women on the Isthmus of Panama." Journal of the West, v. 12, April 1973: 325-334.

1289. Rodas de Villagrán, Lucila. Desarrollo histórico de la educación de la mujer y su situación actual. Guatemala: 1965.

1290. Rodríguez de Fabrega, M., and R. de León de Almillategui. "La educación como factor de determinante en la vida de la mujer." Thesis, Universidad de Panamá, 1973.

Caribbean

1291. Collazo-Collazo, Jenaro. "Participación de la mujer en la fase educativa de la vida puertorriqueña." Education, v. 22 (27), 1969: 41-53.

1292. Perera, Hilda. "Women in a New Social Context in Cuba." International Journal of Adult and Youth Education, no. 3, 1962: 144-149.

Andean Region

1293. Antay, Evangelina. La mujer como factor de la obra de educación nacional. Lima: 1919.

1294. Barrionuevo de Cáceres, Nora. "La mujer, la educación, y el trabajo." Thesis, Pontificia Universidad Católica, Lima, 1967.

1295. Bazante, Julia. "Notas para un planteamiento de la educación de la mujer ecuatoriana." Revista Ecuatoriana de Educación, nos. 54-55, 1964-1965: 168-180.

1296. Castillo Ledón, Amalia C. "Situación general de la mujer en el campo educativo y cultural." Letra y Encajes, v. 26 (308), March 1952: 2489-2494.

1297. Centro de Estudios Sociales con la cooperación de AITEC. "La participación femenina en el sistema educacional venezolano." Documento Técnico no. 2. Caracas: 1975. Available from Centro de Estudios Sociales, Apartado Postal 14.385, Caracas 101, Venezuela.

1298. Escalante Cortijo, Griselda. "Educación de la mujer." Lima: Escuela Normal Urbana, Pontificia Universidad Católica, 1962.

1299. García Vital, Emma Isabel. "Algunas sugerencias para la educación de la mujer peruana." Thesis, Pontificia Universidad Católica, Lima, 1959.

1300. Hoyle Cox de Romero, Miriam. "La mujer peruana en el campo educacional." Thesis, Universidad Nacional Mayor de San Marcos, Lima, 1968.

1301. Ichaso Vásquez, Raquel. La enseñanza a la nación femenina. La Paz: Imp. Intendencia de Guerra, 1927.

1302. Jiménez de Tejada, Sonny. "Surgimiento y desarrollo de la educación femenina en Antioquía." Universidad de Antioquía, v. 41 (158), 1964: 609-624.

1303. Liendo Reyes, Luz. "Una contribución a la educación de la mujer." Thesis, Universidad Nacional Mayor de San Marcos, Lima, 1950.

1304. Mónica Teresa [pseud.]. La mujer, la educación, la cultura. Bogotá: Antares, 1955.

1305. Neyra Farfán, Rosa. "La educación de la mujer peruana." Thesis, Pontificia Universidad Católica, Lima, 1950.

1306. Salinas Lavado, Aurora. "Evolución de la educación de la mujer en el Perú." Thesis, Universidad Nacional Mayor de San Marcos, Lima, 1961.

Chile and the Platine

1307. Argentine Republic. Ministerio de Cultura y Educación. "Conferencia Interamericana Especializada sobre Educación Integral de la Mujer." Buenos Aires: August 1972.

1308. Cien profesiones y oficios para la mujer chilena. Santiago: Imprenta Chile, 1950.

1309. Eichelbaum de Babini, A.M. "La desigualdad educacional en Argentina." In J.F. Marsal, ed., Argentina colectiva: Seis estudios sobre problemas sociales argentinos. Buenos Aires: Paidos, 1972: 19-57.

1310. Garay de Raimondi, Ana Lya. "Mujeres argentinas." Revista de la Instrucción Pública, June-July 1947: 96-97.

1311. Labarca Hubertson, Amanda. Women and Education in Chile. Paris: 1952.

Brazil

1312. Camurca, Zéila Sá. "A presencia de mulher, e educação da mulher." Mimeo. Fortaleza, Brazil: Universidade Federal do Ceará, 1970.

1313. Campos, María M. Malta. "Research on Work and the Education of Women in Brasil." Canadian Newsletter of Research on Women, v. 5 (3), October 1976: 105-107.

1314. _____, and Yara Lucía Esposito. "Relação entre sexo de criança e aspirações educacionais e ocupacionais das mães." Cadernos de Pesquisa, no. 15, December 1975: 37-46.

1315. Mala, Silvia Tigre. "A evolução intelectual feminina no Brazil." Formação, September 1943: 45-51; December 1943: 33-39.

1316. Namo de Mello, Guiomar. "Os estereotipo sexuais na escola." Cadernos de Pesquisa, no. 15, December 1975: 141-144.

1317. Rodriguez, Leda María Pereira. A instrução feminina em São Paulo. São Paulo:Facultade de Filosofia "Sedes Sapientiae," 1966.

1318. Rosemberg, Fulvia. "A escola e as diferenças sexuais." Cadernos de Pesquisa, no. 15, December 1975:78-85.

1319. Vasques de Miranda, Glaura. "A educação da mulher brasileira e sua participação nas atividades econômicas em 1970." Cadernos de Pesquisa, no. 15, December 1975: 21-36.

B. SPECIALIZED TRAINING (Includes rural, technical, literacy, professional, and political education).

Africa - General

1320. "African Women Help in Rural Education and Training." UNESCO Information Bulletin, v. 22, February 1966: 12-13.

1321. Carley, V. African Women Educators' Project. Washington, D.C.:

U.S. Agency for International Development, 1961.

1322. Coulibaly, O. "Sur l'éducation des femmes indigènes." L'Education Africaine, nos. 99-100, 1938: 33-36.

1323. Cleire, Celina, et al. "Cycle d'étude des nations unies sur l'éducation civique et politique de la femme." Revue Sénégalaise de Droit, v. 3 (5), March 1969: 127-135.

1324. Darlow, M. "Education of Women and Children in External Classes." Cahiers de L'Institut Solvay, v. 1, 1951: 17-24.

1325. "Les Femmes africaines et l'éducation des adultes." Revue Internationale de l'Education des Adultes et de la Jeunesse, v. 15 (2), 1963: 90-98.

1326. German Foundation for Developing Countries. "Education, Vocational Training and Work Opportunities for Girls and Women in African Countries." DOK 565 a/a-b, III-S 5/71, v.1, 1971.

1327. "Girls Vocational Training Centres." Advance, v. 42, 1964.

1328. Gordon, Joanna. "Communicating with Women: Classes or Other Means?" Community Development Journal, v. 1, January 1966: 10-21

1329. Harris, B. "Women's Training Centre, Kwadaso." Community Development Bulletin, v. 4 (2), March 1953: 35-36.

1330. International Labour Organization. "Vocational Training for African Women." African Women, December 1962: 4-7; June 1963: 35-.

1331. _____. "The Employment and Vocational Preparation of Girl and Women in Africa." Background Paper. Mimeo. March 1969. U.N Document # E/CN.14/SW/INF/8.

1332. Johnson, Essie. "Mindolo Women's Training Centre." African Women, v. 4 (3), December 1961: 63-65.

1333. Keita, A. "L'Emancipation de la femme et l'éducation de la mère doivent etre au premier plan des préoccupations des gouvernements africains." La Vie Africaine, v. 20, December 1961: 54-55

1334. Shrubsole, A.C. "Some Problems of Teacher Education in a Rapidly Changing African Society." Women Today, v. 6 (5), 1965: 97-99.

1335. United Nations Division of Human Rights. "Seminar on the Civ and Political Education of Women. Accra, Ghana, 19 November to 2 December 1968." United Nations: New York, 1969. U.N. Document ST/TAO/HR/35.

1336. United Nations Economic Commission for Africa. "Report of the Regional Conference on Education, Vocational Training and Work Opportunities for Girls and Women in African Countries, Rabat, May 20-29, 1971." UN Document # DOK565 A/a+b. Report issued 1972.

1337. United Nations Economic Commission for Africa, United Nations, Food and Agricultural Organization and the Netherlands Government. "Report on Five Workshops for Trainers in Home Economics and Other Family-Oriented Fields: Eastern and Southern Africa." 1973. Excerpts only.

West Africa

1338. Arnot, A. S., et al. "Literacy Among Calabar Women." Books for Africa, v. 8 (4), October 1938: 49-52.

1339. Awe, Bolanle. "University Education for Women in Nigeria." Ibadan, no. 18, February 1964: 57-62.

1340. Bellonde, G. "Rural Education and Rural Development Projects in West Africa." Mimeo. Paris: Institut de Recherche et D'Application des Méthodes de Développement, 1974.

1341. Bergeret, Ivette. "A Training Centre for Home and Family Life." International Review of Missions, v. 41 (164), 1952: 496-502.

1342. Betts, V. O. "The Home Development Programme — Sierra Leone." Women Today, v. 6 (3), December 1964: 64-66.

1343. DeGroote, J. "Au Cameroun, animation rurale féminine." Monde et Mission, March 1969: 16-21.

1344. Edme, P. "L'Education ménagère de la femme camerounaise." Bulletin d'Information et de Documentation, v. 115, October 1955: 18-21.

1345. "L'Education de la femme Camerounaise par l'énseignement ménager." Bulletin d'Information Cameroun, v. 47, October 1952: 9-12.

1346. "L'Enseignement féminin du second degré et les professions féminines en Afrique Occidentale Française." Education Africaine, v. 23, 1954.

1347. Foster, J. "Women's Teacher Training in Northern Nigeria." Overseas Education, v. 31 (4), January 1960: 147-155.

1348. Gueye, Marie. "The Education of Women in Rural Areas of Senegal." International Journal of Adult and Youth Education, v. 13 (4), 1961: 190-197.

1349. Hamilton-Hazeley, Lottie E. A. "The Education of Women and Girls in the Provinces." Sierra Leone Journal of Education, v. 1 (1), April 1966: 20-23.

1350. Ivory Coast, Services Communautaires. "Animation féminine rurale en pays Dida." Mimeo. Abidjan, Ivory Coast: Services Communautaires, Projet de Lakota, 1973.

1351. Johnson, Essie. "Ghana Women and Higher Education." Extract from the Report of the Commission on University Education in Ghana, May 1961. African Women, v. 4 (3), December 1961: 62-65.

1352. Prete, Roques. "Éducation et formation professionnelle féminines dans les états africains et malgache d'expression française." Afrique Contemporaire, v. 5, November-December 1965: 18-20

1353. Spence, A. "Adult Education for Women (Calabar Province)." Community Development Bulletin, v. 6 (1), December 1954: 10-12.

1354. Teager, Frances M. "The Women's Centre, Riyom, Northern Nigeria." Overseas Education, v. 20 (3), April 1949: 867-871.

1355. United Nations Economic Commission for Africa. "Country Report on Ghana. Vocational Training Opportunities for Girls and Women." Addis Ababa: Economic Commission for Africa, 1974.

1356. _____. "Country Report for Nigeria. Vocational Training Opportunities for Girls and Women." Addis Ababa: Economic Commission for Africa, 1973.

1357. UNESCO (United Nations Educational, Scientific and Cultural Organization). "Report of the Research Team Appointed by the Sierra Leone Commission for Education, Training, and Employment Opportunities for Women in Sierra Leone, 1974."

1358. Yeld, E. R. "Education amongst Women and Girls in the Kebbi Emirate of Northern Nigeria." In H. N. Weiler, ed., Erziehung und Politick in Nigeria/Educational Politics in Nigeria. Freiburg: Breisgau Verl. Rombach, 1964: 65-79.

Central Africa

1359. Geary, C. L. H. Education of Women and Girls in the Sudan. Zaria: Gaskiya Corporation, 1950: 5490-5498.

1360. Holding, Mary. "Report on Adult Literacy among the Meru Women." Books for Africa, v. 15 (2), April 1945: 17-22.

1361. _____. "Adult Literacy among Meru Women." Colonial Review, v. 4 (3), September 1945: 82-83. Also cited as Congo Mission News, v. 134, April 1946: 16-17.

1362. Lex, B. "Un essai pour l'éducation des femmes adultes par les foyers sociaux." Bulletin du CEPSI, v. 44, March 1959: 52-61.

1363. Mann, M. "Women's Homecraft Classes in Northern Rhodesia." Overseas Education, v. 31 (1), April 1959: 12-16.

1364. Richards, G. E. "Adult Education amongst Country Women: An Experiment at Umm Gerr." Sudan Notes and Records, v. 29 (2), 1948: 225-227.

1365. Royston-Piggott, P. J. "Higher Education for Sudanese Women." Journal of Education, v. 83, 1951: 490.

1366. Sanderson, Lilian. "Careers for Women in the Sudan Today." African Women, v. 5 (2), June 1963: 25-29.

1367. _____. "University Education for Sudanese Women in African Perspectives." Sudan Society, v. 3, 1965: 21-30.

1368. Sohier-Brunard, A. "L'Impréparation de la femme indigène du Congo aux tâches que la vie à notre contact lui impose." In Institut de Sociologie Solvay, ed., L'Énseignement à disposer aux indigènes dans les territoires non-autonomes. Brussels: Editions de la Librairie Encyclopédique, 1951.

1369. Tay, Janet. "The National Women's Training Centre, Pamfokrom." African Women, v. 5 (1), December 1962: 1-3.

1370. Whyms. "L'Education de la femme indigène au Ruanda." Servir, v. 11 (3), 1950: 79-81.

East Africa

1371. "African Women's Progress in Kenya: First Year's Work at Machakos Training College." African World, November 1959: 11.

1372. Awori, Thelma. Adult Education for Women in Uganda. Makerere: Makerere Adult Studies Centre, n.d.

1373. Barghouti, Shawki M. "Reaching Rural Families in East Africa." Programmes for Better Family Living. Handbook Series, no. 1. Nairobi: United Nations Food and Agricultural Organization, 1973.

1374. _____. "Integrated Functional Education in Machakos District." Programmes for Better Family Living. Report Series, no. 13. Nairobi: United Nations Food and Agricultural Organization, 1974. UN Document # FPA/551/KEN/FAO/1.

1375. Bilharz, J. "Social Life in a Ugandan Secretarial School." Mimeo. Paper presented at 50th Annual Central States Anthropological Society Meeting, Detroit, 1971.

1376. Burnet, A. M. "Women at Makerere." African Women, v. 2 (4), June 1958: 78-80.

1377. Cagnolo, C. The Akikuyu: Their Customs, Traditions and Folklore. Nyeri: Consolata Mission Printing School, 1933. English Translation.

1378. "College Aims to help African Women's Development." East African Standard, 28 November, 1958: 7.

1379. Comhaire-Sylvain, Suzanne. "Higher Education and Professional Training of Women in Ethiopia." Women Today, v. 6 (3), 1964: 58-59.

1380. "Education for Womanhood in East Africa." Improving College and University Teaching, v. 22, Winter 1972: 68-70.

1381. "First Women's Teacher Training College in Rift Valley." East African Standard, 16 October 1953: 11.

1382. Heasman, K. "Literacy Programme for the Women of Uganda." Women Today, v. 6 (3), December 1964: 57-58.

1383. Holding, Mary. "Adult Literacy Experience in Kenya." Overseas Education, v. 17 (1), October 1945: 204-208.

1384. Jellicoe, M. R. "An Experiment in Mass Education among Women." Occasional Papers on Community Development no. 1. Dar es Salaam: East African Literary Bureau, 1962.

1385. Ladkin, R. G. "Literacy Progress for the Women of Uganda." Women Today, v. 6 (3), December 1964: 57-58.

1386. Lavers, Anthony. "Masai Girls are Learning New Way of Life." East African Standard, 5 December 1958: 26.

1387. Mhina, Anne R. "Women's Problem in an Adult Education Campaign in Rural Tanzania." Mimeo. Dar es Salaam: Kibaha Education Centre, 1971. Speech given at African Adult Education Association.

1388. "'Miss Masailand' Goes to School." Kenya Today, v. 4 (3), September 1958: 25-27.

1389. "New School for Masai Girls." East African Standard, 5 June 1959: 6.

1390. Pankhurst, Sylvia. "Women's Vocational School." Ethiopia Observer, v. 2 (4), May 1958: 155-156.

1391. Pears, Marjorie. "Sweden and the ILO Help Kenya Train Girls for Office Work." ILO Panorama (International Labour Organization), January-February 1966: 2-9.

1392. Picton-Tubervill, Edith. "Education of Native Women in Kenya." Crown Colonist, v. 4 (36), November 1934: 493.

1393. "Progress in Kenya." African Women, v. 1 (1), December 1954: 14-15.

1394. Saunders, M. M. "Technical Education for Girls in Uganda." African Women, v. 2 (2), June 1957: 30-31.

1395. "The Training of African Women: A Refresher Course at Jeanes School." East African Standard, 3 February 1934: 10.

1396. United Nations Economic Commission for Africa. "Country Report for Kenya. Vocational Training Opportunities for Girls and Women." Addis Ababa, 1972.

1397. United Nations Food and Agricultural Organization. "Integrated Functional Education: An Approach for Rural Education, 1974." FAO Document # FPA/551/KEN/FAO/1. Kenya. Available from Home Economics and Social Programmes Service, UN/FAO, Via delle Terme di Caracalla, 00100, Rome, Italy.

Southern Africa

1398. Jones, N. "Training Native Women in Community Service in Southern Rhodesia." International Review Missions, v. 21, 1932: 556-574.

1399. United Nations Economic Commission for Africa. "Country Report for Lesotho. Vocational Training Opportunities for Girls and Women." Addis Ababa: Economic Commission for Africa, 1972.

Latin America--General

1400. Arias, María Cecilia, Sister. "A Case Study of the Program of the Overseas Education Fund Institute in Leadership Development for Latin American Women in the United States from 1963 to 1970." Ed.D. dissertation, Boston University School of Education, 1972.

1401. Hecker, Monique. "Enseñanza mixta y promoción de la mujer." Crónica de la UNESCO, v. 18 (8-9), August-September 1971.

1402. "Las mujeres del campo aprenden algo nuevo." En Guardia, v. 4 (12), July 1945: 21-23.

1403. Moreau, Kenold J. "La Fonction sociale de l'école rurale dans l'éducation de la famille paysanne." Boletin del Instituto Interamericano del Niño, v. 34 (3), September 1960: 333-343.

1404. UNESCO (United Nations Educational, Scientific and Cultural Organization), "Political Education of Women." New York: 1951.

1405. UNICEF (United Nations Children's Fund.). "Assessment of Projects for the Education of Women and Girls for Family and Community Life." Prepared by UNICEF with the Cooperation of the U.N. Division of Social Development and the Food and Agricultural Organization, 1970. U.N. Document # E/ICEF/L.1275.

Mexico and Central America

1406. Aguerri, Josefa Toledo de. Educación y feminismo. Managua: Impreso de los Talles Nacionales, 1940.

1407. Bopp, Marianne O. de. "La mujer en la universidad." Filosofía y Letras, v. 30 (60-62), 1956: 147-163.

1408. Figueroa, Ana. La mujer ciudadana: Sugestiones para la educación cívica de la mujer. Paris: UNESCO, 1955.

1409. Guatemala. Secretaría de Educación Pública. Programas para las escuelas de artes y oficios femeniles. Guatemala: Tipografía Nacional de Guatemala, 1946.

1410. Hendricks, Herbert W. "Teacher Training at a Mexican Normal School and Its Relevance to Mexico's National Goals." Ph.D. dissertation, Stanford University, 1968.

1411. Herradora, María Luisa. "Temario: Trabajo desarrollado... para enviarlo al Primer Congreso Centroamericano Femenino de Educación, que se reunirá en San José de Costa Rica, del 8 al 15 de septiembre de 1938." Tégucigalpa: Talleres Tipográficos Nacionales, 1938.

1412. Lavalle Urbina, María. "La mujer y su situación legal y de facto. Me daban el asiento pero no el lugar." Los Universitarios, v. 29, 15 July 1974: 8-16.

1413. Llano Cifuentes, Carlos. "La educación superior femenina, como tarea específica." Istmo, v. 58, September-October 1968: 24-28; 30-35.

1414. Morin, Renee. "Mexican Adults Crave Education." Food for Thought, v. 8 (1), October 1947: 5-7.

1415. Oduber Quiros, Daniel. La educación, la mujer, y la política. San José: C. Morúa Carrillo, 1966.

1416. Peres Alvarez, Eduardo. "La evolución profesional de la mujer en la universidad." Espejo, v. 3, 1967: 55-68.

1417. Porras Muñoz, Guillermo. "ESDAI - Oportunidad para la mujer." Istmo, v. 65, 1969: 29-32.

1418. "The Right to Education Means the Right to a Better Living." UNESCO Courier, v. 5 (11), November 1952: 4-5.

1419. Robinson, Michael O. K. "Paradoxes in the Relationships Between Men and Women in the Mexican Middle CLass: And Rural Education in Mexico 1920-1940." Masters report, University of Texas at Austin, 1970.

1420. Wise, Sidney. "Sunday School Under the Trees." Times Educational Supplement, no. 2710, April 1967: 1408-1409.

Caribbean

1421. Aguilar, Onelia. "Escuela para campesinas." Verde Olivo, 12 February, 1961: 16-17.

1422. Avala, V. O. "Home Economics Education in the Caribbean." Caribbean Commission Monthly Information Bulletin, v. 6 (9), April 1953: 199-201.

1423. Benitez, Jaime. "La mujer universitaria en la vida puertorriqueña." La Torre, v. 14 (53), May-August 1966: 11-18.

1424. Cuba. Ministerio de Educación. "Y toda Cuba es una gran escuela: Fidel Castro, informe 1963-64." Ciudad Libertad: n.d.

1425. Cubillas, Vicente. "Las muchachas campesinas se preparan para enseñar." Bohemia, 4 June 1961: 4-8.

1426. "Doce mil campesinas estudiarán en La Habana." INRA, March 1961: 100-101.

1427. Dolz y Arango, María Luisa. La liberación de la mujer cubana por la educación. Habana: 1955.

1428. "FAR Institutes for Women's Combat Training." Translations on Latin America, no. 125, 1969: 50.

1429. Manzano, Matilde. "Apuntes de una alfabetizadora." Casa de las Américas, v. 3 (19), 1963: 91-117.

1430. United Nations Food and Agricultural Organization. "Home Economics Education and Extension in the Caribbean." Rome: FAO, 1952.

1431. "Women's Qualification Schools Created by Ministry of Domestic Trade in the City of Mariano." Translations on Cuba, no. 225, 1965: 11-12.

Andean Region

1432. Adam, Félix, and Pedro Tomás Vásquez. La educación de adultos y los planes de desarrollo económico y social en Venezuela. Caracas: Oficina de Educación de Adultos, 1965.

1433. Adams, Dale W. "Leadership, Education and Agricultural Development Programs in Colombia." Land Tenure Center Reprint no. 45. Madison: Land Tenure Center, University of Wisconsin, 1968.

1434. Alvarez, José. "Preparación de auxiliares de enfermería para puestos de salud rural." Anuario Indigenista, v. 28, August 1969: 133-140.

1435. Aranda Zarzuri, Martha. "La educación secundaria femenina en el Perú." Thesis, Universidad Nacional Mayor de San Marcos, Lima, 1943.

1436. Araoz, María Rosario. "La orientación profesional femenina en el Perú." Servicio Social, v. 11-12 (11-12), 1953-54: 139-159.

1437. Arze Quintanilla, Oscar. "Programa Interamericano de Adiestramiento en Desarrollo de Comunidades Indígenas." Anuario Indigenista, v. 26, December 1966: 97-123.

1438. Bethencourt R., Omar J., and T. S. Nicoletta Solinas. "Algunas consideraciones generales entre educación familiar y la salud pública." Revista de la Universidad de Zulia, v. 4, April-June 1962: 203-215.

1439. Burgess, Elaine. "Role of Women PCV's in Ecuador." Program and Training Journal, September 1973: 31-34.

1440. Chesterfield, Ray A., and Kenneth R. Ruddle. "Nondeliberate Education: Venezuelan Campesino Perceptions of Extension Agents and Their Message." In Thomas La Belle, ed., Educational Alternatives in Latin America: Social Change and Social Stratification. Los Angeles: Latin American Center, UCLA, 1975: 149-168.

1441. Cillonez Portocarrero de Carrión, Consuelo. "Los colegios industriales femeninos urbanos en función de la escuela." Monograph, Pontificia Universidad Católica, Lima, 1949.

1442. Clason, Carla. "Spotlight on the Rural Woman in Colombia." World Education Reports, no. 10, December 1975.

1443. Cohen, Lucy M. Las colombianas ante la renovación universitaria. Bogotá: Ediciones Tercer Mundo, 1971.

1444. D'Brot, Carmela. "La mujer triunfa en las universidades." Siete Días, v. 23 (782), 1973: 60-61.

1445. De Sagasti, Heli Ellen Ennis. "Social Implications of Adult Literacy: A Study Among Migrant Women in Peru." Ph.D. dissertation, University of Pennsylvania, 1972.

1446. "The Education of Women in Official Training Schools." World Education, v. 6 (2), 1941: 190-191.

1447. Espinoza, Teodolinda. "Reflexiones sobre la educación cívica femenina y la posibilidad de su reforma." Thesis, Universidad Nacional Mayor de San Marcos, Lima, 1959.

1448. Filella, James F. "Educational and Sex Differences in the Organization of Abilities in Technical and Academic Students in Colombia, South America." Ph.D. dissertation, Fordham University, 1957.

1449. Fonseca Scaglia, Juanita. "La educación industrial femenina en el Perú." Thesis, Universidad Nacional Mayor de San Marcos, Lima, 1965.

1450. Goetz, Delia. "Education in Venezuela." U. S. Office of Education Bulletin, no. 14. Washington, D.C.: Government Printing Office, 1948.

1451. Goisa Chambilla, Dora Gladys. "Situación socio-laboral de la empleada doméstica emigrada de provincias y aporte de la educadora familiar a las soluciones de los problemas encontrados." Lima: 1968.

1452. International Labour Organization. "Informe al gobierno de Venezuela sobre el proyecto para la integración de las poblaciones indígenas." ILO Document # ILO/TAP/Venezuela/R.9. Geneva: ILO, 1970.

1453. Olivan J., María Milagros. "Importancia y trascendencia de la educación de la mujer en la enseñanza media." Thesis, Pontificia Universidad Católica, Lima, 1953.

1454. Ortiz, Emma. "Reflexiones sobre la educación de la mujer ecuatoriana." Educación, v. 9 (90-97), 1934: 61-68.

1455. Portugal Ada, Esther. "La mujer puneña y la educación secundaria." Thesis, Universidad Nacional Mayor de San Marcos, Lima, 1948.

1456. Silva Torres, Zoila E. "El problema vocacional en la educación industrial femenina." Thesis, Universidad Nacional Mayor de San Marcos, Lima, 1964.

1457. Soles, Roger. "Experiences of a Peace Corps Volunteer Introducing Family Gardening in Colombia." Land Tenure Paper no. 58. Madison: Land Tenure Center, University of Wisconsin, 1968.

1458. Talbot, Dorothy McComb. "Professionalization among Student Nurses in Peru: A Sociological Analysis." Ph.D. dissertation, Tulane University, 1970.

1459. Vallanos-Hernández, Irma. "La educación de la mujer peruana en las Academias Industriales Particulares." Thesis, Pontificia Universidad Católica de San Marcos, Lima, n.d.

1460. Verdesoto de Romo, Raquel. "La mujer y el analfabetismo." Revista Ecuatoriana de Educación, v. 16 (52), May-December 1963: 73-78.

1461. Zapata, Ramón. "Granjas populares para la educación agrícola de la mujer." Senderos, v. 2 (7-8), 1934: 65-76.

Chile and The Platine

1462. Chile. Dirección de Asuntos Indígenas. "Labor actual de la Dirección de Asuntos Indígenas (Chile) y proyectos elaborados por ésta, en favor de la población indígena." Santiago: 1966.

1463. Cien profesiones y oficios para la mujer chilena. Santiago: Imprenta Chile, 1950.

1464. Cortés Carabantes, Waldemar. "Los planos extraordinarios de educación de adultos." Revista de Educación, v. 7, June 1968: 28-35.

1465. "Establishment of Textile Trade Schools in Argentina in 1942." Monthly Labour Review, v. 58 (1), January 1944: 111+.

1466. Fogel, Gerardo. "Programa integrado urbano-rural de desarrollo de la comunidad en Encarnación: Itapúa, Paraguay." Revista Paraguaya de Sociología, v. 6 (14), March 1969: 5-69.

1467. Gissi Bustos, Jorge. "Prejuicios en la educación de la mujer." Familia, v. 1 (2), 1973: 92-95.

1468. Jalon, Ana María. "La mujer y su papel de educadora." Revista Universitaria Nacional de Córdoba, v. 10 (1/2), March-June 1969: 305-318.

1469. Matheros, Ester. "A Salute to the University Women of Chile." Journal of the American Association of University Women, April 1942: 141-144.

1470. "Paraguay's Community Work Center." Practical Home Economics, v. 23 (9), November 1945: 544; 572; 574.

1471. Rigalt, Francisco. "La mujer rural y el Instituto Nacional de Tecnología Agropecuaria." Revista Universitaria Nacional de Córdoba, v. 10 (1-2), 1969: 217-220.

1472. Vasallo Bedoya, Sara. "La función social de la escuela rural en la educación de la familia campesina." Boletín del Instituto Interamericano del Niño, v. 34 (3), September 1960: 312-332.

1473. Vera Manríquez, Sergio. "Situación de la educación para la mujer campesina." Revista de Educación, v. 11, October 1968: 14-15.

1474. "Vocational Education in Argentina." <u>International Labour Review</u>, v. 57 (6), June 1948: 652-654.

Brazil

1475. Barroso, Carmen Lucia de Melo, and Guiomar N. de Mello. "O accesso da mulher ao ensino superior brasileiro." <u>Cadernos de Pesquisa</u>, no. 15, 1975: 47-77.

1476. Ferretti, Celso João. "A mulher e a escolha vocacional." Mimeo. São Paulo: Fundación Carlos Chagas, 1974.

1477. _____. "A mulher e a escolha vocacional." <u>Cadernos de Pesquisa</u>, no. 16, 1976: 20-40.

1478. Gouveia, Aparecida Joly. "Student Teachers in Brazil: A Study of Young Women's Career Choices." Ph.D. dissertation, University of Chicago, 1962.

1479. _____. Professoras de amanha: Um estudo de escolha ocupacional. Rio de Janeiro: Livraria Pioneira, 1970.

1480. Nordin, June Leith. "For Better Living in Brazil." <u>Agriculture in the Americas</u>, v. 4 (8), August 1944: 148-150; 156.

1481. Saffioti, Heleith Iara B. "Profissiona cização femenina: Professoras primarias e operarias." Mimeo. Araraquara: Faculdade de Filosofia, Ciencias e Letras, 1969.

Chapter VI

WOMEN AND THE POLITY

Chapter 6, compiles materials on women's civic and political participation, women as leaders and women in positions of power. References cover both modern and traditional leadership and political roles. Section A, "Various Topics," deals specifically with formal political participation, voting behavior, political attitudes, and power. Section B, "Women in Public Life and As Leaders," concentrates on leadership roles of women. The African references in this section deal with historical roles in general and with the specific roles of notable African women. Latin American references deal with historical roles and more specifically with women as elected officials, diplomats, union leaders, and rural leaders.

The final section, "Women in Revolution and Warfare," focuses on women as revolutionaries, in political protest movements, and in combat. Most entries for this latter section come from Latin America, especially Cuba.

The references on women's participation in feminist movements have been included under chapter 8, section B.

A. VARIOUS TOPICS (Includes participation in parties, voting patterns, etc.)

Africa - General

1482. Brooks, A. E. "Political Participation of Women in Africa South of the Sahara." Annals. American Academy of Political Social Science, v. 375, January 1968: 82-85.

1483. Lebeuf, Annie M. D. "The Role of Women in the Political Organization of African Societies." In Denise Paulme, ed., Women of Tropical Africa. London: Routledge and Kegan Paul, 1963: 93-120.

1484. O'Barr, Jean F. "Making the Invisible Visible: African Women in Politics and Policy." African Studies Review, v. 18 (3), December 1975: 19-28.

1485. Reyher, Rebecca. "Chez le roi aux cent femmes." France Illustration Supplément, v. 152, April 1954: 132.

1486. Ross, Marc, and Venna Thadani. "Why Women and Men Don't Always Participate in Politics in the Same Way for the Same Reasons or With the Same Results: An African Perspective." Paper presented at the annual meeting of the Political Science Association, Chicago, September 1976.

1487. Seabury, R. I. Daughter of Africa. Boston: Pilgrim Press, 1945.

1488. Uba, S. "Women in Politics." Man, v. 16, December 1972: 18-23.

West Africa

1489. Cutler, Virginia F. Woman Power, Social Imperatives, and Home Science. Accra: Ghana Universities Press, 1969.

1490. De la fosse, M. "Coutûmes observées par les femmes en temps de guerre chez les Agni de la Cote d'Avoire." Revue d' Ethnologie et de Sociologie, v. 4, 1913: 266-268.

1491. Derryck, Vivian Lowery. "Liberia: Urban Women and Political Participation." Mimeo. Paper presented to the 14th World Conference of the Society for International Development, Abidjan, Ivory Coast, 1974.

1492. Dobert, Margarita. "Civic and Political Participation of

Women in French-Speaking West Africa." Ph.D. dissertation, George Washington University, 1970.

1493. _____, "Women in French-Speaking West Africa: A Selected Guide to Civic and Political Participation in Guinea, Dahomey, and Mauritania." Current Bibliography of African Affairs, v. 3 (9), September 1970: 5-21.

1494. Lewis, Barbara C. "Female Strategies and Public Goods: The Ivory Coast." Paper presented at the Wellesley Conference on Women and Development, June 1976. Available from Wellesley Center for Research on Women, 828 Washington St., Wellesley, Massachusetts 02181.

1495. M'Baye, Annette. "Une victoire des Sénégalaises." Jeune Afrique, v. 367, 21 January, 1968: 34-35.

1496. Price, J. H. "Some Notes on the Influence of Women in Gambian Politics." In Nigerian Institute of Social and Economic Research, Conference Proceedings, 1958. 1959: 151-158.

1497. Reyher, Rebecca H. The Fon and His Hundred Wives. New York: Doubleday and Co., 1952.

1498. Richard, Madeleine. "Histoire, tradition et promotion de la femme chez les Batanga (Cameroun)." Anthropos, v. 65 (3-4), 1970: 369-443; v. 65 (5-6), 1970: 881-947.

1499. du Sacré Coeur, Marie-André, Sister. "L'Activité politique de la femme en Afrique noire." Revue Juridique et Politique de L' Union Francaise, v. 8, October-December 1954: 476-497.

1500. Steady, Filomena C. "Female Power in African Politics: The National Congress of Sierra Leone." Munger Africana Library Notes, no. 31, August 1975.

1501. Van Allen, Judith. "Sitting on a Man: Colonialism and the Lost Political Institutions of Igbo Women." Canadian Journal of African Studies, v. 6 (2), 1972: 165-182.

Central Africa

1502. Al-Shahi, A. S. "Politics and the Role of Women in a Shaiqiya Constituency (1968)." Sudan Society, v. 4, 1969: 27-38.

1503. Darlow, Mary. "The African Townswoman in Northern Rhodesia." African Women, v. 1 (3), 1955: 57-59.

1504. De Heusch, L. <u>Essai sur le symbolisme de l'inceste royal en Afrique</u>. Brussels: Institut de Sociologie Solvay, 1958. Chapter III.

1505. Descampe, E. "Note sur les Bayanzi." <u>Congo</u>, v. 1 (5), 1935: 685-688.

1506. Netting, Robert M. "Women's Weapons: The Politics of Domesticity Among the Kofyar." <u>American Anthropologist,</u> v. 71 (6), December 1969: 1037-1046.

1507. Plessers, R.P. "Des Bakaji ba mpinga (femmes de remplacement) chez les Baluba du Lubilash." <u>Bulletin des Juridictions indigènes et du Droit Coutumier Congolais</u>, no. 5, 1945: 130-132.

1508. du Sacré Coeur, Marie André, Sister. "Évolution de la femme africaine." <u>Grand Lacs</u>, v. 188, 1956-57: 16.

1509. Soyer, D. "Le Vote des femmes au Congo." <u>La Femme et le Congo</u>, v. 30 (168), January 1960: 5-10.

1510. Storme, M. "Ngankabe, la prétendue reine des Baboma." <u>Memoires de L'Académic Royale des Sciences Coloniales</u>, v. 7 (2), 1956.

1511. Tew, D. "A Form of Polyandry among the Lele of the Kasai." <u>Africa,</u> v. 21 (1), 1951: 1-12.

1512. Youlou-Kouya, H. "Une Adoratrice du Nkoué mbali." <u>Liaison</u>, no. 57, 1957: 27-28; no. 58, 1957: 54-56.

East Africa

1513. Bromhead, W. S. "Shall Women Vote in British East Africa?" <u>Reveille</u>, v. 3, 1917: 189-206.

1514. Earthy, E. Dora. "The Role of the Father's Sister among the Valenge." <u>South African Journal of Science</u>, v. 22, 1925: 526-529.

1515. Heasman, K. "Kenya African Women's Seminar." <u>Women Today</u>, v. 6 (1), December 1963: 5-6.

Southern Africa

1516. Ehrenfels, U. R. "The African Woman: Apartheid and Its Significance to Mankind." <u>United Asia</u>, v. 14, January 1962: 76-80.

1517. Falls, C. "Grave Trouble in Natal." London News, v. 235, 29 August 1959: 126.

1518. "La Femme dans la sagese bantoue. (Interview du R. P. Mveng)." Vivante Afrique, v. 243, March-April 1966: 3-7.

Latin America--General

1519. Cebotarev, E. A. "Rural Women in Non-Familial Activities: Credit and Political Action in Latin America." Paper presented at the Wellesley Conference on Women and Development, June 1976. Available from Wellesley Center for Research on Women, 828 Washington St., Wellesley, Massachusetts 02181.

1520. Jaquette, Jane. "Female Political Participation in Latin America." In June Nash and Helen I. Safa, eds., Sex and Class in Latin America. New York: Praeger, 1976: 221-224.

1521. Vekemans, Roger. Familia, modernización política y mutación cultural en América Latina. Santiago: DESAL/CELAP, 1965.

Mexico and Central America

1522. Aviel, Jo Ann. "Changing the Political Role of Women: A Costa Rican Case Study." In Jane Jaquette, ed., Women in Politics. New York: John Wiley and Sons, 1974: 281-303.

1523. Blough, William J. "Political Attitudes of Mexican Women; support for the Political System among a Newly Enfranchised Group." Journal of Inter-American Studies, v. 14, May 1972: 201-224.

1524. _____. "Political Participation in Mexico: Sex Differences in Behavior and Attitudes." Ph.D. dissertation, University of North Carolina, 1967.

1525. Bonilla de Ulloa, Janina. "La mujer costarricense en el mundo de hoy." Revista de la Universidad de Costa Rica, v. 29, 1970: 81-86.

1526. Fagen, Richard R., and William S. Tuohy. Politics and Privilege in a Mexican City. Stanford: Stanford University Press, 1972.

1527. Jaquette, Jane, ed., Women in Politics. New York: John Wiley and Sons, 1974.

1528. Lewis, Samuel, Jr. "La mujer panameña y la política." Lotería, v. 6- June 1948.

1529. Oller de Mulford, Juana. "Influencia de la mujer en el sostenimiento de nuestra independencia nacional." Tierra y Dos Mares, v. 8 (43), January-February 1969: 8, 21, 24, 40, 51.

1530. Talamantes, María Esther. "La mujer y la política." Filosofía y Letras, v. 30 (60-62), 1956: 109-118.

Caribbean

1531. Benglesdorf, Carollee. "The 'Frente Femenino.'" Cuban Review, v. 4, September 1974: 27-28.

1532. Castro, Fidel. The Revolution Has in Cuba Women Today An Impressive Political Force. La Habana: Editorial de Ciencias Sociales, 1974.

1533. Domínguez, Ofelia. "La niñita." Noticias de Hoy, 7 July 1938: 2.

1534. Guayaves Martínez, María A. "La mujer en las luchas de la clase obrera." Revolución y Cultura, v. 26, 1974: 9-15.

1535. Gudjonsson, Petur. "Women in Castro's Cuba." Progressive, v. 36, August 1972: 25-29.

1536. Infante, Isa María. "Women in Revolutionary Politics in the Dominican Republic." Paper presented at the Wellesley Conference on Women and Development, June 1976. Available from the Wellesley Center for Research on Women, 828 Washington St., Wellesley, Massachusetts 02181.

1537. Mota, Vivian M. "El feminismo y la política en la República Dominicana." Boletín Documental Sobre las Mujeres, v. 4 (4), 1974: 50-60.

1538. Pico de Hernández, Isabel. "Sexual Ideologies and Women's Participation in the Puerto Rican Political Process." Paper presented at the Wellesley Conference on Women and Development, June 1976. Available from Wellesley Center for Research on Women, 828 Washington St., Wellesley, Massachusetts 02181.

1539. Safa, Helen I. "Class-Consciousness among Working Class Women in Latin America: Puerto Rico." In June Nash and Helen I Safa, eds., Sex and Class in Latin America. New York: Praeger, 1976: 69-85. Also cited as Politics and Society, v. 5 (3), 1975.

Andean Region

1540. Centro Femenino Popular. El Marxismo, Maritegui, y el movimiento femenino. Lima: Editorial Pedagógico, 1974.

1541. Gueiler Tejada de Moller, Lydia. La mujer y la revolución. La Paz: Los Amigos del Libro, 1959.

1542. Meneses, Rómulo. Aprismo femenino peruano. Lima: Editorial Cooperativa Aprista "Atahualpa," 1934.

1543. Nash, June C. "Women in Resistance Movements in Bolivia." In R. R. Leavitt, ed., Cross-Cultural Perspectives on the Women's Movement and Women's Status. The Hague: Mouton, 1976.

1544. _____. "Resistance as Protest: A Role of Women in Struggles Against Oppression in Bolivian Tin Mines." Mimeo, n.d.

1545. Ospina, O. D. de. "El poder político de la mujer." Revista del Centro de Estudios Colombianos, v. 5, 1972: 61-66.

1546. Portal, Magda. El aprismo y la mujer. Lima: Editorial Cooperativa Aprista "Atahualpa," 1934.

1547. _____. "La mujer en el partido del pueblo. Primera Convención Nacional de Mujeres Apristas Reunidas del 14 al 24 de noviembre de 1946." Lima: 1948.

1548. Schmidt, Steffen W. "Women in Colombia." Journal of Interamerican Studies and World Affairs, v. 17 (4), November 1975.

1549. Villanueva y Saavedra, Etelvina. Acción socialista de la mujer en Bolivia (La Paz). La Paz: Cooperativa de Artes Gráficas E. Burillo, 1970.

Chile and the Platine

1550. Bambirra, Vania. "La mujer chilena en la transición al socialismo." Punto Final, v. 133, 22 June 1971.

1551. Bauer, Alfredo. La mujer en el socialismo. Buenos Aires: Sílaba, 1974.

1552. _____. La mujer: Ser social y conciencia. Buenos Aires: Ed. Sílaba, 1970.

1553. Castillo, Carmen. "Women in the Chilean Resistance." NACLA's Latin America and Empire Report, v. 9 (6), September 1975: 26-29.

1554. Chaney, Elsa M. "The Mobilization of Women in Allende's Chile." In J. Jaquette, ed., Women in Politics. New York: John Wiley and Sons, 1976.

1555. _____. "Women and Change: The Mobilization of Women in Three Cultures: Cuba, Chile, and North Vietnam." In R. R. Leavitt, ed., Cross-Cultural Perspectives on the Women's Movement and Women's Status. The Hague: Mouton, 1976.

1556. Cohen, Paul M. "Men, Women, and the Latin American Political System: Paths to Political Participation in Uruguay." Paper presented at the annual meeting of the American Political Science Association, University of Florida, 1974.

1557. Correa Morande, María. La guerra de las mujeres. Santiago: Ed. Universitaria Técnica del Estado, 1974.

1558. Edelman, Fanny J. Conferencia Nacional de Mujeres comunistas. Buenos Aires: Ed. Anteo, 1959.

1559. Floria, Carlos ALberto. "La mujer argentina y la política." Mimeo. Buenos Aires: Centro Nacional de Documentación e Información Educativa, 1972.

1560. Gómez, Ema, et al. "Mujeres en la lucha por el progreso y la felicidad." In Documentos del XIII Congreso Nacional del Partido Comunista de Chile. Folleto No. 5. Santiago: 1965.

1561. Mattelart, Michele. "When Bourgeois Women Take to the Streets." NACLA's Latin America and Empire Report, v. 9 (6), September 1975: 14-25.

1562. Moreau de Justo, Alicia. "Participación de la mujer en la política nacional." Revista Universitaria Nacional de Córdoba, v. 10 (1-2), March-June 1969: 283-304.

1563. Partido Revolucionario Febrerista. Departamento de Asuntos Femeninos. Idearío de la mujer febrerista. Buenos Aires: 1962.

1564. Prado, Danda. "Mujer y Política." Punto Final, v. 7 (174), 1973: 17-20.

1565. Velíz, Brunilda. "Women's Political Behavior in Chile." Master's thesis, University of California, Berkeley, 1964.

Brazil

1566. Blachman, Morris J. "Eve in an Adamocracy: Women and Politics in Brazil." New York: New York University, Ibero-American Language and Area Center, 1973.

1567. _____. "Women and Politics: The Brazilian Mixture." Cadernos, Centro de Estudos Rurais e Urbanos, v. 6, 1973: 147-173.

1568. Miller, Francesca. "Brazilian Women's Participation in International Movements." Paper presented at the annual meeting of the Pacific Coast Council on Latin American Studies, Arizona, October 1976.

B. WOMEN IN PUBLIC LIFE AND AS LEADERS

Africa--General

1569. De La Rue, A. "The Rise and Fall of Grace Ibingira." New African, v. 5 (10), December 1966: 207-208.

1570. De Santi, Dominique. "Les Femmes africaines--Marie-Thérese, c'est un 'Monsieur'." Jeune Afrique, v. 141, 1-7 July 1963: 44-45.

1571. Hoffer, Carol P. "Women's Role: What Male Anthropologists Say vs. What Women Paramount Chiefs Do." Paper presented at the 70th Annual Meeting of the American Anthropological Association, New York, 1970.

1572. Krige, E. J., and J. D. Krige. The Realm of a Rain-Queen. Oxford: Oxford University Press, 1943. Chapters X, XI.

1573. Lagarde, Dominique. "Electrices et séducteurs." Jeune Afrique, no. 697, May 1974: 46-47.

1574. "Le Role de la femme africaine dans la vie publique." Jeune Afrique, no. 554, 17 August 1971: 37.

1575. Possett, F. "The Story of the Princess Mepo." Nada, v. 7, 1929: 115-117.

1576. Thompson, Nora B. Africa to Me: Some Women Leaders of Tropical Africa. Dexter, Missouri: Candor Press, 1963.

1577. United Nations Food and Agricultural Organization. "Women's Leadership in Rural Development." Rome: FAO, 1975. Available from UNIPUB, Box 433, Murray Hill Station, New York 10016.

1578. Walters, Joseph Jeffrey. Guanya Pau: A Story of an African Princess. Cleveland: Lauer and Mattell, 1891.

West Africa

1579. Alima, J. B. "Une Grande interview d'une grande africaine: Madame Delphine Tsanza." Jeune Afrique, v. 513, 3 November 1970: 42-45.

1580. Baker, Tanya. "Women Elites in Western Nigeria." Ph.D. dissertation, Edinburgh University, 1957.

1581. Dugast, Rene. "Autobiographie d'une femme Banen: recueillie par Mme. R. Dugast." Bulletin de la Société d'Études Camerounaises, v. 6, June 1944: 73-84.

1582. Harris, Jack S. "The Position of Women in a Nigerian Society." Transactions of the New York Academy of Science, series 2, v. 2 (5), March 1940: 141-148.

1583. Hoffer, Carol P. "Mende and Sherba Women in High Office." Canadian Journal of African Studies, v. 6 (2), 1972: 151-164.

1584. Jeffreys, M. D. W. "Mary Slessor--Magistrate." West African Review, June 1950: 628-629; July 1950: 802-805.

1585. "Lady Paramount Chief: Mme. Ella Koblo Gulama, from the Mende of Sierra Leone." West Africa, no. 2141, 1958: 391.

1586. Leith-Ross, Sylvia. "The Rise of a New Elite amongst the Women of Nigeria." African Women, v. 2 (3), December 1957: 51-56. Also cited as International Social Science Bulletin, v. 8 (3), 1956: 481-488. Also in D. L. Van den Berghe, ed., Africa: Social Problems of Change and Conflict. San Francisco: Chandler, 1965: 221-229.

1587. "Madame Ahidjo, Première Dame du Cameroun." Afrique, v. 5, October 1961: 40-41.

1588. Oppong, Christine; Christine Okali; and Beverly Houghton. "Woman Power: Retrograde Steps in Ghana." African Studies Review, v. 18 (3), December 1975: 71-84.

1589. "Togo Woman Leader." Ebony, v. 18, April 1963: 44+.

1590. Westermann, D. Autobiographies d'Africains. Paris: Payot, 1943.

Central Africa

1591. Colin, P. M. "Trois femmes congolaises." Voix du Congolais, v. 119, 1956: 125-132.

1592. De Leeuwe, J. "On Former Gynaecocracy among African Pygmies." Acta Ethnographica, v. 11 (1-2), 1962: 85-118.

1593. Fortes, M. The Dynamics of Clanship among the Tallensi. Oxford: Oxford University Press, 1945: 147-153.

1594. Iyeki, J. F. "Un Pas de plus ver la promotion de la femme noire." Voix du Congolais, v. 12 (129), 1956: 859-863.

1595. Martin, J. "Fille de roi, fille de Dieu." Grand Lacs, v. 52 (5-6), 1936: 313-320.

1596. Munongo, A. "Mort de la Mugoli (reine) Mahanga, ancienne femme du Mwami Msiri et mère du chef Mafinge Mulongo." Bulletin du CEPSI, v. 17, 1951: 260-263.

1597. Ould Daddah, Madame. "La Politique au féminin." Continent 2000, v. 10-11, July-August 1970: 54-62.

1598. "Sophie Lihau-Kanza, premier en tout." Jeune Afrique, v. 308, 4 December 1966: 34-45.

East Africa

1599. Fuller, H. W. "Visit With Jomo's Daughter." Negro Digest, v. 12, September 1963: 49-50.

1600. Hathaway, Margaret. "The Special Burden of Leadership For African Women. [Priorities Facing Young Women's Christian Association Work in Kenya, Uganda, Tanzania, Zambia, and Rhodesia]." YWCA Magazine, v. 60, April 1966: 8-9.

1601. Homberg, Michael. "Women May Lead the Way Back." East African Standard, 24 June 1955: 32.

1602. Pankhurst, Sylvia. "Empress Menen." Ethiopia Observer, v. 6 (1), 1962: 2.

1603. _____. "Three Notable Ethiopian Women. (Empress Eieni, Sabla Wangeĭ, Metuab)." Ethiopia Observer, v. 1 (3), February 1957: 84-90.

Southern Africa

1604. Akeley, M. L. J. "The Swazi Queen at Home: Intimate Observations on Love, Life, and Death in South Africa's Timeless Swaziland." Natural History, June 1938: 21-32.

1605. Bazeley, W. Selwyn. "Manyika Headwomen." Nada, v. 17, 1940: 3-5.

1606. Biebuyck, D. "The Chieftainship in Basutoland." African Studies, v. 4 (4), 1945: 157-179.

1607. Blumber, M. "Betty Kaunda." Guardian, 24 April 1963: 6.

1608. Butler, Lorna M. "Bases of Women's Influence in the Rural Malawian Domestic Group." Ph.D. dissertation, Washington State University, 1976.

1609. "The Chieftainship in Basutoland." African Studies, v. 4 (4), 1945: 157-159.

1610. Jacques, A. A. "Genealogy of Male and Female Chiefs of a Sotho Tribe." Bantu Studies, v. 8, 1934: 377-382.

1611. Joseph, H. "Women and Passes." Africa South, v. 2 (2), 1958: 26-31.

1612. Kuper, H. "The Marriage of a Swazi Princess." Africa, v. 15 (3), 1945: 145-156.

1613. Mpashi, Stephen A. Betty Kaunda, Wife of the President of the Republic of Zambia: Her Story as Told to and Reproduced by Stephen A. Mpashi. Lusaka: Longmans of Zambia, 1969.

1614. Reyher, Rebecca H. Zulu Woman (Her Autobiography, Christina Sibiya). New York: Columbia University Press, 1948.

1615. Saakse, J. "The Visit to Mujaji, the Rain-Queen." Nada, v. 29, 1952: 83-86.

1616. "Women Paramount Chiefs of Basutoland." African Studies, v. 2, 1943: 168-169.

Mexico and Central America

1617. Jiménez de López, G. Participación de la mujer en la vida pública. Panama City: Estrella de Panamá, 1960.

1618. Ruíz Olvera, Estela. "La mujer mexicana y la diplomacia." Thesis, Universidad Nacional Autónoma de México, 1963.

Caribbean

1619. Collado, María. "La mujer cubana en el parlamento." In Album del Cincuentenario. La Habana: Ed. Lex, 1953: 123-125.

1620. Mota, Vivian M. "La mujer en la historia dominicana." Unpublished manuscript, 1972.

1621. Rivera Alvarado, Carmen. "La contribución de la mujer al desarrollo de la nacionalidad puertorriqueña." In J.A. Silen and N. Zayas, eds., La mujer en la lucha hoy. Rio Piedras: Ed. Kikiriki, 1972.

Andean Region

1622. Colombia Women in Public Affairs. "La ciudadana femenina en el Congreso de Colombia y en la Asamblea Internacional de Mujeres." Mireya, October 1946: 3-4.

1623. Crespi, Muriel. "Mujeres campesinas como líderes sindicales: La falta de propiedad como calificación para puestos públicos." Estudios Andinos, v. 5 (1), 1976: 151-170.

1624. Festini, Nelly. "Women in Public Life in Peru." Annals of the American Academy of Political and Social Science, no. 375, January 1968: 48-60.

1625. Hecht, Annie. "New Leaders For a Nation (Venezuela's Women Build the Future of Their Country)." Pan American, January 1948: 26-28.

1626. Soler, Luis. Presencia de la mujer en la diplomacia. Quito: Casa de Cultura Ecuatoriana, 1956.

Chile and The Platine

1627. Bunster, Ximena. "The Emergence of a Mapuche Leader: Chile." In June Nash and Helen I. Safa, eds., Sex and Class in Latin America. New York: Praeger, 1976: 302-319.

1628. Hollander, Nancy Caro. "Women: The Forgotten Half of Argentine History." In Ann Pescatello, ed., Female and Male in Latin America: Essays. Pittsburgh: University of Pittsburgh Press, 1973.

1629. Johnson, Ann H. "The 'Unexciting' Woman in Chile." Paper presented at the Pacific Coast Council on Latin American Studies Conference on Revolution in the Americas, 1776-1976. Arizona, October 1976.

1630. Vergara de Chamudas, Marta. "Chilean Women in Public Life." Inter-American, v. 11, March 1943: 28-29.

Brazil

1631. Servicio de Documentação. A Mulher no serviço público Rio de Janeiro: Departamento de Imprensa Nacional, 1957.

C. WOMEN IN REVOLUTION AND WARFARE

West Africa

1632. Ritzenthaler, Robert E. "Anlu: A Women's Uprising in the British Cameroons." African Studies, v. 19 (3), 1960: 151-156. Also cited as Zaire, v. 14 (5/6), 1960: 481-490. Also African Abstracts, v. 13 (1), 1962: 22.

1633. Urdang, Stephanie. "Fighting Two Colonialisms: The Women's Struggle in Guinea-Bissau." African Studies Review, v. 18 (3), December 1973: 29-34.

Central Africa

1634. Krapf-Askari, Eva. "Women, Spears, and the Scarce Good: A Comparison of the Sociological Function of Warfare in Two Central African Societies (Zande and Nzakara)." In A. Singer, et al., eds. Zande Themes. London: Oxford University Press, 1972: 19-40.

1635. Lobban, Carolyn Fleuhr. "Women in Radical Political Movements in the Sudan." Paper presented at the Wellesley Conference on Women and Development, June 1976. Available from Wellesley Center for Research on Women, 828 Washington St., Wellesley, Massachusetts 02181.

1636. Wright, Robin. "Women on the March." Foreign Affairs Research Newsletter. September 1975.

East Africa

1637. Liberation Support Movement Information Center. "The Mozambican Woman in the Revolution." Mimeo. Richmond, British Colombia: Liberation Support Movement Information Center, 1974.

1638. Machel, Josina. "The Mozambican Women in the Revolution: Frelimo Women's Detachment." Mimeo. Richmond, British Columbia: Liberation Support Movement, 1969.

Latin America -- General

1639. Jaquette, Jane. "Women in Revolutionary Movements in Latin America." Journal of Marriage and the Family, v. 35, May 1973: 344-354.

1640. Puga, Carmela, ed., La mujer y la revolución. Discursos, entrevistas, artículos, ensayos. Lima: Ed. Causachun, 1972.

1641. "Revolution within the Revolution: Women in Latin America." Action Latin America, v. 1 (3), 1972.

Mexico and Central America

1642. Batalla de Bassols, Clementina. La mujer en la revolución mexicana. Mexico City: 1960.

1643. Mendieta Alatorre, María de los Angeles. "Galería de mujeres mexicanas en la revolución." Revista de la Universidad de México, v. 28 (3), 1973: 15-21.

1644. _____. La mujer en la revolución mexicana. México: Talleres Gráficos de la Nación, 1961.

1645. Rascón, María Antonieta. "La mujer mexicana como hecho político: La precursora, la militante." La Cultura en México, no. 569, 3 January 1973: 9-12.

1646. Rodríguez Cabo, Mathilde. "La mujer y la revolución." Thesis, Universidad Nacional Autónoma de México, 1937.

1647. Turner, Frederick C. "Los efectos de la participación femenina en la revolución de 1910." Historia Mexicana, v. 16, 1967: 602-620.

Caribbean

1648. Castro, Fidel, and Linda Jenness. Women and the Cuban Revolution. New York: Pathfinder Press, 1970.

1649. Chaney, Elsa M. "Women and Change. The Mobilization of Women in Three Cultures: Cuba, Chile, and North Vietnam." In R. R. Leavitt, ed., Cross Cultural Perspectives on the Women's Movement and Women's Status. The Hague: Mouton, 1976.

1650. "El Frente de Mujeres Martianas formula declaraciones." El Mundo, 13 January 1955: A7.

1651. Hernández Vidaurreta, Manuel. "La mujer en la revolución." Humanismo, v. 7 (53-54), January-April 1959: 383-387.

1652. Horrego Estuch, Leopoldo. "La mujer en la revolución cubana." Carteles, v. 30 (36), 4 September 1949: 22-23.

1653. Marsan Sánchez, Gloria. "La mujer en la lucha insurrectional cubana del 53 al 59." OCLAE, August 1972: 7-12.

1654. Ponte Domínguez, Francisco J. "La mujer en la revolución de Cuba." Revista Bimestre Cubana, March-April 1933: 276-300.

1655. "Protestan Mujeres Martianas." El Mundo, 7 January 1955: A7.

1656. Rodríguez, Javier. "Las mujeres que se alzaron el en Escambray." Bohemia, 9 August 1968: 12-16.

1657. Rowbotham, Sheila. "Colony within the Colony." In Sheila Rowbothan, ed., Women, Resistance, and Revolution. A History of Women and Revolution in the Modern World. New York: Random House, 1974: 220-233.

1658. Sarabia, Nydia. "Mujeres guerrilleras en la batalla de Guisa." Bohemia, 24 November 1967: 50-55.

1659. _____. "La mujer santiguerra en la lucha revolucionaria Revolución, 30 July, 1962: 11.

1660. _____. "La mujer villareña en la lucha Patria." Bohemia, 19 July 1968: 16-20; 26 July 1968: 16-23.

1661. _____. "La mujer y el 30 de noviembre." Bohemia, 20 December 1968: 100-115.

1662. Vignier, Enrique. "Cronología, apuntes de las primeras rebeldías y las luchas patrióticas de la mujer en Cuba." Revolución y Cultura, v. 26, 1974: 66-80.

1663. Zell, Rosa Hilda. "Mosáico en rojo y negro; presencia femenina en el 26 de julio de 1953." Lunes de Revolución, 26 July 1959: 8-11.

Andean Region

1664. Gueiler Tejada de Moller, Lydia. "Importancia de la mujer en la acción revolucionaria." <u>Abril</u>, v. 2, January 1964: 39-43.

1665. _____. "La mujer en Bolivia." <u>Combate</u>, v. 3, September-October 1961: 33-41.

1666. Vega, Juan José. <u>Micaela Bastidas y las heroínas Tupamaristas</u>. La Cantuta: Ed. Universidad Nacional de Educación, 1972.

Chile and The Platine

1667. "Never is a Woman as Equal to a Man as when She's Behind a Colt 45." <u>Action Latin America</u>, v. 1 (3), 1972: 17-19.

Chapter VII

WOMEN AND ORGANIZATIONS

This brief chapter represents a sampling of materials on participation in women's organizations, associations, and movements. Section A, "Organizations, Voluntary Associations, and Societies," consists of references on women's roles and activities in cooperative societies, traditional secret societies, and women's groups associated with development schemes. Most references come from African research. Section B, "Feminist Movements," deals with women's participation in women's liberation movements, cross-cultural perspectives on women's liberation, and the relationship between feminine liberation and the class struggle. Most references in this section come from Latin American research.

A. ORGANIZATIONS, VOLUNTARY ASSOCIATIONS, AND SOCIETIES

Africa--General

1668. Afro-Asian Women's Conference. Cairo: Amalgamated Press of Egypt, 1961.

1669. Forde, D. "Ward Organization Among the Yakö." Africa, v. 20, 1950: 267-289.

1670. "Fostermothers in Africa (lactatio serotina)." Africa, v. 11 (1), 1938: 108-109.

1671. Holding, E. M. "Women's Institutions and the African Church." International Review of Missions, v. 31 (123), 1942: 290-300.

1672. Keirn, Susan Middleton. "Voluntary Associations Among Urban African Women." In Brian M. du Toit, ed., Culture Change in Contemporary Africa. Communications from the African Studies Center. Vol. 1. Gainesville: University of Florida, 1970.

1673. Organization of Angolan Women. "Report of the Seminar of the All-African Women's Conference." Dar-es-Salaam: July 1972.

1674. Talbot, D. A. Women's Mysteries of a Primitive People. London: Cassell, 1915.

1675. United Nations Food and Agriculture Organization. "Women's Groups in Rural Development." Rome: FAO, 1975. Available from UNIPUB, Box 433, Murray Hill Station, New York, 10016.

1676. "Women's Work." Advance, v. 48, October 1965: 1-32.

West Africa

1677. Balde, S. "Les associations d'âge chez les Foulbé du Fouta-Djallon." Bulletin de L'IFAN, v. 1 (1), 1939: 89-109.

1678. Butt-Thompson, F. West African Secret Societies. London: Witherby, 1929.

1679. Chilver, E. M., and P. M. Kaberry. "The Kingdom of Kom in West Cameroon." In D. Forde and P. N. Kaberry, eds., West African Kingdoms in the Nineteenth Century. London: Oxford University Press for the International African Institute, 1969.

1680. Donner, Etta. "Togba, a Women's Society in Liberia." Africa, v. 11, 1938: 109-111.

1681. Ema, A. J. Udo. "Fattening Girls in Oron, Calabar Province." Nigeria, v. 21, 1940: 386-389.

1682. Jaulin, Robert. "Questions Concerning Women. Eléments et aspects divers de l'organisation civile et pénale des groupes du Moyen-Chari: Groupe sara madjingaye et groupe mbaye." Bulletin de L'IFAN, v. 20, B (1-2), 1958: 170-184.

1683. Jawara, A. "The Gambia Women's Federation." Women Today, v. 6 (4), June 1965: 79-81.

1684. Jeffreys, M. D. W. "The Nyama Society of the Ibibio Women." African Studies, v. 15 (1), 1956: 15-29.

1685. Jellicoe, M. R. "Women's Groups in Sierra Leone." African Women, v. 1 (2), June 1955: 35-43.

1686. Kaberry, P. M. Aboriginal Women: Sacred and Profane. London: Routledge and Keagan Paul, 1939.

1687. "Lagos Women's Play." Nigeria, v. 58, 1958: 225-237.

1688. Little, Kenneth L. "The Poro Society as an Arbiter of Culture (Sierra Leone)." African Studies, v. 7 (1), 1948: 1-15.

1689. _____. "Two West African Elites." International Social Science Bulletin, v. 8 (3), 1956: 495-498.

1690. _____. "Voluntary Associations and Social Mobility among West African Women." Canadian Journal of African Studies, v. 6 (2), 1972: 275-288.

1691. MacCormack, Carol. "Cultural Control of Biological Events and the Organizational Potential for Development: Sierra Leone." Paper presented at the Wellesley Conference on Women and Development, June 1976. Available from Wellesley Center for Research on Women, 828 Washington St., Wellesley, Massachusetts 02181.

1692. Maclatchy, A. "The Women's Society. L'Organisation sociale de la région de Mimongo (Gabon)." Bulletin de L'Institut d'Études Centrafricaines, v. 1 (1), 1945: 81-82.

1693. Mauny, R. "Masques mende de la société bundu (Sierra Leone)." Notes Africaines, v. 81, 1959: 8-13.

1694. O'Kelly, E. "Corn Mill Societies in Southern Cameroons." African Women, v. 1 (1), 1955: 33-35.

1695. Rouch, J., and E. Bernus. "Notes sur les prostituées toutou de Treichville et d'Adjamé." Études Eburnéennes, v. 6, 1957: 231-242.

1696. Tastevin, Constant. Société secrète féminine chez les Bakoko (Cameroun). Brussels: 16th International Congress of Anthropology and Prehistoric Archeology, 1935: 901-906.

Central Africa

1697. Brausch, G. E. J. B. "Les Associations prenuptiales dans la Haute Lukenyi." Bulletin des Juridictions Indigènes et du Droit Coutumier Congolais, v. 4, 1947: 109-129.

1698. Burton, W. F. P. "The Secret Societies of Lubaland (Congo Belge)." Bantu Studies, v. 4 (4), 1930: 217-250.

1699. Dricot, F. "Jeuness-féminine dans un camp de travailleurs au Katanga." Cahiers des Auxiliaires Laïques des Missions, v. 3, 1951: 25-35.

1700. Even, A. "Les Confréries secrètes chez les Babamba et les Mindassa d'Okondja." Bulletin de la Société de Recherches Congolaises, v. 23-24, 1937: 51-72.

1701. _____. "Les Propriétés maléfiques et bénéfiques du sexe de la femme selon des croyanees des Babamba et des Mindassa (Moyen Congo, A. E. F.)." Bulletin et Mémoires de la Société d'Anthropologie de Paris, v. 10 (1-3), 1939: 51-72.

1702. Holding, E. M. "Some Preliminary Notes on Meru Age-Grades." Man, v. 42, 1942: 58-65.

1703. "La Programme d'action sociale de la femme au Ruanda." Servir, v. 25 (1), 1964: 36-37.

1704. Pedrals, D. P. de. "Une Curieuse fondation, le Yéhoué." Encyclopédie Mensuelle d'Outre-Mer, v. 4 (43), 1954: 107-108.

1705. Rademaekers, Mlle M. "Activités pour femme adults au foyer social de L'U. M. H. K. à Panda-Jadotville." Bulletin du CEPSI, v. 44, March 1959: 43-51.

1706. Zugnoni, J. "Yilede, a Secret Society among the Gbaya (Kreish), Aja, Banda Tribes of the Western District of Equatoria." Sudan Notes and Records, v. 26 (1), 1945: 105-111.

East Africa

1707. Curley, Richard T. Elders, Shades, and Women: Ceremonial Change in Lango, Uganda. Berkeley: University of California Press, 1973.

1708. Hastie, P. "Womens' Clubs in Uganda." Mass Education Bulletin, v. 2 (1), December 1950: 4-6.

1709. Interantional Co-operative Alliance. "Report of the Proceedings of the ICA Regional Women Co-operators Seminar, Kampala." Mimeo. Moshi, Tanzania: ICA Regional Office for East and Central Africa, January 1974.

1710. Juma, Waziri. "The Sukuma Societies for Young Men and Women." Tanganyika Notes and Records, v. 54, 1960: 27-29.

1711. Lambert, H. E. Kikuyu Social and Political Institutions. Oxford: Oxford University Press, 1956. Chapters IV, VI, VII, IX.

1712. Nelson, N. "Network for Survival." Ceres, v. 8 (2), April 1975: 42-45.

1713. Pankhurst, Sylvia. "Ethiopian Women's Welfare Association." Ethiopia Observer, v. 4 (2), March 1960: 45-47.

1714. Stuart, Mrs. "Uganda Mothers." Union Books for Africa, v. 14 (3), July 1944: 40-42.

1715. Wainwright, Bridget. "I Was a Homecraft Officer." Corona, v. 6 (8), August 1954: 297-298.

1716. _____. "Women's Clubs in the Central Nyanza District of Kenya." Community Development Bulletin, v. 4 (4), September 1953: 77-80.

1717. Wipper, Audrey. "The Maendeleo Ya Wanawake Movement: Some Paradoxes and Contradictions." African Studies Review, v. 18 (3), December 1975: 99-120.

1718. _____. "The Maendeleo Ya Wanawake Movement in the Colonial Period." Rural Africana, Winter 1975-1976.

1719. "Women's International Club." Ethiopia Observer, v. 4 (2), March 1960: 58.

Southern Africa

1720. Blacking, J. "Fictitious Kinship among Girls of the Venda of the Northern Transvaal." Man, v. 59, 1959: 155-157.

1721. Michelman, Cherry. The Black Sash of South Africa. Oxford: Oxford University Press, 1975.

1722. Silberbauer, G. B. "Marriage and the Girls' Puberty Ceremony of the G/wi Bushmen." Africa, v. 22 (1), January 1963: 12-24.

Latin America--General

1723. Cannon, Mary Minerva. "Women's Organizations in Ecuador, Paraguay, and Peru." Bulletin of the Pan American Union, v. 77, 1943: 601-607.

1724. "Declaración de principios de la Comisión Interamericana de Mujeres." Ciencia Interamericana, v. 16 (3-4), July-December 1975: 9.

1725. Frederick, William F. "Two Organizations Advance Women's Status in Latin America." Labor Developments Abroad, v. 15 (6), 1970: 4-10.

1726. Labarca Hubertson, Amanda. "La Asamblea Internacional de Mujeres de Sur América." Ciencia, September-October 1947: 277-283.

1727. Pan American Union. "Women's Cooperative Banking and Industrial Society Has Recently Been Organized: Purposes of the Society." Bulletin, v. 64, October 1936: 107.

1728. Ware, Caroline F. "Mujeres ciudadanas." Americas, v. 20 (1), 1968: 30-34.

Mexico and Central America

1729. Dotson, Floyd. "A Note on Participation in Voluntary Associations in a Mexican City." American Sociological Review, v. 18 (4), 1953: 380-386.

1730. Muriel de la Torre, Josefina. Los recogimientos de mujeres. Mexico City: Universidad Nacional Autónoma de Mexico, Instituto de Investigaciones Históricas, 1974.

1731. "Unión de Ciudadanas de Panamá." Tierra y Dos Mares, v. 7 (39), 1968: 8-9, 38, 44.

Caribbean

1732. Aguilar, Onelia. "La Federación de Mujeres Cubanas." Verde Olivo, 3 September 1960: 74-75.

1733. "The Federation of Cuban Women: A Decisive Force of Our Revolution." Granma Weekly Review, 29 August 1971: 3.

1734. Steffens, Heidi. "F. M. C.: Feminine, not Feminist." Cuba Review, v. 4 (2), 1974: 22-24.

1735. _____. "F. M. C. at the Grass Roots." Cuba Review, v. 4 (2), 1974: 25-26.

Andean Region

1736. Gillin, Helen N. "The Other Half: Women in Colombian Life." In A. C. Wilgus, ed., The Caribbean: Contemporary Colombia. Gainesville: University of Florida Press, 1962: 234-250.

1737. Misch, Marion Ruth, and Joseph B. Margolin. "Rural Women's Groups as Potential Change Agents: A Study of Colombia, Korea, and the Philippines." Mimeo. Washington, D.C.: George Washington University, Program of Policy Studies in Science and Technology, 1975.

1738. Schipske, Evelyn G. "An Analysis of the Consejo Nacional de Mujeres del Peru." Journal of Interamerican Studies and World Affairs, v. 17 (4), November 1975: 426-438.

1739. Unión de Mujeres de Bolivia. Orientación revolucionaria del Unión de Mujeres de Bolivia: Primer Congreso Nacional, La Paz, 1966.

1740. Villanueva y Saavedra, Etelvina. "Acción socialista de la mujer en Bolivia." La Paz: 1970.

Chile and the Platine

1741. Newhall, Beatrice. "Feminist Union of Chile." Bulletin of the Pan American Union, v. 67, February 1933: 142-143.

1742. Pan American Union. "Activities of the National Council of Women (Argentina)." Bulletin of the Pan American Union, v. 65, January 1931: 104.

1743. _____. "Argentine Federation of University Women." Bulletin of the Pan American Union, v. 73, January 1939: 59.

B. FEMINIST MOVEMENTS

Africa--General

1744. Awobajo, Theophilus D. "African Version of Women's Liberation." African Progress Magazine, v. 1, September-October 1971: 21-22.

1745. Awori, Thelma. "For African Women Equal Rights Are Not Enough." UNESCO Courier, March 1975.

1746. Femmes et mères d'Afrique: Congrés Africain au mouvement mondial des mères. Paris: Bibliographie Ethnographique de l'Afrique Sud-Saharienne, 1962.

1747. Gillespie, Iris S. "Sex War in a Developing Country." Mimeo. 1970. Available from the author at 60 Northcourt Ave., Reading, England.

1748. Kiba, Simon. "Avant de partir en guerre pour liberer la femme africaine." Afrique Nouvelle, v. 20 (992), 11-17 August 1966: 16.

1749. Nabaraoui, Céza. "African Women Seek Independence and Peace." Freedomways, v. 1, Spring 1961: 102-106.

1750. Somal, M. "La Femme dans la nation." Trait d'Union. (Fiches de Documentation), v. 70 (6), August 1961: 1-3.

1751. Spinks, M. "Do African Women Want Emanicipation?" African World, December 1968: 6-7.

1752. Wipper, Audrey. "The Politics of Sex." African Studies Review, v. 14 (3), 1971: 463-482.

West Africa

1753. Aiyfola, L. "Speaking with One Voice." Flamingo, v. 5 (5), February 1966: 51-53.

1754. "Calabar." Nigeria, v. 52, 1956: 70-88.

1755. Dobert, Margarita. "Liberation and the Women of Guinea." Africa Report, v. 15 (7), October 1970: 26-28.

1756. Esike, S. O. "The Aba Riots of 1929." African Historian, no. 3, March 1965: 7-13.

1757. Gailey, H. The Road to Aba. London: University of London Press, 1971.

1758. Ifeka-Moller, Caroline. "Female Militancy and the Colonial Revolt: The Women's War of 1929, Eastern Nigeria." In Shirley Ardener, ed., Perceiving Women. London: Malaby Press, 1975: 127-157.

1759. Ogundpipe-Leslie, Omolara. "Women's Protest Movements in West Africa." Paper presented at the Wellesley Conference on Women and Development, June 1976. Available from Wellesley Center for Research on Women, 828 Washington St., Wellesley, Massachusetts 02181.

1760. Paulme, Denise. "Un Mouvement féminin en pays kissi." Notes Africaines, v. 46, April 1950: 43-44.

1761. Retif, André. "Vers la libération de la femme camerounaise." Études, v. 284 (1), January 1955: 8-88.

1762. Urdang, Stephanie. "Towards a Successful Revolution: The Women's Struggle in Guinea-Bissau (for Women's Liberation)." Objective Justice, v. 11, January-March, 1975: 11-17.

1763. Van Allen, Judith. "Sitting on a Man: Colonialism and the Lost Political Institutions of Igbo Women." Canadian Journal of African Studies, v. 6 (2), 1972: 165-182.

1764. _____. "Memsahib, Militante, femme libre: Political and Apolitical Styles of Modern African Women." In Jane S. Jaquette, ed., Women in Politics. New York: John Wiley and Sons, 1974: 304-321.

Central Africa

1765. "La Femme congolaise et son émancipation." Assistance aux Maternités et Dispensaires de L'Afrique Centrale, v. 27, October 1970: 7-19.

1766. Kashif, H. "The Sudanese Women's Movement." African Women, v. 3 (3), December 1959: 55-56.

1767. Nzeza, A. M. "La Libération de la femme africaine." Remarques Africaines, v. 8 (275), 20 October 1966: 512-515.

East Africa

1768. Alport, C. J. M. "Kenya's Answer to the Mau-Mau Challenge." African Affairs, v. 53, 1954: 241-247.

1769. Berman, Sanford. "Women/Sexism/the Feminist Movement: A Roster of Material at the Makarere Institute of Social Research Library." Paper no. 28. Kampala, Uganda: Makarere Institute of Social Research, 1972.

1770. "International Feminists Congratulate Ethiopian Women." Ethiopia Observer, v. 1 (7), August 1957: 211-212.

1771. Malcomson, Margaret. "The Emancipation of African Women." East African Annual, 1945-1946: 85-86.

1772. _____. "Kikuyu Women Prove Their Right to Emancipation." East African Standard, 8 April 1949: 15.

1773. Wipper, Audrey. "Equal Rights for Women in Kenya?" Journal of Modern African Studies, v. 9 (3), October 1971: 463-476.

Southern Africa

1774. Bernstein, Hilda Watts. For Their Triumphs and for Their Tears: Conditions and Resistance of Women in Apartheid South Africa. London: International Defence and Aid Fund, 1975.

1775. Clay, G. "The Demonstrations in South Africa. What Makes the Women March?" New York Herald Tribune, 10 September 1959.

1776. Dhlamini, Z. "Women's Liberation: A Black South African Woman's View." Sechaba, v. 6 (9), September 1972: 4-8.

1777. Malama, Duncan S. "Zambian Women Get into New Struggle against Their Men." Outlook, September 1968: 12-13.

Latin America--General

1778. Dickmann, Enrique. Emancipación civil, política y social de la mujer. Buenos Aires: 1935.

1779. Dussel, Enrique. "Towards a Methodology of Women's Liberation, Latin American Style." Boletin Documental Sobre las Mujeres, v. 0 (1), 1970.

1780. García Gradilla, Natividad. "Liberación de la mujer en América Latina." Summa, v. 52, 1972: 13-14.

1781. _____. "Realité et utopie d'un mouvement de liberation des femmes en Amérique Latine." Revue des Temps Modernes, v. 29, 1974: 2723-2735.

1782. Henault, Mirta; Peggy Morton and Isabel Larguia, eds., Las mujeres dicen basta! Buenos Aires: Ed. Nueva Mujer, 1972.

1783. Inman, Samuel Guy. "The Feminist Movement in Latin America." Bulletin of the Pan American Union, v. 54 (353): 1922.

1784. Larguía, Isabel, and John Demoulin. "Toward a Science of Women's Liberation." NACLA's Latin America and Empire Report, v. 6 (10), 1972: 3-20.

1785. Leavitt, R. R., ed., Cross-Cultural Perspectives on the Women's Movement and Women's Status. The Hague: Mouton, 1976.

1786. Mañon, Darío A. Orientaciones feministas para las mujeres de América. Mexico City: Ed. Ibero-Mexicana, 1956.

1787. Moro, America. "La liberación de la mujer latinoamericana." Fichas de ISAL, v. 4 (46), 1973: 1-18.

1788. Nelson, Jas. F. "Some Causes and Consequences of Female Liberation Attitudes in Two Latin American Metropolises: A Causal Analysis of Non-Interval Data." Ph.D. dissertation, University of Chicago, 1975.

1789. Sánchez Morales, Aurelia Gpe. "La liberación de la mujer en América Latina." Boletin Documental sobre las Mujeres, v. 5 (2), 1975: 3-17.

1790. Shokina, Izabella. "El movimiento femenino en América Latina." América Latina, v. 4, 1975: 65-81.

1791. Stevens, Evelyn P. "The Prospects for a Woman's Liberation Movement in Latin America." Journal of Marriage and the Family, v. 35 (2), 1973: 313-321.

1792. "The Women of Latin America and the Fight for Equality." Development Forum, v. 3 (8), 1975: 4.

Mexico and Central America

1793. Acevedo, Marta. "Sobre el sexismo mexicano; I. Primeras consideraciones." La Cultura en Mexico, no. 553, 13 September 1972: 8-9.

1794. Campuzano, Felipe. "Antisexismo; de la liberación de la mujer como abolición del trabajo invisible." La Cultura en Mexico, no. 600, 1973: 13-14.

1795. Figueiredo, Mariza, ed., La liberación de la mujer; dossier. Mexico City: Ed. Asociados, 1974.

1796. Gonzalez de Behringer, C. Orientación feminista. Panama City: Revista, 1925.

1797. Laurell, Cristina. "Sobre el sexismo mexicano; II. La ofensiva patriarcal y el movimiento de la mujer." La Cultura en Mexcio, no. 553, 13 September 1972: 10.

1798. Moncada, Raul. "Si las mujeres mandasen (el movimiento feminista de México)." Hoy, 23 June 1945: 22-23.

1799. Montes, Segundo. "La liberación femenina." Estudios Centroamericanos, v. 30 (316-317), 1975: 115-128.

1800. "Mujeres en Acción Solidaria." Punto Crítico, v. 2 (24), 1974: 50-51.

1801. Parroquia de Somoto, Nicaragua. "Material de trabajo para la concientización de la mujer campesina." (n.d.)

1802. Zendejas, Adelina. "El movimiento femenil mexicano (breve reseña historica)." Boletin Documental Sobre las Mujeres, v. 5 (2), 1975: 27-35.

Caribbean

1803. Cambre Mariño, Jesús. "La concientización sociopolítica de la mujer." Revista de Ciencias Sociales, v. 16, December 1972: 475-490.

1804. "Feminismo Balaguerista: a Strategy of the Right." NACLA's Latin America and Empire Report, v. 8 (4), 1974: 28-32.

1805. Fernandez Cintrón, Celia, and Marcia Rivera Quintero. "Bases de la sociedad sexista en Puerto Rico." Interamerican Review, v. 4 (2), 1974: 239-245.

1806. Gordon, Linda. "Speculations on Women's Liberation in Cuba." Women: A Journal of Liberation, v. 1 (4), 1970: 14-15.

1807. Lara Fernandez, Carmen. Historia del feminismo en la República Dominicana. Ciudad Trujillo: Imp. Arte y Cine, 1946.

1808. Lopez, Olga. "La rebeldía de la mujer cubana." Cuba Internacional, March 1972: 4-11.

1809. Madrigal, Stasia. "Cuba's Radical Feminists." Direct from Cuba, 15 March 1973: 1-4.

1810. Mortizen, Julius. "Political Emancipation of Dominican Women: A National Asset." The Dominican Republic, January-February, 1943: 14-15.

1811. Pogolotti, Graziella. "Revolución, lucha de clases, y condición feminina." Casa de las Américas, v. 14 (82), 1974: 169-171.

Andean Region

1812. Aguirre Elorriaga, Manuel. "La promoción de la mujer." SIC: Revista Venezolana de Orientación, v. 31 (303), 1968: 117-119.

1813. Blanco-Fombona, Miriam. "Venezuela's Feminist Movement Is Still in Its Early Stages, But the Future for Women in the Republic is a Bright One." Latin American World, v. 28 (30), August 1947.

1814. Cáceres, Zoila Aurora. Estatutos y reglamentos del feminismo peruano. Lima: 1938.

1815. _____. Feminismo peruano. Lima: 1924.

1816. Lopez Civiera, Francisca. "A cincuenta años del Primer Congreso de Mujeres." Bohemia, 17 August 1972: 100-103.

1817. Marpons, Josefina. "La mujer en la lucha por la libertad." Revista de America, April 1946: 41-45.

1818. Martinez M., María Esther. "El problema feminista en el Ecuador." Nuevos Horizontes, v. 7 (27), November 1933.

1819. Uribe de Acosta, Ofelia. Una voz insurgente. Bogotá: Ed. Guadalupe, 1963.

Chile and the Platine

1820. Anzóategui, Yderla G. La mujer y la política; Historia del feminismo. Buenos Aires: Ed. Mendoza, 1953.

1821. Arenales, Miguel. "Igualdad y libertad para la mujer." Dinámica Social, v. 11 (135), January-March 1962: 27+.

1822. Bambirra, Vania. "La mujer chilena en la transición al socialismo." Punto Final, v. 5 (133), 1971.

1823. _____. "Women's Liberation and Class Struggle." Translated by B. Bayer and C. Krels. Review of Radical Political Economics, v. 4 (3), 1972: 75-84.

1824. Chaney, Elsa M. "Old and New Feminists in Latin America: Peru and Chile." Journal of Marriage and the Family, v. 35 (2), 1973: 331-343.

1825. Labarca Hubertson, Amanda. Feminismo contemporáneo. Santiago: Zig-Zag, 1947.

1826. _____. "Trayectoria del movimiento feminista en Chile." Diagonal, 18 October 1945: 6.

1827. Little, Cynthia Jeffries. "The Development of the Argentine Feminist Movement and its Role in the 1926 Reform of the Civil

Code." Paper presented at Berkshire Conference on Women's History, March 1973.

1828. _____. "Moral Reforms and Feminism: A Case Study." Journal of Interamerican Studies and World Affairs, v. 17 (4), November 1975: 386-397.

1829. Machado Bonet, Ofelia. Hacia la revolución del siglo. Montevideo: Edit. Goes, 1972.

1830. Pan American Union. "Chile's First National Congress of Women." Bulletin, v. 79, March 1945: 176-177.

1831. _____. "Congress of Uruguayan Women." Bulletin, v. 79, April 1945: 246-247.

1832. Vidal, Virginia. "La emancipación de la mujer." Santiago: 1972.

1833. Yañez, Anabella T., ed., "Acerca de la mujer en el proceso de liberación." Documento de trabajo no. 1. Mendoza, Arg.: Ed. IASYF, 1973.

Brazil

1834. Austregesilo, Antonio. Pérfil da mulher brasileira (esboco a cerca do feminismo no Brasil). Rio de Janeiro: Ed. Guanabara, 1938.

1835. da Silva, María Lucia Carbalho. "Algumas considerações sobre e emancipação da mulher." Mimeo. São Paulo: Serviço Social do Comercio, 1970.

1836. d'Eca, Raúl. "Feminism in Brazil." Bulletin, v. 70, December 1936: 981-982.

1837. Mitchell, Juliet. "Mulheres: A revolução mais longa." Revista Civilização Brasileira, v. 14, July 1967: 5-6.

Editors' Note: For references on suffrage see Pan American Union. Index to Latin American Periodical Literature, 1921-1960. 8 vols.; and Supplement 1961-1965, 2 vols. See also "Politics and Revolutionary Movements." In Meri Knaster, ed., Women in Spanish America: An Annotated Bibliography. Boston: G. K. Hall, 1977: 524-560.

Chapter VIII

WOMEN AND THE ECONOMY

Chapter 8 deals with women's participation in both the informal and formal sectors of the economy, the political economy of women's roles, and the social aspects of women's labor. Section A, "The Political Economy of Women's Roles," covers such topics as access to technology, the impact of industrialization on traditional productive roles and the changing status of women in developing economies. Section B, "The Informal Sector," includes references on home labor, handicrafts, domestic service, prostitution and the division of labor by sex in rural areas. Rural labor and prostitution predominate as topics for Africa, while Latin American entries emphasize handicraft production — particularly weaving — and domestic service.

Section C, "Marketing and Commerce," considers women in peasant marketing systems and as urban vendors. References on women's participation in industry, labor unions, and the professions comprise section D, "The Formal Sector." Section E, "Social Aspects of Women's Labor," contains entries on role incompatibility, factors affecting labor force participation, e.g., educational attainment and marital status, problems of the working mother, and the exploitation of female labor.

This chapter is biased in favor of Latin American materials; some sections contain twice as many entries for this region as for Africa. This can be attributed to the greater interest in the formal employment of women in Latin America and in the tensions resulting from the conflicting roles of mother and worker.

For further references on the employment of educated women and specialized job training, see Chapter 5.

A. THE POLITICAL ECONOMY OF WOMEN'S ROLES

Africa--General

1838. Aberle, David F. "Matrilineal Descent in Cross-Cultural Perspective." In David M. Schneider and Kathleen Gough, eds., Matrilineal Kinship. Berkeley: University of California Press, 1961: 655-727.

1839. Colson, Elizabeth. "The Impact of the Colonial Period on the Definition of Land Rights." In Victor W. Turner, ed., Colonialism in Africa, 1870-1960. Cambridge: Cambridge University Press, 1971: 193-215.

1840. Douglas, Mary T. "Is Matriliny Doomed in Africa?" In Mary T. Douglas and Phyliss Kaberry, eds., Man in Africa. London: Tavistack, 1969: 121-135.

1841. Gluxman, Max. Politics, Law, and Ritual in Tribal Society. Chicago: Aldine, 1965.

1842. Gugler, Joseph. "The Second Sex in Town." Canadian Journal of African Studies, v. 6 (2), 1972: 289-302.

1843. Lancaster, Chet S. "Women, Horticulture, and Society in Sub-Saharan Africa." American Anthropologist, v. 78 (3), September 1976: 539-564.

1844. Leacock, Eleanor B. "Introduction." In Eleanor B. Leacock, ed., The Origin of the Family, Private Property, and the State, by Friedrich Engels. New York: International Publishers, 1972: 7-67.

1845. Lee, Richard B., and Irven DeVore, eds., Man the Hunter. Chicago: Aldine, 1968.

1846. Mbilinyi, Marjorie J. "Women's Education, Labor Force Participation, and Underdevelopment." Paper presented at the Wellesley Conference on Women and Development, June 1976. Available from Wellesley Center for Research on Women, 828 Washington Street, Wellesley, Massachusetts 02181.

1847. _____. "Women as Labour in Underdevelopment." Paper presented at the Wellesley Conference on Women and Development, June 1976. Available from Wellesley Center for Research on

Women, 828 Washington Street, Wellesley, Massachusetts 02181.

1848. Phillips, John F. V. <u>Agriculture and Ecology in Africa</u>. London: Faber & Faber, 1959.

1849. Sacks, Karen Helen Brodkin. "Economic Bases of Sexual Equality: A Comparative Study of Four African Societies." Ph.D. dissertation, University of Michigan, 1971.

1850. Sow, F. "Dépendence et développement: Le Statut de la femme en Afrique moderne." Unpublished manuscript, 1972.

1851. Schmidt, W. "The Position of Women with Regard to Property in Primitive Society." <u>American Anthropologist</u>, v. 37, 1935: 244-256.

1852. Schneider, David M. "The Distinctive Features of Matrilineal Descent Groups." In David M. Schneider and Kathleen Gough, eds., <u>Matrilineal Kinship</u>. Berkeley: University of California Press, 1962: 1-29.

1853. Schneider, Harold K. "A Model of African Indigenous Economy and Society." <u>Comparative Studies in Society and History</u>, v. 7, 1964: 37-55.

1854. _____. "Turu Ecology: Habitat, Mode of Production, and Society." <u>Africa</u>, v. 36, 1966: 254-268.

1855. Van Allen, Judith. "Women in Africa: Modernization Means More Dependency." <u>The Center Magazine</u>, v. 7 (3), May-June 1974: 60-67.

West Africa

1856. Urdang, Stephanie. "Fighting Two Colonialisms: The Women's Struggle in Guinea-Bissau." <u>African Studies Review</u>, v. 18 (3), December 1975: 29-34.

Central Africa

1857. Lancaster, Chet S., and Anatole Pohorilenko. "Ingombe Ilede and the Zimbabwe Culture." <u>International Journal of African Historical Studies</u>, v. 9, 1976.

1858. Richards, Audrey I. "Mother-Right Among the Central Bantu." In E. E. Evans-Pritchard et al., eds., <u>Essays Presented to C. G. Seligman</u>. London: Kegan Paul, Trench, and Truber, 1934: 267-279.

1859. _____. <u>Land, Labour and Diet in Northern Rhodesia</u>. London: Oxford University Press, 1939.

East Africa

1860. Mbilinyi, Marjorie J. "Barriers to the Full Participation of Women in the Socialist Transformation of Tanzania." Mimeo. University of Dar-es-Salaami, Tanzania: 1974.

1861. Schneider, Harold K. The Wahi Wanyaturu: Economics in an African Society. Viking Fund Publications in Anthropology, 1970.

Southern Africa

1862. Kolata, Gina B. "!Kung Hunter — Gatherers: Femininism, Diet, and Birth Control." Science, v. 185, 1974: 932-934.

Latin America--General

1863. Chaney, Elsa M. and Marianne Schmink. "Women and Modernization: Access to Tools." In June Nash and Helen I. Safa, eds., Sex and Class in Latin America. New York: Praeger, 1976: 160-187. Also cited as "Las mujeres y la modernización: Acceso a la tecnología." La mujer en America Latina, v. 1. Mexico City: Sepsetentas, 1975.

1864. Chaney, Elsa M.; Marianne Schmink; and Gloria Galotti. "Going From Bad to Worse: Women and Modernization." Paper presented at the Conference on Feminine Perspectives in Social Science Research in Latin America, Buenos Aires, 1974.

1865. Larguía, Isabel. "La mujer." In M. Herrault et al., eds., Las mujeres dicen basta. Buenos Aires: Ediciones Nueva Mujer, 1972: 71-128.

1866. Larguía, Isabel, and John Demoulin. "Aspects for the Conditions of Women's Labor." NACLA Latin America and Empire Report, v. 9 (6), September 1975: 2-9.

1867. Saffioti, Heleith Iara B. "Women, Mode of Production, and Social Formation." Latin American Perspectives, v. 4 (1-2), Winter-Spring 1977: 27-37.

1868. Wasserspring, Lois. "Inequality and Development: Women in Latin America." Paper presented at the Wellesley Conference on Women and Development, June 1976. Available from Wellesley Center for Research on Women, 828 Washington Street, Wellesley, Massachusetts 02181.

Mexico and Central America

1869. Chinchilla, Norma. "Industrialization, Monopoly Capitalism, and 'Women's Work' in the United States and Guatemala." Paper presented at the Wellesley Conference on Women and Development, June 1976. Forthcoming in SIGNS, Fall 1977. Available from Wellesley Center for Research on Women, 828 Washington Street, Wellesley, Massachusetts 02181.

Andean Region

1870. Bourque, Susan C., and Kay B. Warren. "Campesinas y comuneras: Subordinación en la sierra peruana." Estudios Andinos, v. 5 (1), 1976: 77-98.

1871. Chaney, Elsa M. "Women at the Marginal Pole of the Economy: The Case of Peru." Paper presented at the Wellesley Conference on Women and Development, June 1976. Available from Wellesley Center for Research on Women, 828 Washington Street, Wellesley, Massachusetts 02181.

1872. Deere, Carmen Diana. "Changing Social Relations of Production and Peruvian Peasant Women's Work." Latin American Perspectives, v, 4 (1-2), Winter-Spring 1977: 48-69.

Brazil

1873. Aguiar, Neuma. "The Impact of Industrialization on Women's Work Roles in Northeast Brazil." In June Nash and Helen I. Safa, eds., Sex and Class in Latin America. New York: Praeger, 1976: 110-128. Also cited as Studies in Comparative International Development, v. 10 (2), Summer 1975: 78-94.

1874. Saffioti, Heleith Iara B. A mulher na sociedade de classe: mito e realidade. Saõ Paulo: Quatro Artes, 1969.

1875. _____. "Relaciones de sexo y clases sociales." In La mujer en América Latina, Vol. II. Mexico City: Sepsetentas, 1975: 35-59. Also cited (in English) as "Relationships of Sex and Social Class in Brazil." In June Nash and Helen I. Safa, eds., Sex and Class in Latin America. New York: Praeger, 1976: 147-157.

B. THE INFORMAL SECTOR (Includes home labor, handicrafts, rural participation, prostitution, and domestic service.)

Africa--General

1876. Allan, William. The African Husbandman. New York: Basic

Books, 1965.

1877. Baumann, Hermann. "The Division of Work According to Sex in African Hoe Agriculture." Africa, v. 1, 1928: 289-319.

1878. Belcher, A. "The Future of Pottery for African Women." African Women, v. 2 (2), 1957: 28-29.

1879. Bunbury, Isla. "Women's Position as Workers in Africa South of the Sahara." Civilizations, v. 11 (2), 1961: 159-168.

1880. Cleave, John H. African Farmers: Labor Use in the Development of Smallholder Agriculture. New York: Praeger, 1974.

1881. Cornet, R. P. La Femme en régime matriarcal; Rapports et Comptes rendus de la XX Semaine de Missiologie de Louvain, 1950. Brussels: Ed. Universelle, 1951: 192-209.

1882. Dupire, Marguerite. "The Position of Women in a Pastoral Society." In Denise Paulme, ed., Women of Tropical Africa. London: Routledge and Kegan Paul, 1963: 47-92.

1883. Dyson-Hudson, V. R. "Men, Women, and Work in a Pastoral Society." Natural History, v. 69 (10), December 1960: 42-57.

1884. Goody, Jack, and Joan Buckley. "Inheritance and Women's Labour in Africa." Africa, v. 43 (2), April 1973: 108-121.

1885. LeVine, Robert A. "Sex Roles and Economic Change in Africa." Ethnology, v. 5, April 1966: 186-193.

1886. Marris, P. "The Social Barriers to African Entrepreneurship." Mimeo Series, no. 22. Brighton: University of Sussex, Institute of Development Studies, 1969.

1887. Mbilinyi, Marjorie J. "The Participation of Women in African Economies." Paper ERB 71.12. Dar-es-Salaam: University Economic Research Bureau, 1971.

1888. Moore, M. P. "Some Economic Aspects of Women's Work and Status in the Rural Areas of Africa and Asia." IDS Discussion Paper, no. 43. Mimeo. Brighton: University of Sussex, Institute of Development Studies, 1974.

1889. Paulme, Denise. "La Femme Africaine au travail." Présence Africaine, v. 13, 1952: 116-123.

1890. Read, M. Migrant Labour in Africa and Its Effects on Tribal Life. Montreal: International Labour Office, 1943.

1891. Robalino, I. "La Femme travailleuse en Equateur." Labor, v. 5, 1967: 257-262.

1892. "Unemployment in Forest Regions: Servitude of Women." In René Dumont, ed., False Start in Africa. New York: Praeger, 1966: 227-230.

1893. United Nations Economic Commission for Africa. Human Resources Development Division. Women's Programme Unit. "Selected Projects in Handicrafts and Other Small Industries in English-Speaking African Countries." Mimeo. Mindolo, Zambia: 1974.

1894. Walker, K. E., and H. M. Hauck. "Women's Work in Changing Villages." Journal of Home Economics, v. 56, April 1964: 233-238.

1895. Wantz, Marja-Liisa. "Women and Land: Basic Problems." Sunday News, Dar-es-Salaam, 18 August 1975.

West Africa

1896. Abell, H. Home Economics Aspects of the FAO Socio-Economic Survey of Peasant Agriculture in Northern Nigeria. Rome: United Nations Food and Agriculture Organization, 1962.

1897. Ames, D. "The Economic Base of Wolof Polygyny." Southwestern Journal of Anthropology, v. 11 (4), 1955: 391-403.

1898. Appia-Dabit, B. "Quelques Artisans Noirs." Bulletin de L'IFAN, v. 3 (3-4), 1941: 1-44.

1899. Beurnier, R. "Artisans et artisanes de Saint-Lours-de-Sénégal." Outre-Mer, December 1937: 279-300.

1900. Binet, Jacques. "Condition des femmes dans la région Cacaoyère du Camerous." Cahiers Internationaux de Sociologie, v. 20, January-June 1956: 109-123. Also cited as African Abstracts, v. 8 (2), 1957: 74.

1901. Burnley, Gwen E. "Woman's Work in West Cameroun." Women Today, v. 6 (2), June 1964: 34-35.

1902. Cardew, Michael. "Firing the Big Pot at Kwali." Nigeria Magazine, v. 70, September 1961: 199-205.

1903. Curryer, W. H. S. "Mothercraft in Southern Nigeria." United Empire, v. 18 (2), February 1927: 78-81.

1904. DuBois, Victor D. Prostitution in the Ivory Coast. New York: American Universities Field Staff, 1967. Also cited as West African Series, v. 10 (2), 1967.

1905. Gaudry, M. "Une exposition de travaux d'art féminine indigènes." L'Afrique Française, v. 8, August 1933: 461-466.

1906. Harris, Jack S. "Papers on the Economic Aspect of Life Among the Ozuitem Ibo." Africa, v. 14 (1), January 1943: 12-23.

1907. Helleiner, G. Peasant Agriculture, Government and Economic Growth in Nigeria. New Haven: Yale University Press, 1972.

1908. Hill, Polly. "Women Cocoa Farmers." Ghana Farmer, v. 2 (2), May 1958: 70-71; 76.

1909. International Labour Organization. Sénégal, l'action dans la domaine de l'économie familiale rurale. Geneva: International Labour Organization, 1971.

1910. Kaberry, Phyllis M. Women of the Grassfields. A Study of the Economic Position of Women in Bamenda, British Cameroons. London: H. M. Stationary Office, 1952.

1911. Kouaovi, B. M. "Les Tagalakoy ou Porteuses d'eau du Niger." Encyclopédie Mensuelle d'Outre-Mer, v. 5 (53), 1955: 46-47.

1912. Koulaseli. "La Levée chez les femmes du clan forgeron (Dikodougou, Côte d'Ivoire)." Notes Africaines, v. 103, July 1964: 81-83.

1913. Leger, A. "Le Chasseur et son chien, l'homme et la femme, Contes du pays Bamiléké au Cameroun." Togo-Cameroun, January 1932: 81.

1914. Leis, Nancy Boric. "Economic Independence and Ijaw Women: A Comparative Study of Two Communities in the Niger Delta." Ph.D. dissertation, Northwestern University, 1964.

1915. Lestrange, M. de. "La Journée de Madame Nemmé, femme Coniagui de la Guinée Française." Geographia, v. 1, 1951: 43-47.

1916. Liger, Z. "La Pêche des jeunes filles bozo et somuno à Kouakourou." Notes Africaines, v. 88, October 1960: 121-122.

1917. Marshall, Gloria. "In a World of Women: Field Work in a Yoruba Community." In Peggy Golde, ed., Women in the Field: Anthropological Experiences. Chicago: Aldine, 1970: 167-194.

1918. Murray, K. C. "Women's Weaving among the Yorubas at Omuaran in Ilorin Province." The Nigerian Field, v. 5 (4), 1936: 182-191.

1919. Norman, D. W. "Economic Analysis of Agricultural Production and Labour Utilization among the Hausa in the North of Nigeria." African Rural Employment Paper no. 4. East Lansing: Michigan State University, African Rural Employment Program, 1973.

1920. Okala, C., and S. Mabey. "Women in Agriculture in Southern Ghana." Manpower and Unemployment Research in Africa, v. 8 (2), November 1975.

1921. O'Kelly, Elizabeth. "Working Women in the Southern Cameroons." Corona, v. 13 (2), February 1961: 67-71.

1922. Opoku, Andrew A. "The Women of Ghana's Place in Agriculture." The Ghana Farmer, v. 9 (1), February 1965: 28-29.

1923. Oppong, Christine; Christine Okali; and Beverley Houghton. "Woman Power: Retrograde Steps in Ghana." American Sociological Review, v. 13 (3), December 1975: 71-84.

1924. Ottenberg, Phoebe. "The Changing Economic Position of Women Among the Afikpo Ibo." In William R. Bascome and Melville J. Herskovits, eds., Continuity and Change in African Cultures. Chicago: University of Chicago Press, 1959: 205-223.

1925. "Pottery in Ghana." African Women, v. 2 (4), 1958: 84-85.

1926. Poynor, Robin. "The Social Significance of Traditional Textiles in Owo, Nigeria." Paper presented at the annual meeting of the African Studies Association, San Francisco, October-November 1975.

1927. Sai, Florence Aleeno. "Market Women in the Economy of Ghana." Master's thesis, Cornell University, 1971.

1928. Schmidt, Agathe. "Field Researches into the Life of Women in the Grasslands of the Cameroons 1938-1939." Achiv für Völkerkunde, v. 4, 1949: 165-185.

1929. Simmons, Emmy Bartz. "The Small-Scale Rural Food Processing Industry in Northern Nigeria." Food Research Institute Studies, v. 14 (2), 1975.

1930. Spencer, D. S. C. "The Economics of Traditional and Semi-Traditional Systems of Rice Production in Sierra Leone." In Proceedings of the WARDA Seminar on the Socio-Economic Aspects of Rice Cultivation in West Africa, Monrovia, Liberia, 1974.

1931. _____. "Micro-Level Farm Management and Production Economics Research Among Traditional African Farmers: Lessons from Sierra Leone." African Rural Employment Paper no. 3. East Lansing: Department of Agricultural Economics, Michigan State University, 1972.

1932. "Travail coutumier et la situation sociale en Afrique noire française." Bulletin de l'Institute Inter-Africain du Travail, December 1953: 528-543.

1933. Wahlman, Maude, and Enyinna Chuta. "Sierra Leone Resists Dyed Textiles." Paper presented at the annual meeting of the African Studies Association, San Francisco, October-November 1975.

1934. Well, P. M. "Wet Rice, Women, and Adaptation in the Gambia." Rural Africana, v. 19, Winter 1973: 20-29.

Central Africa

1935. Abeele, Marcel Van Den. "Le Rôle de la femme dans le développement de la sériciculture au Congo Belge." Bulletin de L'Union des Femmes Coloniales, v. 8 (118), July 1947: 2-3.

1936. Davidson, Basil. "The 'Free Women' of Congo City." In Jacob Drachler, ed., African Heritage. New York: Colliers Books, 1973: 230-241.

1937. La Fontaine, Jean S. "The Free Women of Kinshasa: Prostitution in a City in Zaire." in J. Davis, ed., Choice and Change. London: Athlone Press, 1974: 89-113. Also cited as New York: Humanities Press, 1974.

1938. Maquet, E., and R. de Wilde. "Lés Tâches quotidiennes de la paysanne ruandaise." La Femme et le Congo, v. 27 (158), 157: 6-9.

1939. Mobe, A. M. "Encore un mot an sujet de la prostitution." Voix du Congolais, v. 95: 82-87.

1940. Pauwels, M. "Les Couleurs et les dessins du Ruanda." Anthropos, v. 47 (3-4), 1952: 474-482.

1941. Spelman, N. G. "Women's Work in the Gezira, Sudan." Overseas Education, v. 26 (2), July 1954: 66-69.

1942. "Sudan's Donkey-Back Midwives." Today's Health, January 1968: 16-18.

1943. Vincent, Jeanne-Françoise. "Le Travail des femmes à Tonkama, Village Lari." Annales du Centre de L'Enseignement Supérieur de Brazzaville, v. 2, 1966: 17-31.

1944. Wassa, F. "Liberté de la femme noire et prostitution." Voix du Congolais, v. 4 (23), February 1948: 71-72.

East Africa

1945. Bondestam, Lars. "Prostitution in Addis Ababa." Addis Ababa, 1972.

1946. Bujra, Janet M. "Women 'Entrepreueurs' of Early Nairobi." Canadian Journal of African Studies, v. 9 (2), November 1975: 213-234.

1947. Carlebach, Julius. Juvenile Prostitutes in Nairobi. East African Studies no. 16, 1962.

1948. Dyson-Hudson, Rada, and Neville Dyson-Hudson. "The Food Production System of a Semi-Nomadic Society: The Karimojong of Uganda." In P. M. McLaughlin, ed., African Food Production Systems: Cases and Theory. Baltimore: The Johns Hopkins Press, 1970: 91-123.

1949. Elam, Yitzchak. The Social and Sexual Roles of Hima Women: A Study of Nomadic Cattle Breeders in Nyabushozi County, Ankole, Uganda. Manchester: Manchester University Press, 1973.

1950. Fischer, J. The Anatomy of Kikuyu Domesticity and Husbandry. London: Department of Technical Cooperation, 1956.

1951. Fosbrooke, Jane. "Masai Women and Their Work." Crown Colonist, v. 14 (150), May 1944: 313-314.

1952. Hayley, T. T. Steiger. "Wage Labour and the Desire for Wives Among the Lango." Uganda Journal, v. 8 (1), September 1940: 15-18.

1953. Koeume, E. The African Housewife and Her Home. Nairobi: Eagle Press, 1952.

1954. Nsimbi, M. B. "Village Life and Customs in Buganda." Uganda Journal, v. 20 (1), 1956: 27-36.

1955. Olmstead, Judith. "Women and Work in Two Southern Ethiopian Communities." American Studies Review, v. 18 (3), December 1975: 85-98.

1956. Parkyns, Mansfield, and Charles Johnston. "Women's Life and Work in Old-Time Ethiopia." Ethiopia Observer, v. 2 (1), February 1958: 29-32.

1957. Staudt, Kathleen A. "Agricultural Policy, Political Power and Women Farmers in Western Kenya." Ph.D. dissertation, University of Wisconsin, 1976.

1958. Strange, Bertha F. "Kenya Women in Agriculture." Women Today, v. 6 (1), December 1963: 7-9.

1959. UNICEF (United Nations Children's Fund). "Womanpower in Kenya." UNICEF News, no. 51.

1960. Wills, Jane. "A Study of Time Allocation by Rural Women and Their Place in Decision Making: Preliminary Findings from Embu District." Rural Development Research Paper, no. 44, Makerere University College, 1967.

1961. "Women Farmers and Inequities in Agricultural Services." Rural Africana, v. 29, Winter 1975-76.

Southern Africa

1962. Clark, Barbara A. "The Work Done by Rural Women in Malawi." Zomba: Ministry of Agriculture and Natural Resources, 1972.

1963. _____. "Work Done by Rural Women in Malawi." East African Journal of Rural Development, v. 8 (1-2), 1975: 80-91.

1964. Gluckman, Max. "Zulu Women in Hoe Culture Ritual." Bantu Studies, v. 9, 1935: 255-271.

1965. Sibisi, Harriet. "How African Women Cope with Migrant Labour in South Africa." Paper presented at the Wellesley Conference on Women and Development, June 1976. Available from Wellesley Center for Research on Women, 828 Washington St., Wellesley, Massachusetts 02181.

1966. South African Institute of Race Relations. "The Employment of Native Girls Trained in Domestic Service at Native Training Institutions." South African Outlook, v. 62, 1932: 6-9.

Latin America--General

1967. Cebotarev, E. A. "Rural Women in Non-Familial Activities: Credit and Political Action in Latin America." Paper presented at the Wellesley Conference on Women and Development, June 1976. Available from Wellesley Center for Research on Women, 828 Washington St., Wellesley, Massachusetts 02181.

1968. Darling, Martha. The Role of Women in the Economy: A Summary Based on Ten National Reports. Paris: Organisation for Economic Cooperation in Development, 1975.

1969. International Labour Organization. "Protection of Women Home Workers in Latin America." Industry and Labour Information, 6 November 1939: 159-161.

1970. Jelin, Elizabeth. "Labor Migration and Female Labor Force Participation in Latin America: The Case of Domestic Service in the Cities." Paper presented at the Wellesley Conference on Women and Development, June 1976. Available from Wellesley Center for Research on Women, 828 Washington St., Wellesley, Massachusetts 02181.

1971. La mujer en America Latina, vols. I and II. Mexico City: Sepsetentas, 1975.

1972. Murdock, George P., and Caterina Provost. "Factors in the Division of Labor by Sex: A Cross-Cultural Analysis." Ethnology, v. 12 (2), 1973: 203-225.

1973. Nash, June C., and Helen I. Safa, eds., Sex and Class in Latin America. New York: Praeger, 1976.

1974. Nelson, Linda. "La economía del hogar en la reforma agraria." Desarrollo Rural en las Américas, v. 4 (3), 1972: 279-287.

1975. O'Callaghan, Sean. Damaged Baggage: The White Slave Trade and Narcotics Trafficking in the Americas. London: Hale, 1969.

1976. United Nations Economic Commission for Latin America. "Socio-Cultural Determinants of Economic Activities of Women." Staff Paper no. 5. Caracas: 1975. Available from United Nations Center for Social and Humanitarian Affairs, United Nations Development Programme, New York.

Mexico and Central America

19//. Arauz Aguilar, Federico G. "El trabajo a domicilio en la doctrina y en nuestro derecho." Thesis, Universidad de San Carlos, Guatemala, 1951.

1978. Arizpe, Lourdes. "'Las Marías' y la migración indígena a la ciudad de Mexico." Mexico City: Instituto Nacional de Antropología e Historia, 1974.

1979. _____. Indígenas en la Ciudad de México. El caso de las "Marías." Mexico City: Secretaría de Educación Pública, 1975.

1980. _____. "Women in the Informal Labor Sector in Mexico City: A Case of Unemployment or Voluntary Choice?" Paper presented at the Wellesley Conference on Women and Development, June 1976. Available from Wellesley Center for Research on Women, 828 Washington St., Wellesley, Massachusetts 02181. Revised version will be published in fall issue of SIGNS, 1977.

1981. Arosemena de Tejeira, Otilia. La mujer en la vida panameña. Panama City: Editorial de la Universidad de Panamá, 1966.

1982. Behrman, Daniel. "The Mayans Modernize." UNESCO Courier, v. 7 (12), May 1955: 16-17.

1983. _____. When the Mountains Move: Technical Assistance and the Changing Face of Latin America. Paris: UNESCO, 1954.

1984. Chiñas, Beverly C. The Isthmus Zapotecs: Women's Roles in Cultural Context. New York: Holt, Rinehart & Winston, 1973.

1985. _____. Mujeres de San Juan: La mujer zapoteca en la economía. Mexico City: Secretaría de Educación Pública, 1975.

1986. de la Torre, Josefina Muriel. "Los recogimientos de mujeres: Respuesta a una problemática social novo-hispana."

Thesis, Universidad Nacional Autónoma de México, 1974.

1987. "Domestic Workers in the Dominican Republic." Industry and Labour, v. 2 (7), October 1949: 303-304.

1988. Elmendorf, Mary Lindsay. Nine Mayan Women: A Village Faces Change. Cambridge, Massachusetts: Schenkman Pub. Co., 1975.

1989. Fabrega, Horacio, Jr. "Begging in a Southeast Mexican City." Human Organization, v. 30 (3), 1971: 277-287.

1990. Graue Díaz González, Desiderio. "La prostitución en la Ciudad de México, causas y efectos sociales." In Congreso Nacional de Sociología. Estudios sociológicos. Mexico City: UNAM, 1950: 131-159.

1991. Hagan, Alfred J. "An Analysis of the Hand Weaving Sector of the Guatemalan Economy." Ph.D. dissertation, University of Texas, 1970.

1992. Hatch, D. Spencer. Toward Freedom from Want: From India to Mexico. Bombay: Oxford University Press, 1949.

1993. Hunt, Robert. "The Developmental Cycle of the Family Business in Rural Mexico." In June Helry, ed., Essays in Economic Anthropology. Seattle: University of Washington Press, 1965: 54-79.

1994. Jopling, Carol F. "Women Weavers of Yalalag: Their Art and Its Process." Ph.D. dissertation, University of Massachusetts, 1973.

1995. _____. "Woman's Work: A Mexican Case Study of Low Status as a Tactical Advantage." Ethnology, v. 13 (2), April 1974.

1996. Kelly, Isabel. "An Anthropological Approach to Midwifery Training in Mexico." Journal of Tropical Pediatrics, v. 1, 1956: 200-205.

1997. Kinzer, Nora Scott. "A Feminist Analysis of Oscar Lewis' Culture of Poverty Concept." Paper presented at the Central States Anthropological Meeting, April 1972.

1998. Litzler, Beverly Newbold. "Women of San Blas Atempa: An Analysis of the Economic Role of Isthmus Zapotec Women in Relation to Family and Community." Ph.D. dissertation, University of California at Los Angeles, 1968.

1999. Lomnitz, Larissa. "The Role of Women in an Informal Economy." Paper presented at the Wellesley Conference on Women and Development, June 1976. Available from Wellesley Center for Research on Women, 828 Washington St., Wellesley, Massachusetts 02181.

2000. López, César Emilio. "Nuestro problema social de la prostitución." Ateneo, v. 42 (202), 1954: 32-54.

2001. López Legaspi, Fortino. "El problema del trabajo a domicilio en México." Jus. Revista de Derecho y Ciencias Sociales, v. 22 (130), May 1949: 367-381.

2002. Lópezllera, Cristina de. "Trabajadoras auxiliares del hogar en México." Boletín Documental sobre las Mujeres, v. 0 (1), 1970: 51-57.

2003. Mercado, Isabel. "Trabajadoras auxiliares del hogar en México." Boletín Documental sobre las Mujeres, v. 1 (1), 1970: 51-57.

2004. Montalban, L. "La prostitución aborígena en Nicaragua." Nicaragua Indígena, v. 3, 1968: 34-39.

2005. Morales, Hugo I. "El rabajo a domicilio." Revista Mexicana de Trabajo, v. 11 (2), June 1953: 115-120.

2006. Nash, Manning. Machine Age Maya: The Industrialization of a Guatemalan Community. American Anthropological Association Memoir, no.87. Menasha, Wisconsin: 1958.

2007. Paul, Lois, and Benjamin D. Paul. "The Maya Midwife as Sacred Specialist: A Guatemalan Case." American Ethnologist, v. 2 (4), November 1975: 707-726.

2008. Plattner, Stuart. "Occupation and Marriage in a Mexican Trading Community." Southwestern Journal of Anthropology, v. 28 (2), 1972: 193-206.

2009. Quezada, F. Ventura. "Problemas del servicio doméstico en Honduras." Trabajo, v. 1 (9), 1958: 13-14.

2010. Reina, Rubén C. In Chinautla, a Guatemalan Indian Community. A Study of the Relationship of Community Culture and National Change. New Orleans: Tulane University, 1972: 68-74.

2011. Roebuck, Julian, and Patrick McNamara. "Ficheras and Free-Lancers: Prostitution in a Mexican Border City." Archives of Sexual Behavior, v. 2 (3), 1973: 231-244.

2012. Rojas González, Francisco. "La familia rural mejicana y su industria doméstica." In Congreso Nacional de Sociología. Estudios Sociológicos. Mexico City: UNAM, 1950: 69-76.

2013. Ruiloba, N. M. "Estudio de las condiciones sociales y laborales de 103 trabajadoras domésticas investigadas en la Ciudad de Panamá." Thesis, Universidad de Panamá, 1967.

2014. Salviano Faria, and Nino Velázquez. "La participación de la esposa campesina en la toma de decisiones y en la producción agropecuaria." Agrociencia, v. 12, 1973: 57-68.

2015. Solis Quiroga, Hector. "La prostitución en México hasta 1957." Criminalia, v. 30 (4), 1964: 271-277.

2016. Vargas-Baron, Emily Ann. "Development and Change of Rural Artisanry: Weaving Industries of the Oaxaca Valley, Mexico." Ph.D. dissertation, Stanford University, 1968.

2017. Villela, Enrique. "Sobre prostitución en México." In Congreso Nacional de Sociología. Estudios sociológicos. Mexico City: UNAM, 1951: 217-229.

2018. "Voluntary Manual Labor in Mexico." Times Educational Supplement, no. 2040, June 1954: 555.

2019. Young, Kate. "El aporte económico de la mujer a la economía campesina." Mexico City: Instituto Nacional de Estudios del Trabajo, 1976.

2020. _____. "Women's Work in a Rural Community in Colonial and Modern Mexico." History Workshop Journal, v. 4, 1977.

Caribbean

2021. Acevedo, Arturo. "La mujer de hoy en nuestros campos." INRA, April 1961: 54-59.

2022. "Agricultural Batallions Gain 2597 Women Members." Translations on Latin America, no. 89, 1968: 42-43.

2023. Aloma, Daura. "Hacia una nueva vida." Bohemia, 1 January 1963: 40-43.

2024. Ayala, Esther. "Facilita el MINCIN incorporación de la mujer a tareas productivas." Juventud Rebelde, 18 May 1966: 4.

2025. Bravet, Rogelio Luis. "Mujeres: Tomates y divisas." Bohemia, 6 January 1967: 30-35.

2026. Cabrera, Luis R. "La peligrosa organización de explotadores de menores." Bohemia, 17 June 1956: 56-57.

2027. "Compañera doméstica." Verde Olivo, 3 December 1961: 33.

2028. "Cuba Steps Up Mobilization of Women for Labor." New York Times, 15 December 1968.

2029. Duvallón, Georgina. "Las pioneras de la agricultura en Cuba." Verde Olivo, 8 October 1961: 47-49.

2030. _____. "La revolución en el servicio doméstico." Verde Olivo, 15 October 1961: 28-31.

2031. Fernández, Olga. "Las Marianas." Cuba Internacional, April 1973: 34-41.

2032. Gil de Lamadrid, José. "Mujeres en la fábrica, en el campo." Bohemia, 3 March 1967: 16-19.

2033. González, Manet E. "El trabajo y la mujer." Bohemia, 3 December 1963: 18-19.

2034. "Oriente Women Participate in Agricultural Work (Cuba)." Translations on Latin America, no. 33, 1968: 83-89.

2035. "Prostitution in Cuba." Translations on Cuba, no. 575, 1967: 16-22.

2036. Reckord, Barry. "Sex, Work and Motivation in Castro's Cuba." The Washington Monthly, May 1971: 44-53.

2037. Sánchez Lalebret, Rafael. "Entusiasta contribución de la mujer." Bohemia, 26 April 1968: 26-29.

2038. Senande, Ramón. "La superación de las domésticas." Verde Olivo, 19 November 1961: 28-31.

2039. "Women Increasing in Agricultural Work (Cuba)." Translations on Latin America, no. 102, 1968: 86-90.

Andean Region

2040. Adams, Richard N. A Community in the Andes. American Ethnological Society Monograph, no.31. Seattle: University of Washington Press, 1959.

2041. Ardila, Alfredo, et. al. Psicología y problemas sociales en Colombia. Tunja: Universidad Pedagógica y Tecnológica de Colombia, 1971.

2042. Beaglehole, Ernest. "A Technical Assistance Mission in the Andes." International Labour Review, v. 67 (6), June 1953: 520-534.

2043. Cárdenas Vargas de Matto, Morayma. "Encuesta realizada en cien familias de empleadas en servicio doméstico particular." Servicio Social, v. 3 (3), 1945: 133-135.

2044. Castro, Mercedes. "La nueva situación de las empleadas de casas particulares." Rikchay, v. 2 (3), 1972: 36-38.

2045. Davalos y Lisson, Pedro. La prostitución en la ciudad de Lima. Lima: Imp. La Industria, 1909.

2046. Deere, Carmen Diana. "The Division of Labor by Sex in Agriculture: Peasant Women's Subsistence Production on the Minifundios." Ph.D. research essay, University of California, Berkeley, 1975.

2047. _____. "Division of Labor by Sex on the Minifundio: Familial Labor Deployment Strategies and Technological Change." Rural Development Project Working Paper, no. 8. Los Angeles: California Agricultural Experiment Station, University of California at Los Angeles, June 1975.

2048. _____. "Rural Women's Subsistence Production in the Capitalist Periphery." Journal of Radical Political Economics, v. 8, Spring 1976: 9-17.

2049. Fortún, Julia Elena. "La mujer aymará. Algunos problemas relacionados con su incorpación." Abril, v. 2, 1964: 50-59.

2050. Goisa Chambilla, Dora Gladys. Situación socio-laboral de la empleada doméstica emigrada de provincias y aporte de la educadora familiar a las soluciones de los problemas encontrados. Lima: 1968.

2051. Grisanti de Luigi, Isabel Ceicelia. La prostitución y el juego como anomalías sociales. Valencia: Universidad de Carabobo, 1973.

2052. Helfer, Ruth. "El problema social de la empleada doméstica." Thesis, Escuela Normal Superior de Mujeres de San Pedro, Lima, 1966.

2053. International Labor Organization. "Assistance to Home Workers in Peru." Industrial and Labour Information, 7 June 1937: 417.

2054. Ismodes Cairo, Aníbal. "Estudios sobre la prostitución en Lima." Mimeo. Paper presented at the Conference on Family Planning, Lima, 1967.

2055. Instituto Ecuatoriano de Antropología y Geografía. "La Misión Andina en el Ecuador." América Indígena, v. 20 (1), June 1960: 35-51.

2056. Johnson, Orna R., and Allen Johnson. "Male/Female Relations and the Organization of Work in a Machiguenga Community." American Ethnologist, v. 2 (4), November 1975: 634-648.

2057. Martínez Maxera, Napoleón. "El trabajo femenino y la realidad social moderna." Thesis, Universidad Nacional Mayor de San Marcos, Lima, 1950.

2058. Matos Mar, José. "Three Indian Communities in Peru." In Jean Meynaud, ed., Social Change and Economic Development. New York: UNESCO, 1963.

2059. Nett, Emily. "The Servant Class in a Developing Country: Ecuador." Journal of Inter-American Studies, v. 8 (3), July 1966: 437-452.

2060. Rutté García, Alberto. Simplemente explotadas. El Mundo de las empleadas domésticas de Lima. Lima: DESCO, 1973.

2061. Sepúlveda Niño, Saturnino. La prostitución en Colombia; una quiebra de las estructuras sociales. Bogotá: Ed. Andes, 1970.

2062. Smith, Margo Lane. "Institutionalized Servitude: The Female Domestic Servant in Lima, Peru." Ph.D. dissertation, Indiana University, 1971.

2063. _____. "Domestic Service as a Channel of Upward Mobility for the Lower Class Woman: The Lima Case." In Ann Pescatello, ed., Female and Male in Latin America: Essays. Pittsburgh: University of Pittsburgh Press, 1973: 191-208.

2064. _____. "The Female Domestic Servant and Social Change: Lima, Peru." In R. R. Leavitt, ed., Cross Cultural Perspectives on the Women's Movement and Women's Status. The Hague: Mouton, 1976.

2065. Tello Figueroa, María. "Algunos determinantes sociales de la prostitución en Lima." Thesis, Universidad Nacional Mayor de San Marcos, Lima, 1973.

2066. Vaca, Victor Hugo. La prostitución en el Ecuador. Quito: Editorial Universitaria, 1954.

2067. Vásquez, Jesús María, O. P. El servicio doméstico en Lima. Lima: Centro Arquidiocesano Pastoral, 1970.

2068. Venezuela. Consejo de Bienestar Rural. Problemas económicos y sociales de los Andes Venezolanos. Part II. Caracas: Consejo de Bienestar Rural, 1956.

2069. Watson-Franke, Marie-Barbara. "A Woman's Profession in Guajiro Culture: Weaving." Antropológica, v. 37, 1974: 24-40.

2070. Wellin, E. "Pregnancy, Childbirth and Midwifery in the Valley of Ica, Peru." Health Information Digest for Hot Countries, v. 3, 1956: 1-15.

Chile and the Platine

2071. Eriksson, N. "The Argentine Woman: Her Social, Political and Economic Role." Review of the River Plate, no. 152, December 1972: 959-961, 985-988.

2072. Garrett, Patricia. "Some Structural Constraints on the Agricultural Activities of Women: The Chilean Hacienda." Paper presented at the Wellesley Conference on Women and Development, June 1976. Available from Wellesley Center for Research on Women, 828 Washington St., Wellesley, Massachusetts 02181. Also cited as Land Tenure Center Research Paper, no. 70. Madison: Land Tenure Center, University of Wisconsin, 1976.

2073. Hermitte, Esther. "Ponchos, Weaving and Patronclient Relations in North West Argentina." In Arnold Stricken and Sidney M. Greenfield, eds., Structure and Process in Latin America. Albuquerque: University of New Mexico Press, 1972: 159-177.

2074. Hollander, Nancy Caro. "Women in the Political Economy of Argentina." Ph.D. dissertation, University of California at Los Angeles, 1974.

2075. Ielpi, Rafael Oscar y Hector Nicolas Zinni. Prostitución y rufianismo. Buenos Aires: Ed. Encuadre, 1974.

2076. Leban de Cavia, Lucía N. "La mujer como recurso humano no reconocido en el medio rural." Boletín Documental Sobre las Mujeres, v. 4 (3), 1974: 42-48.

2077. Nores de Cafferata, Teresa. "Valorización del ama de casa." Revista Universitaria Nacional de Córdoba, v. 10 (1/2), March-June 1969: 209-216.

2078. Pareja, Ernesto M. La prostitución en Buenos Aires: Factores antopológicos y sociales. Buenos Aires: Edit. Tor, 1937.

2079. Ríos, Raúl Arturo. "Valorización del ama de casa." Revista Universitaria Nacional de Córdoba, v. 10 (1/2), March-June 1969: 197-207.

2080. Service, Elman R., and Helen Service. Tobatí: Paraguayan Town. Chicago: University of Chicago Press, 1954. Parts 2, 3 and 4.

2081. Thomson, R. Educational Aspects of Community Development. South Pacific Commission Technical Paper, no. 74. Noumea, New Caledonia: 1955.

2082. Torre Palma, Atilio de la. El trabajo a domicilio. Santiago: Universidad de Chile, 1948.

Brazil

2083. Alves, Eliseu Roberto de Andrade. "An Econometric Study of the Agricultural Labor Market in Brazil: A Test of Subsistence and Commercial Family Farm Models." Ph.D. dissertation, Purdue University, 1972.

2084. Fontanelle, L. F. Raposo. A dinâmica dos grupos domésticos no Arraial do Cabo (Cabo Frio). Rio de Janeiro: Ministerio de Agricultura, Serviço Social Rural, 1960.

2085. García, Afranio R., Jr., and Beatriz Alasia de Heredia. "Trabalho familiar e campesinato." America Latina, v. 14 (1/2), January-June 1971: 10-19.

2086. García, Evaldo da Silva. "O trabalho da mulher no campo." O Observador, v. 15 (170), March 1950: 116-120.

2087. "Impact of Industrialization on Women's Work in North East Brazil." Studies in Comparative International Development, Summer 1975: 78-94.

2088. Lagenest, H. D. Barruel de. Lenocínio e prostituição no Brasil; estudo sociologice. Rio de Janeiro: AGIR, 1960.

2089. _____. Mulheres em leilão; um estudo da prostituição no Brasil. Petropolis: Ed. Vozes, 1973.

2090. Pereira, Armando. Sexo e prostituição. Rio de Janeiro: Gráfica Record Ed., 1967.

2091. Teixeira, Teotonio. "Resource Efficiency and the Market For Family Labor: Small Farms in the Sertão of Northeast Brazil." Ph.D. dissertation, Purdue University, 1976.

Editors' Note: For references on prostitution as a psychological or socialization problem rather than as an economic activity, see "Law-female Delinquency and Penal Institutions" in Meri Knaster, Women in Spanish America: An Annotated Bibliography. Boston: G. K. Hall, 1977: 410-425.

C. MARKETING AND COMMERCE

West Africa

2092. Aguessy, D. "La Femme dakaroise commerçante au détail sur le marché. In M. Sankale; L. V. Thomas; and P. Fougeyrollas, eds., Dakar en devenir. Paris: Présence Africaine, 1968: 395-421.

2093. Awosika, Keziah. "Nigerian Women in Distributive Trade." Paper presented at the Wellesley Conference on Women and Development, June 1976. Available from Wellesley Center for Research on Women, 828 Washington St., Wellesley, Massachusetts 02181.

2094. Balandier, George. "Note sur l'exploitation du sel par les vielles femmes du Bargny." Notes Africaines, v. 32, 1946: 22.

2095. Bauer, P. T. West African Trade. London: Cambridge University Press, 1954.

2096. Comhaire, Jean. "La Vie religieuse à Lagos." Zaïre, v. 3 (5), 1949: 549-556.

2097. Comhaire-Sylvain, Suzanne. "Le Travail des femmes à Lagos, Nigeria." Zaïre, v. 5 (2), 1951: 169-187; v. 5 (5), 1951: 475-502.

2098. Ekejiuba, F. "Omu Okwei: Merchant Queen of Ossomari." Nigeria, v. 90, 1966.

2099. Gore-Clough, R. Oil Rivers Trader: Memories of Iboland. London: University of London Press, 1971.

2100. Handwerker, W. P. "Changing Household Organization in the Origins of Market Places in Liberia." Economic Development and Cultural Change, v. 22, January 1974: 229-248.

2101. _____. "Kinship, Friendship and Business Failure Among Market Sellers in Monrovia, Liberia, 1970." Africa, v. 43, October 1973: 288-301.

2102. Hill, Polly. "Hidden Trade in Hausaland." Man, v. 4 (3), 1969: 332-409.

2103. Institute de Science Economique Appliquée Dakar. "La Femme africaine et les marchées dakarois." Processed. Dakar: 1963.

2104. Johnson, Eleanor J. "Marketwomen and Capitalist Adaptation: A Case Study in Rural Benin, Nigeria." Ph.D. dissertation, Michigan State University, 1973.

2105. Kiers, Eric J. "Madame Mercedes-Benz: Merchant of Togo." Ms., v. 5 (10), April 1977: 112-117.

2106. Leith-Ross, Sylvia. "Women of Affairs." Journal of the Royal African Society, v. 37 (149), October 1938: 477-482.

2107. Leonard, A. G. The Lower Niger and Its Tribes. London: Macmillan, 1906.

2108. Lewis, Barbara. "Female Strategies and Public Goods: Market Women in the Ivory Coast." Paper presented at the Wellesley Conference on Women and Development, June 1976. Available from Wellesley Center for Research on Women, 828 Washington St., Wellesley, Massachusetts 02181.

2109. Magbogunje, Akin L. "The Market-Women." Ibadan, v. 11, February 1961: 14-17.

2110. Marshall, Gloria A. "The Marketing of Farm Produce: Some Patterns of Trade among Women in Western Nigeria." Proceedings of Conference at the Nigerian Institute of Social and Economic Research, Ibadan. 1962: 88-99.

2111. _____. "Women, Trade, and the Yoruba Family." Ph.D. dissertation, Columbia University, 1964.

2112. McCall, Daniel. "Trade and the Role of Wife in a Modern West African Town." In A. W. Southall, ed., Social Change in Modern Africa. Oxford: Oxford University Press, 1961.

2113. Meillassoux, Claude, ed., The Development of Indigenous Trade and Markets in West Africa. London: Oxford University Press, 1971.

2114. Nypan, Astrid. Market Trade. A Sample Study of Market Traders in Accra. Legon: College of Ghana, 1960.

2115. Ocloo, Esther. "The Ghanaian Market Woman." Mimeo. Paper presented at the Society for International Development, 14th Annual Conference, Abidjan, Ivory Coast, August 1974.

2116. Remy, Dorothy. "Social Network and Patron — Client Relations: Ibadan Market Women." Mimeo. Washington, D.C.: Federal City College, Department of Urban Studies, 1974.

2117. Robertson, Claire. "Economic Woman in Africa. Profit-Making Techniques of Accra Market Women." Journal of Modern African Studies, v. 12 (4), December 1974: 657-664.

2118. _____. "Twentieth Century Changes in the Organization of the Fish Trade in Accra." Paper presented at the Wellesley Conference on Women and Development, June 1976. Available from Wellesley Center for Research on Women, 828 Washington St., Wellesley, Massachusetts 02181.

2119. Sai, Florence Aleeno. "The Market Woman in the Economy of Ghana." Master's thesis, Cornell University, 1971.

2120. Sudarkasa, Niara. Where Women Work: A Study of Yoruba Women in the Marketplace and in the Home. Ann Arbor: University of Michigan Press, 1973.

2121. Talbot, P. A. Life in Southern Nigeria. London: Cass, 1923.

2122. _____. The Peoples of Southern Nigeria, v. 1, 2, 3, 4. Oxford: Oxford University Press, 1926.

2123. Van Der Vaeren-Aguessy, D. "Les Femmes commerçantes au détail sur les marchés dakarois." International African Seminar, v. 279, 1964: 244-255.

2124. Williams, David. "Women Traders in West African Markets." Times British Colonies Review, v. 36, 1959: 11.

2125. "Women as Traders Playing Leading Role in Togo Economy." International Commerce, v. 72, February 1966: 33.

2126. "Women of Ghana Make Successful Traders." Ghana To-day, v. 3 (19), 1959.

Central Africa

2127. Duvieusart, E. "Congolese Women in Trade." Problèmes Sociaux Congolais, v. 45, 1959: 80-81.

2128. Santos, Ana de Sousa. "Quitandas e quitandeiras de Luanda. (Markets and Market Women in Luanda)." Boletin do Instituto de Investigação Científica de Angola, v. 4 (2), 1967: 89-112.

Latin America--General

2129. Mintz, Sidney Wilfred. "Men, Women and Trade." Comparative Studies in Society and History, v. 13, 1971: 247-269.

2130. _____. "Peasant Market Places and Economic Development in Latin America." Occasional Paper, no. 4. Nashville: Vanderbilt University, Graduate Center for Latin American Studies, 1964.

Mexico and Central America

2131. Beals, Ralph Leon. The Peasant Marketing System in Oaxaca, Mexico. Berkeley: University of California Press, 1975.

2132. _____. "Zapotec 'Viajeras' of the Isthmus." In S. Cook and M. Diskin, eds., Markets and Society in Oaxaca: Essays on a Regional Peasant Economy in Mexico. Austin: University of Texas Press, 1976.

2133. Hagen, Margaret. "Notes on Public Market Distribution Systems and Networks of Managua." Managua: INCAE, 1972.

2134. _____. Public Markets and Marketing Systems of Managua. Managua: Instituto Centroamericano de Administración de Empresas, 1973.

2135. Kuehler, Gregory Wulfe. "The Role of Woman in Culture Change and the Role of Traditional Marketing Systems in Developing Nations: Integration of Marginalization." Master's thesis, University of Texas, 1972.

2136. Litzler, Beverly Newbold. "Role Perception and Marketing Among Isthmus Zapotecs." Paper presented at the 68th Annual Meeting of the American Anthropological Association, 1969.

2137. Smith, Carol Ann Gulley. "The Domestic Marketing System in Western Guatemala: An Economic, Locational and Cultural Analysis." Ph.D. dissertation, Stanford University, 1972.

Caribbean

2138. Norvell, Douglass G. "Food Marketing in an Urban Place in the Dominican Republic." Caribbean Studies, v. 9 (3), 1969: 104-110.

Andean Region

2139. Alfaro Calle, Victor. La mujer comerciante. Lima: 1910.

2140. Beals, Ralph Leon. "Community in Transition: Nayón, Ecuador." Los Angeles: Latin American Center, University of California, 1966.

2141. Buechler, Judith-Marie Hess. "Las negociantes contratistas en los mercados bolivianos." Estudios Andinos, v. 5 (1), 1976: 57-76.

2142. _____. "Peasant Marketing and Social Revolution in the Province of La Paz, Bolivia." Ph.D. dissertation, McGill University, 1972.

2143. Michigan State University, Latin American Studies Center. "Market Processes in La Paz, Bolivia." East Lansing, Michigan: 1969.

2144. Sagasti, Heli. "La mujer vendedora ambulante." Informe final (Ford Foundation Project). Lima: Fundación Ford, August 1974.

D. THE FORMAL SECTOR (Includes women in industry and the professions)

Africa--General

2145. Bahoken, J. C. "Le Rôle économique de la femme en Afrique." La Vie Africain, v. 57, April 1965: 22-25+.

2146. Barthel, Diane. "The Rise of a Female Professional Elite." African Studies Review, v. 18 (3), December 1975: 1-18.

2147. Bridgman, F. B. "Social and Medical Work for Native Women and Girls in Urban Areas." In <u>The Realignment of Native Life on a Christian Basis</u>. Lovedale: Institution Press, 1928: 58-70.

2148. Comhaire-Sylvain, Suzanne. "Participation of Women in Industry and Commerce in African Towns South of the Sahara." Paper presented at the Workshop on Urban Problems, Lagos, Nigeria, September 1963. Addis Ababa: United Nations Economic Commission for Africa, 1963. U.N. Document #E/CN.14/URB/14.

2149. Dackey, Michelle. "Place de la femme dans le monde du travail." <u>Afrique Nouvelle</u>, v. 20 (1031), 11-17 May 1967, 11. v. 20 (1032), 18-24 May 1967, 11. v. 20 (1033), 25-31 May 1967, 11.

2150. Davies, Richard L. "Women in African Economies." <u>SAIS Review</u>, v. 5 (1), Autumn 1960: 15-19.

2151. "D'Innombrables carrières s'ouvrent aux femmes africaines." <u>Afrique Nouvelle</u>, v. 22 (1097), 15-21 August 1968: 10.

2152. "Employment of African Women." <u>Labour Gazette</u>, v. 64, November 1964: 985.

2153. Ford, Eric. "A New Deal for the Women of Africa: Wider Opportunities in Industry and the Professions." <u>African World</u>, August 1962.

2154. Guelfi, L. <u>La Femme noire et les formes modernes du travail</u>. Paris: Conseil National des Femmes Françaises, October 1957: 7-14.

2155. Hauferlin, C. "La Femme africaine: Une Méconnue." <u>Marco Polo</u>, v. 28, 1957: 59-68.

2156. International Labour Organization. "Women Workers in a Changing World." Geneva: International Labour Organization, 1963.

2157. _____. "The Employment and Conditions of Work of African Women. Part 2." Geneva: International Labour Organization, 1964. Also cited as <u>Overseas Quarterly</u>, v. 4 (6), 1965: 176-178.

2158. _____. "The Employment and Vocational Preparation of Girls and Women in Africa." Mimeo. Geneva: International Labour Organization, 12 March 1969. U.N. Document #E/CN.14/SW/INF/8.

2159. Kisosonkole, Pumla, and Paymond Smyke. "International Women's Year and African Teachers." Convergence, v. 8 (1), 1975: 25-33.

2160. Lee, Annabelle. "African Nuns: An Anthropologist's Impressions." New Blackfriars, v. 49 (576), May 1968: 401-409.

2161. "Native Progress in the British Empire." International Labour Review, v. 25, June 1932: 290-295.

2162. Ntsan'wisi, B. "The African Woman and Her Place in Society, with Special Reference to University-Trained Women." Ministry, v. 8 (1), January 1968: 21-22.

2163. Oluoch, Justus. "African Women in Industry." Heshima, v. 6 (50), November 1956: 294.

2164. Samuels, Annette. "Life Style of An African Career Woman." Tuesday, January 1973: 9-14.

2165. Sanon, B. "Travail des femmes dan les villes en Afrique." Construire Ensemble, v. 3, May-June 1968: 11-18.

2166. Trenoum, Marguerite. "La Femme africaine dans le monde du travail." Afrique Nouvelle, v. 21 (1047), 31 August-6 September, 1967, 8-9. v. 21 (1048), 7-13 September 1967, 11. v. 21 (1049), 14-20 September 1967, 11.

2167. Vries, M. G. de. "Les Femmes, l'emploi et le développement." Finances et Développement, v. 8 (4), December 1971: 3-9.

2168. "Women at Work." Manufacturer, v. 14 (7), July 1964: 15-26.

West Africa

2169. "Au Mali, les femmes représentent le moitié de la population active." Afrique Nouvelle, v. 20 (1014), 12-18 January 1967, 11.

2170. Awosika, Keziah. "Nigerian Women in the Labor Force: Planning for Effective Participation in the Development Process." Paper presented at the Wellesley Conference on Women and Development, June 1976. Available from Wellesley Center for Research on Women, 828 Washington St., Wellesley, Massachusetts 02181.

2171. Barthel, Diane L. "The Rise of a Female Professional Elite: The Case of Senegal." African Studies Review, v. 18 (3), December 1975: 1-17.

2172. "Cameroon: Employment of Women and Children." International Labour Review, v. 102, October 1970: 403-406.

2173. "Career Women of West Africa." West African Review, v. 26 (331), April 1955: 290-297.

2174. Carter, M. "Professional Women of Sierra Leone." African Women, v. 3 (2), June 1959: 41-42.

2175. Chuta, Enyinna, and Carl Liedholm. "The Role of Small Scale Industry in Employment Generation and Rural Development: Initial Research Results from Sierra Leone." African Rural Employment Paper, no. 11. East Lansing, Michigan: Michigan State University, 1975

2176. "Economic Position of Cameroon Women." Nature, v. 172, 25 July 1953: 152.

2177. Faladé, Solange. "Women of Dakar and the Surrounding Urban Area." In Denise Paulme, ed., Women of Tropical Africa. London: Routledge and Kegan Paul, 1963: 217-230.

2178. Grandmaison, Collete Le Coeur. "Activités économiques des femmes dakaroises." Africa, v. 39 (2), April 1969: 138-152.

2179. Greenstreet, M. "Le Travail des femmes au Ghana." Revue Internationale du Travail, v. 103 (2), February 1971: 133-147. Also cited (in English) as "Employment of Women in Ghana." International Labour Review, v. 103, February 1971: 117-129.

2180. Kirsch, Martin. "Le Travail de la femme dans les états membres de la communauté, la République du Togo et L'Etat sous Tutelle du Cameroun." Industries et Travaux d'Outre-Mer, v. 7 (69), August 1959: 572-575.

2181. Liedholm, Carl, and Enyinna Chuta. "An Economic Analysis of Small-Scale Industry in Sierra Leone." Mimeo. East Lansing: Michigan State University, Department of Agricultural Economics, African Rural Development Program, 1976.

2182. Lucas, David. "Women in the Nigerian Labour Force." Paper presented at the African Population Conference, Accra, Ghana, December 1971. Available from United Nations Commission for Africa. U.N. Document #M71-2985.

2183. Nemo, J. "The Economic Role of Women. Contributions à l'étude démographique et sociologique d'une ville du Togo: Palimé." Documents et Statistiques, no. 22, 1958: 67-74. Paris: Ministère de la France d'Outre-Mer.

2184. Oppong, Christine. "Ghanaian Women Teachers as Workers, Kin, Wives, and Mothers: A Study of Conjugal Family Solidarity--Norms, Reality and Stress." Paper presented at the Wellesley Conference on Women and Development, June 1976. Available from Wellesley Center for Research on Women, 828 Washington St., Wellesley, Massachusetts 02181.

2185. Peil, Margaret. "Female Roles in West African Towns." Paper presented at the VIIIth World Congress of the International Sociological Association, Toronto, Canada, August 1974.

2186. Sierra Leone Education Department. "Welfare Work Among Women." Forschungen und Fortschritte, v. 6 (1), January-March 1945: 31-33.

Central Africa

2187. "Business Women in Northern Rhodesia." African Women, v. 3 (4), June 1960: 89-90.

2188. Capelle, M. "The Employment of African Women in Undertakings in the Belgian Congo." Bulletin of the Inter-African Labour Institute, v. 6 (2), March 1959: 46-61.

2189. _____. "The Industrial Employment of Women in the Belgian Congo." African Women, v. 3 (3), December 1959: 59-61.

2190. Cunha, A. Ameida F. "Generalidades sobre o trabalho das mulheres em Angola." Trabalho, v. 4, 1963: 173-182.

2191. Gould, Terri F. "A New Class of Professional Zairian Women." Paper presented at the annual meeting of the African Studies Association, San Francisco, October-November 1975.

2192. _____. "The Educated Woman in a Developing Country: Professional Zairian Women in Lubumbashi." Ph.D. dissertation, Union Graduate School, 1976.

2193. Hellman, E. "Rooiyard Economic Life: Revenue Contributed by Women." In Rooiyard: A Sociological Survey of an African Slum Yard. The Rhodes-Livingstone Papers, no. 3, 1948: 37-53.

2194. "La Femme congolais au travail." Congo Magazine, February 1967: 7-8.

2195. Lomboto, J. F. "L'Emploi et les conditions de travail des femmes africaines." Cadicec, v. 7 (31), 1965: 19-21.

2196. Manwanna, Oscar. "Le Travail des femmes africaines." Documents pour L'Action, February 1965: 51-55.

2197. Marthey, J. "L'Oeuvre missionaire pour la population féminine au Congo." Revue de L'Histoire des Colonies, v. 44 (154), 1957: 79-101.

2198. Robalino, I. "La Femme travailleuse en Equateur." Labor, v. 5, 1967: 257-262.

2199. Schwartz, Alfred. "Illusion d'une émancipation et aliénation réelle de l'ouvrière zairoise." Canadian Journal of African Studies, v. 6 (2), 1972: 183-212.

2200. Strangeway, A. K. "The Advance of African Women in Angola." African Women, v. 1 (4), June 1956: 79-84.

2201. Suleiman, S. M. "Women in the Sudan Public Service." Sudan Journal of Administration and Development, v. 2, January 1966: 37-53.

2202. "Le Travail de la femme au Congo (Kinshasa)." Afrique Nouvelle, v. 22 (1123), 13-19 February, 1969: 11.

2203. "Women Teachers in Northern Rhodesia." African Women, v. 4 (1), December 1960: 10-11.

East Africa

2204. Byangwa, Margaret. "The Muganda Woman's Attitude Toward Work Outside the Home." Makerere University, 1968.

2205. Elkan, Walter. "Employment of Women in Uganda." Conference paper, East African Institute of Social Research, Makerere University College, January 1955.

2206. _____. "The Employment of Women in Uganda." Bulletin of the Inter-African Labour Institute, v. 4 (4), July 1957: 8-23. Also cited in African Women, v. 6 (1), December 1956: 6-9.

2207. "Ethiopian Women's Welfare Work." Ethiopia Observer, v. 1 (1), December 1956: 28-29.

2208. Evans, David R. "Image and Reality: Career Goals of Educated Ugandan Women." Canadian Journal of African Studies, v. 6 (2), 1972: 213-232.

2209. Kinyanjui, Kabiru. "Education and Formal Employment Opportunities for Women in Kenya. Some Preliminary Data." Kenya Education Review, December 1975: 6-25.

2210. Lindsay, Beverly. "Socio-Cultural Factors Influencing Kenyan Women's Career Choices: Some Preliminary Findings." Paper presented at the Conference on Comparative and International Education, Toronto, February 1976.

2211. Matheson, Alastair. "In Ethiopia Highland Nurses on Horseback." New York: UNICEF, ca. 1975. UNICEF Document #F/68/6.

2212. Otieno, Hilda. "Women Worker's Problems in Kenya." ICFTU Free Labour World, v. 151, January 1963: 16-18.

2213. Pankhurst, Richard. "Employment of Ethiopian Women." Ethiopia Observer, v. 1 (5), February 1957: 98-102.

2214. Stichter, Sharon B. "Women and the Labor Force in Kenya: 1895-1964." Paper presented at the annual meeting of the African Studies Association, San Francisco, October-November 1975. Also cited as Rural Africana, v. 29, Winter 1976.

2215. _____. "Women in the Urban Labor Force in Kenya: Problems and Prospects." Paper presented at the Wellesley Conference on Women and Development, June 1976. Available from Wellesley Center for Research on Women, 828 Washington St., Wellesley, Massachusetts 02181.

2216. Triuizi, Gloria. "Women Factory Workers in Ethiopia." Unpublished manuscript, 1972.

2217. "What is Being Done in the East African Territories: Opportunities of Advancement for African Women." East Africa and Rhodesia, v. 27 (1384), 1951: 893-906.

2218. Whiting, Beatrice B. "The Kenyan Career Woman: Traditional and Modern." Annals of the New York Academy of Sciences, no. 208, March 1973: 71-75. Also cited in Ruth Bukundsin, ed., The Anatomy of Achievement. New York: William Morrow, 1974.

Southern Africa

2219. Brandel, M. "The African Career Woman in South Africa." African Women, v. 2 (2), 1957: 36-38.

2220. Cheater, A. P. "Marginal Elite? African Registered Nurses in Durban, South Africa." African Studies, v. 32 (3), 1974: 143-158.

2221. Hubback, J. C. "Native Women Teachers in South Africa." United Empire, v. 22 (11): 612-613.

2222. Pons, V. G. "A Study of Absenteeism amongst Women in Commerce. 1948, Capetown, Cape of Good Hope." South African Journal of Economics, v. 18, June 1950: 178-189.

2223. Sibisi, Harriet. "Zulu Women in a Migrant Labor Situation in South Africa." Paper presented at the Wellesley Conference on Women and Development, June 1976. Available from Wellesley Center for Research on Women, 828 Washington St., Wellesley, Massachusetts 02181.

2224. Wessels, Dina M. "Part-Time Work for Married Women: Demand and Supply in Pretoria." Mimeo. Pretoria: South African Human Sciences Research Council, Institute for Manpower Research, 1971.

2225. _____. "The Employment Potential of Graduate Housewives in the PWV Region — Part I: Part-time Employment." Pretoria: South African Human Sciences Research Council, Institute for Manpower Research, 1972.

2226. _____. "Manpower Requirements and the Utilization of Women: The Views of Fifty Employers in Nine Major Industry Groups." Mimeo. Pretoria: South African Human Sciences Research Council, Institute for Manpower Research, 1975.

Latin America--General

2227. Blitz, Rudolph C. "An International Comparison of Women's Participation in the Professions." Journal of Developing Areas, v. 9, July 1975: 499-510.

2228. Cannon, Mary Minerva. "La mujer que trabaja y la legislación social." Noticias de la Oficina de Información Obrera y Social, April 1946: 3-5.

2229. Collver, Andrew, and Eleanor Langlois. "The Female Labor Force in Metropolitan Areas: An International Comparison." Economic Development and Cultural Change, v. 10 (4), July 1962: 367-385.

2230. Denti, Ettore. "Sex-Age Patterns of Labor Force Participation." International Labour Review, v. 98 (6), December 1968: 525-550.

2231. Durand, John. "Regional Patterns in International Variations of Women's Participation in the Labor Force." Paper presented at the annual meeting of the Population Association of America, 22-24 April 1971.

2232. Elizaga, Juan C., and Roger Mellon. "Factores que inciden en la participación femenina." In Juan C. Elizaga and Roger Mellon, eds., Aspectos demográficos de la mano de obra en América Latina. Santiago: Centro Latinoamericano de Demografía, 1971: 78-89.

2233. Elizaga, Juan C. "Participation of Women in the Labor Force of Latin America: Fertility and Other Factors." International Labour Review, v. 109, 1974: 519-538.

2234. Geist, Harold. "Comparación entre las razones para eligir ocupaciones en mujeres de cinco paises latinoamericanos de habla castellana." Revista Latinoamericana de psicología, v. 7 (1), 1975: 87-95.

2235. Gendell, Murray, and Guillermo Rossell. "Economic Activity of Women in Latin America." Washington, D.C.: Organization of American States, Interamerican Commission of Women, 1967. OAS Document #DCAA/Doc 21.

2236. _____. "The Trends and Patterns of the Economic Activity of Women in Latin America During the 1950's." Estadística, v. 26, 1968.

2237. Gereb, Sandor. "La OIT y el trabajo femenino." Revista Mexicana del Trabajo, v. 16 (3), September 1969: 64-68.

2238. Gil, Elena. "La mujer en el mundo del trabajo." In J. L. Vega; Elena Gil; and W. V. Costanza, eds., Tres temas en la América Latina, Hoy. San José, C. R.: Centro de Estudios de Demografía de América Latina, 1970.

2239. Gomes del Rey de Kybal, E. "Womanpower — Untapped Resources for Latin America's Economic Growth." National Businesswoman, v. 38, 1959: 8-9.

2240. Inter-American Commission of Women, 14th Assembly. "Economic Activity of Women in Latin America." Washington, D.C.: Pan American Union, General Secretariat, 1967.

2241. International Labour Organization. "Utilization of Women Workers in Latin America." Industry and Labour, v. 8 (10), May 1955.

2242. _____. "Seminar on the Utilisation of Women's Work in Latin America." Industry and Labour, v. 13 (10), 1955: 437-442.

2243. _____. "Women's Employment in Latin America." International Labour Review, v. 73 (2), February 1956: 177-193.

2244. _____. "La OIT y el trabajo femenino." Revista Mexicana de Trabajo, v. 13 (2), April-June 1966: 67-81.

2245. Klein, Viola. Women Workers: Working Hours and Services: A Survey in Twenty-One Countries. Paris: Organisation for Economic Cooperation in Development, 1965.

2246. Llach, Guillermina. "La enfermera y la trabajadora social." Filosofía y letras, v. 30 (60-62), 1956: 223-234.

2247. Keremitsis, Dawn. "The Expendables: Women Textile Workers in Mexico, Colombia, and Chile." Paper presented at the 5th National Meeting of the Latin American Studies Association, San Francisco, 1974.

2248. "La mujer en la fuerza de trabajo en America Latina." Ciencia Interamericana, v. 16 (3-4), July-December 1975: 14+.

2249. O'Hagan, Mary Ann. "Distribution of Economically Active Women in Major Industrial and Occupational Sectors in Latin America." Master's thesis, University of Texas, 1968.

2250. Pan American Union. "Women and Labor in Latin America." Bulletin of the Pan American Union, v. 79, April 1945: 206-210.

2251. Peek, Peter. "Female Employment and Fertility." International Labour Review, v. 112 (1-3), August-September, 1975.

2252. Pizarre, María Josefa. "Informe de la reunión técnica sobre utilización de la mano de obra femenina en los paises Latinoamericanos celebrada en Lima, diciembre de 1954." Revista del Trabajo (Caracas), v. 4 (17), October-December 1954: 107-134.

2253. Rodríguez, Aída, and Susana Schkolnik. "Chile y Guatemala: Factores que afectan la participación femenina en la actividad económica." Series C, no. 156. Santiago: Centro Latinoamericano de Demografía, 1974.

2254. Safa, Helen I. "The Changing Composition of the Female Labor Force in Latin America." Paper presented at the Wellesley Conference on Women and Development, June 1976. Available from Wellesley Center for Research on Women, 828 Washington St., Wellesley, Massachusetts 02181.

2255. Santa Cruz Ossa, Elvira. "Latin American Women as Industrial Workers." Bulletin of the Pan American Union, v. 61, 1927: 259.

2256. Synon, Mary. "La mujer en el trabajo financiero de la guerra." Interamerica, v. 2 (4): 213-219.

2257. United Nations Economic Commission for Latin America. "Participation of Women in Development in Latin America." Paper presented at the International Women's Year Conference, Mexico City, 1975. U.N.Document #E/Conf.66/BP/8/Add.1.

2258. Van den Boomen, Josephus. Algunos aspectos de la actividad económica de la mujer en América Latina. Santiago: Centro Americano de Demografía, 1963.

2259. Youssef, Nadia H. Women and Work in Developing Societies. Population Monograph Series, no. 15. Berkeley: University of California, 1974.

2260. _____. "Interaction Between Female Employment and Family Planning in Latin America." Paper presented at the University Seminar on Latin American Population, University of California at Los Angeles, May 1975.

Mexico and Central America

2261. Aragon, Agustin. "La mujer mexicana en la ingeniería." Revista Mexicana de Ingeniería y Arquitectura, May 1938: 273-276.

2262. Elu de Leñero, María del Carmen. "Estructura familiar, trabajo, y fecundidad." Boletín Documental sobre las mujeres, v. 4 (3), 1974: 36-41.

2263. _____. "Education and Labor Force Participation of Women in Mexico: Some Significant Relationships." Paper presented at the Wellesley Conference on Women and Development, June 1976. Available from Wellesley Center for Research on Women, 828 Washington St., Wellesley, Massachusetts 02181.

2264. "El trabajo de la mujer: La mujer en la fábrica." Boletín Mensual del Departamento del Trabajo, v. 1 (1), March 1923: 46-51. Reprinted from "La mañana" newspaper, Montevideo, Uruguay.

2265. Encuentro de mujeres. "La mujer y el trabajo." Punto Crítico, v. 12, 1972: 35-39.

2266. Gasnell, C. "La participación laboral de la mujer en Panamá." Panama City: Instituto Panameño de Estudios Laborales, Ministerio de Trabajo, 1975.

2267. Gonzalez Salazar, Gloria. "La participación de la mujer en la actividad laboral en Mexico." In La mujer en América Latina, v. 1. Mexico City: Sepsetentas, 1975.

2268. _____. "Participación laboral y educación de la mujer en México." Boletín documental sobre las mujeres, v. 4 (3), 1974: 14-22.

2269. _____. "Participation of Women in the Mexican Labor Force." In June Nash and Helen I. Safa, eds., Sex and Class in Latin America. New York: Praeger, 1976: 183-201.

2270. Ibarra Olivares, Felipe. "El trabajo y el salario de la mujer." Trabajo y Previsión Social, April 1946: 19-47.

2271. Hernández, Ana María. La mujer mexicana en la industria textil. Mexico City: Tipografía Moderna, 1940.

2272. IFARHU. La mano de obra femenina en Panamá. Panama City: 1975.

2273. International Labour Organization. "Empleo de mujeres en los ferrocarriles mexicanos." Revista Internacional del Trabajo, November-December 1946: 450-451. Also cited as: International Labour Review, July-December 1946: 372-373.

2274. _____. "Employment of Women in El Salvador." Industrial and Labour Information, 27 March 1939: 394.

2275. Matamaros, M. "El papel de la mujer en el movimiento sindical panameño." Planificación y Cambio Social, v. 1, 1974: 104-108.

2276. Moore, Brian Edward Arthur. "Some Working Women in Mexico City: Traditionalists and Modernists." Ph.D. dissertation, Washington University, 1970.

2277. Moreno Contreras, Carmen. "Consideraciones generales sobre la mano de obra femenina en México." Revista del Instituto Técnico de Administración de Trabajo, v. 8, 1959: 106-121.

2278. Pedrero Nieto, Mercedes. "Labor Force in Mexico. A Study of Regional Variations 1950-1960." Ph.D. dissertation, University of Pennsylvania, 1973.

√ 2279. Pérez Peña Tellez, Bertha. "La desorganización familiar cuando la madre trabaja." Thesis, Universidad Nacional Autónoma de Mexico, 1962.

2280. Piho, Virve. "Life and Labor of the Female Textile Worker in Mexico City." In R. R. Leavitt, ed., Cross Cultural Perspectives on the Women's Movement and Women's Status. The Hague: Mouton, 1976.

2281. "Recomendaciones para el empleo de mujeres en la industria." Boletín Mensual del Departamento del Trabajo, v. 1 (3), March 1922.

2282. Rendón, Teresa. "Alternativas para la mujer en el mercado del trabajo en México." In Mercados Regionales de Trabajo. Mexico City: Instituto Nacional de Estudios del Trabajo and United Nations, 1976.

2283. Rivera, María Amalia Inás de, and Irma Violeta Alfaro de Carpio. "Guatemalan Working Women in the Labor Movement." Latin American Perspectives, v. 4 (1-2), Winter-Spring 1977: 194-202.

2284. Riz, Liliana de. "El problema de la condición femenina en America Latina. La participación de la mujer en los mercados de trabajo: El caso de Mexico." Mimeo. Caracas: United Nations Development Programme, 1975.

2285. Rojas P. Palacios, Alfonso. "El salario de la madre." Puericultura, v. 6 (3), May-June 1955: 85-87.

2286. Royer, Fanchon. "Working Women of Mexico." Americas, v. 6 (2), October 1949: 167-172.

2287. Schofield, Kenneth. "Seasonal, Female Work Participation Rates in Costa Rica." Medford, Massachusetts: Fletcher School of Law and Diplomacy, Tufts University, 1974.

2288. Tienda, Marta. "Diferencias socio-económicas regionales y tasas de participación de la fuerza de trabajo femenina: El caso de México." Revista Mexicana de Sociología, 1975.

2289. _____. "Economic Development and the Female Labor Force: The Mexican Case." Master's thesis, University of Texas, 1975.

2290. Tinajero González, María Esperanza. "La mujer mexicana en la industria textil fronteriza: Experiencia de trabajo social en la fábrica de pantolones 'Hicks-Ponder'." Thesis, Universidad Nacional Autónoma de México, 1966.

2291. Torres de Arauz, Reina. "Profesionalismo femenino en Panamá: Proyecciones económicas y sociales." Paper presented at the Conference on Feminine Perspectives in Social Science Research in Latin America, Buenos Aires, 1974.

2292. Valdelamar, Emilia. "Mujeres panameñas participando en el trabajo." Boletín Documental sobre las Mujeres, v. 4 (3), 1974: 60-61.

2293. Valdivia, María Angela. "La larga marcha de las obreras de 'Medalla de Oro'." La Cultura en México, no 580, 21 March 1973: 11-14.

Caribbean

2294. Aiguesvives, Eduardo. "Presencia de la mujer cubana en la organización militar del pueblo." Bohemia, 19 January 1963: 9+.

2295. Benglesdorf, Carolee, and Alice Hageman. "Mujer y trabajo en Cuba: Dando el paso al frente." Boletín Documental sobre las Mujeres, v. 4 (4), 1974: 3-8.

2296. Biaggi Monzón, Nelly. "Situación de la mujer en el sistema científico-tecnológico de la Republica Dominicana." Ciencia Interamericana, v. 16 (3-4), July-December 1975: 2-8.

2297. Carleton, R. "Labor Force Participation: A Stimulus to Fertility in Puerto Rico." Demography, v. 2, 1965.

2298. Díaz Castro, Tania. "Las enfermeras en la revolución (Cuba)." Bohemia, 8 September 1967: 4-9.

2299. Espin, Vilma. "La mujer en el desarrollo económico del país." Verde Olivo, 15 September 1968: 10-13.

2300. McBride, N. W. "Women Workers of Puerto Rico." International Socialist Review, v. 18, June 1971.

2301. Manning, Caroline. The Employment of Women in Puerto Rico. Washington: U. S. Government Printing Office, 1934.

2302. "Mujeres matanceras ayudan a construir 117 casas de campo." Revolución, 10 October 1959:12-13.

2303. Pico-Vidal de Hernández, Isabel. "La mujer puertorriqueña y la recesión económica." Mimeo. Paper presented at the Seminar on Women in Development, Mexico City, 1975.

2304. Puerto Rico. Bureau of Labor Statistics. Employment Status of Women in Puerto Rico for 1962, 1956, and 1950. San Juan: 1963.

2305. Rodríguez, Mirta. "Los planes artesanales: Un paso más en la integración de las mujeres a la producción." Bohemia, 9 June 1967: 12-17.

2306. Roman, Georgina. "The Women Workers of Cuba and Labour Throughout the World." Free Labour World, v. 7 (70), April 1956: 22-24.

2307. Silvestrini-Pacheca, Blanca. "Women in the Trade Unions of Puerto Rico." In R. R. Leavitt, ed., Cross Cultural Perspectives on the Women's Movement and Women's Status. The Hague: Mouton, 1976.

2308. Torres, Lázaro. "La mujer: Factor de éxito en la artesanía." Bohemia, 23 February 1968: 30-33.

2309. Torriente, Loló de la. "Una mirada a la actividad de la mujer cubana." Universidad de la Habana, v. 27 (163), September-October 1963: 53-69.

2310. U. S. Department of Labor. Report on Puerto Rico: The Needlework Industry. Washington, D.C.: U. S. Government Printing Office, 1950.

2311. Veigas, José. "La mujer en la plástica Cubana." Revolución y Cultura, v. 26, 1974: 21-31.

2312. Weller, Robert H. "The Employment of Wives, Role Incompatibility, and Fertility: A Study Among Lower and Middle-Class Residents of San José, Puerto Rico." Milbank Memorial Fund Quarterly, v. 66, 1968: 507-527.

2313. _____. "A Historical Analysis of Female Labor Force Participation in Puerto Rico." Social and Economic Studies, v. 7, March 1968: 60-69.

Andean Region

2314. Almoina de Carrera, Pilar. "Apuntes sobre formas tradicionales populares de trabajo de la mujer venezolana." Archivos Venezolanos de Folklore, v. 7 (10-11), 1961-1962: 269-275.

2315. Araos, María Rosario. "La orientación profesional femenina en el Perú." Servicio Social, no. 11/12, December 1953-January 1954: 139-159.

2316. Bamberger, Michael. "Changing Patterns of Female Labor Force Participation in Venezuela, 1950-1971. Part I." Working Paper, no. 1. Caracas: Centro de Estudios Sociales, 1973.

2317. Barrionuevo de Cáceres, Nora. "La mujer, la educación, y el trabajo." Thesis, Pontificia Universidad Católica, Lima, 1967.

2318. Cannon, Mary Minerva. Women Workers in Peru. Washington, D.C.: U. S. Department of Labor, 1947.

2319. Centro de Estudios de Participación Popular. "Como vive la mujer trabajadora en el Perú." Lima: May 1974.

2320. Centro de Estudios Sociales con la Cooperación de AITEC. "La mujer y el trabajo." Mimeo. Documento Tecnico, no. 1. Caracas: 1975. Available from CES, Apartado 14.385, Caracas 101, Venezuela.

2321. Chaplin, David. The Peruvian Industrial Labor Force. Princeton: Princeton University Press, 1967.

2322. _____. "Labour Turnover in the Peruvian Textile Industry." British Journal of Industrial Relations, v. 6, March 1968: 58-78.

2323. Cohen, Lucy M. "Patrones de prática profesional en mujeres." Educación Médica y Salud, v. 2, 1968: 1-22.

2324. _____. "Women's Entry to the Professions in Colombia." Journal of Marriage and the Family, v. 35 (2), May 1973: 322-330.

2325. de Becerra, Magdalena. La mujer y el trabajo. Caracas: Imprenta del Congreso de la República, 1971.

2326. Escuela Sindical Autónoma de Lima. Mujeres trabajadoras, ciudadanas. Lima: 1960.

2327. Finn, Michael, and Carol Jusenius. "La posición de la mujer en la fuerza laboral del Ecuador." Estudios Andinos, v. 5 (1), 1976: 99-118.

2328. Fucaraccio, Angel. "El trabajo femenino en Bolivia. Un estudio de caso." Mimeo. Santiago: Centro Latinoamericano de Demografía, 1974.

2329. Gurrieri, Adolfo. La mujer joven y el trabajo. Santiago: ILPES, 1969.

2330. _____. "La mujer joven y el trabajo." In A. Gurrieri, et al. Estudios sobre la juventud marginal latinoamericana. Mexico City: Siglo Veintiuno Ed. 1971: 66-194.

2331. Hague, Juan. "El salario de la mujer en el Perú." Voz Rotario, 16 August 1941: 115-128.

2332. Ibero, Norma. La señorita empleada. Bogotá: Talleres Gráficos de la Penitenciaría Central, 1952.

2333. "Inspectores femeninos en Perú." Revista Internacional del Trabajo, January-February 1946: 123.

2334. International Labour Organization. Towards Full Employment: A Program for Colombia. Geneva: International Labor Organization, 1970.

2335. Nash, June C. "Women in the Mining Communities of Bolivia." Paper presented at the IX International Congress of Anthropological and Ethnological Sciences, Chicago, 1973.

2336. _____. "Mi vida en las minas: La autobiografía de una mujer boliviana." Estudios Andinos, v. 5 (1), 1976: 139-150.

2337. Rincón, Ovidio. "El trabajo femenino en Colombia." Economía Colombiana, v. 3 (8), December 1954: 299-307.

2338. Rivera, Ana. "Estudios de mano de obra femenina en dos centros urbanos en diferentes etapas de desarrollo: Lima Metropolitana e Iquitos." Documento de Trabajo. Santiago: CELADE, 1967.

2339. Sánchez, Antonio María. "Mujeres que trabajan." Economía Colombiana, v. 12 (35), March 1957: 443-454.

2340. Schmink, Marianne. "Dependent Development and the Division of Labor by Sex: Venezuela." Paper presented at the 5th National Meeting of the Latin American Studies Association, November 1974.

2341. Stycos, J. Mayone. "Female Employment and Fertility in Lima, Peru." Milbank Memorial Fund Quarterly, v. 63, January 1965: 42-54.

Chile and the Platine

2342. Alvarez de Harvey, Delia. "Importancia de la incorporación de la mujer al campo de lo social." ECA, v. 4 (10), 1962: 23-58.

2343. Argentine Republic. División de Estadísticas Sociales. "Incidencia salarial y ocupacional de la mano de obra femenina en las convenciones colectivas de trabajo." Buenos Aires: 1969.

2344. _____. Secretaría de Estado de Trabajo. Dirección Nacional de Recursos Humanos. Oficina Nacional de la Mujer. "Evolución de la mujer en las profesiones liberales en Argentina, 1900-1965, Segunda Edición." Supplement to the Boletín de la Oficina Nacional de la Mujer, Series A: "La mujer economicamente activa." Buenos Aires: 1970.

2345. Barbieri, María Teresita de. "Acceso de la mujer a las carreras y ocupaciones tecnológicas de nivel medio." Mimeo. Santiago: UNESCO and Escuela Latinoamericana de Sociología, 1972.

2346. Campo, Guillermina del. "Oportunidad y protección en el trabajo." Revista Universitaria Nacional de Córdoba, v. 10 (1-2), March-June 1969: 93-104.

2347. Cannon, Mary Minerva. "Women Workers in Argentina, Chile, and Uruguay." Bulletin of the Pan American Union, v. 76, March 1942: 148-154.

2348. _____. Women Workers in Paraguay. Washington, D.C.: U. S. Department of Labor, 1946.

2349. Deveali de Landín, Gabriela. El trabajo de las mujeres. Buenos Aires: Bibliografía Omeba, 1967.

2350. Ducci, Angélica; Margarita Gili; and Marta Illanes. "El trabajo, ¿un nuevo destino para la mujer chilena?" Santiago: Instituto Laboral y de Desarrollo Social, 1972. Also cited as Familia, v. 1 (2), 1973: 84-88.

2351. Gamboa de Alvarado, Graciela; Haydee Cuello de Mateluna; and Alicia Petit Alcaíno. "El trabajo de la mujer en la industria y sus consecuencias." Servicio Social, v. 30 (2), 1956: 3-28.

2352. Gonella, Nieves. "Participación de la mujer en la empresa." Revista Universitaria Nacional de Córdoba, v. 10 (1-2), March-June 1969: 267-282.

2353. Guido, Francisco Alberto. "La mujer en la vida sindical argentina." Mimeo. Buenos Aires: Centro Nacional de Documentación e Información Educativa, 1972.

2354. Infante Garmendia, Inés. "Estudio comparativo del trabajo de la mujer en la fábrica en el año 1939." Servicio Social, January-March 1940: 1-58.

2355. Kinzer, Nora Scott. "Women Professionals in Buenos Aires." In Ann Pescatello, ed., Female and Male in Latin America: Essays. Pittsburgh: University of Pittsburgh Press, 1973: 159-190.

2356. Lamperein, Lina Vera. "Trabajo femenino." Thesis, Universidad de Chile, 1936.

2357. MacAuliffe, Ana. "Desempeño profesional de la visitadora social." Servicio Social, v. 24 (1), 1950: 3-17.

2358. Martínez Vivot, Julio José. Trabajo de menores y de mujeres. Buenos Aires: Ediciones Depalma, 1964.

2359. Paraguay. Ministerio de Justicia y Trabajo. Dirección General de Recursos Humanos. "Participación de la mujer en la fuerza de trabajo." Mimeo. Asunción: Ministerio de Justicia y Trabajo, 1975.

2360. Perón, María Estela de. La Vicepresidente habla a la mujer que trabaja. Buenos Aires: 1974.

2361. Rabinovich de Pirosky, Rosa. "Participación de la mujer en la investigación científica." Revista Universitaria Nacional de Córdoba, v. 10 (1-2), March-June 1969: 363-378.

2362. Ribeiro, Lucía, and María Teresita de Barbieri. "La mujer obrera chilena." Cuadernos de la Realidad Nacional, v. 16, 1973: 167-201.

2363. Simone, José A. de. "En favor del acceso de la mujer a carreras técnicas." Revista de Educación, v. 24-25, 1970: 72-75.

2364. Stabile, Blanca. "The Working Woman in the Argentine Economy." International Labour Review, v. 85 (2), February 1962: 122-128.

2365. Waisman, Marina. "La mujer en la arquitectura." Revista Universitaria Nacional de Córdoba, v. 10 (1/2), March-June 1969: 379-393.

2366. Zuzunaga Florez, Carlos. Cultura y profesión de la mujer. Buenos Aires: 1958.

Brazil

2367. Alcantara, Glete. A enfermagem moderna como categoria professional: Obstáculos à sua expansão na sociedade brasileira. São Paulo: Universidade de São Paulo, 1966.

2368. Alterman Blay, Eva. "Trabalho industrial e trabalho doméstico. A ideologia no trabalho feminino." Cadernos de Pesquisa, no. 15, December 1975: 8-20.

2369. Barroso, Carmen Lucia de Melo. "A participação da mulher no desenvolvimiento científico brasileiro." Ciência e Cultura, v. 27 (6), 1975: 613-620.

2370. _____. "Por que tão poucas mulheres exercem atividades científicas?" Ciência e Cultura, v. 27 (7), 1975: 703-710.

2371. _____, and Guiomar N. de Mello. "Moças do Rio e São Paulo preferem as carreiras tipicamente femininas." O Globo, 31 December 1974: 7.

2372. Berlinck, Manoel Tosta. "Algumas percepções sobre a mudança do papel ocupacional da mulher na cidade de São Paulo." Master's thesis, Fundação Escola de Sociologia e Política de São Paulo, 1964.

2373. Blay, Eva Alterman. "A participação da mulher na industria paulista." America Latina, v. 10 (1), January-March 1967: 81-95.

2374. _____. "A mulher e o trabalho qualificado na industria paulista." Ph.D. dissertation, Universidade de São Paulo, 1972.

2375. Bulcao Vianna, María Sophia. "Evolución del trabajo de la mujer en el Brasil." Spanish Bulletin, v. 72, January 1938: 13-18.

2376. Cannon, Mary Minerva. Women Workers in Brazil. Washington, D.C.: U. S. Department of Labor, 1946.

2377. Cardone, Marly A. "Subsidios do Direito do Trabalho para um debate sobre a situação da mulher." Cadernos de Pesquisa, no. 15, December 1975: 124-131.

2378. Ferreira-Santos, Celia Almeida. A enfermagem como profissão: Estudo num hospital-escola. São Paulo: Ed. da Universidade de São Paulo, 1973.

2379. Hahner, June. "Changing Structure of Women's Employment in Brazilian Cities: An Historical Perspective." Paper presented at the Wellesley Conference on Women and Development, June 1976. Available from Wellesley Center for Research on Women, 828 Washington St., Wellesley, Massachusetts 02181.

2380. _____. "Women and Work in Brazil, 1850-1920." In Dauril Alden and Warren Dean, eds., Essays Concerning the Socio-Economic History of Brazil and Portuguese India. Gainesville: University of Florida Press, 1977.

2381. Instituto de Desenvolvimento de Guanabara. Guanabara: Mão de obra feminina. Rio de Janeiro: Instituto de Desenvolvimento de Guanabara, 1973.

2382. Jelin, Elizabeth. "La bahiana en la fuerza de trabajo: Actividad doméstica, producción simple, y trabajo asalariado en Salvador, Brazil." Mimeo. Paper presented at the Conference on Feminine Perspectives in Social Sciences Research in Latin America, Buenos Aires, 1974.

2383. _____. "The Bahiana in the Labor Force in Salvador, Brazil." In June Nash and Helen I. Safa, eds., Sex and Class in Latin America. New York: Praeger, 1976: 129-146.

2384. _____. "Formas de organização de atividade econômica e estrutura ocupacional." Estudios CEBRAP, v. 9, 1974: 51-78. Also cited as "Formas de organización de la actividad económica y estructura ocupacional: El caso de Salvador, Brazil." Desarróllo Económico, v. 14 (53), April-June 1974.

2385. Johnston, Henry T. "Ladies Can So Count Cruzeiros." Brazilian Business, v. 43 (12), December 1963: 34-37.

2386. Madeira, Felicia R., and Paul Singer. "Estrutura de emprego e trabalho feminino no Brasil: 1920-1970." Cadernos CEBRAP, v. 13, 1973. Also cited (in English) as Journal of Interamerican Studies and World Affairs, v. 17 (4), November 1975: 490-496.

2387. Mala, Silvia Tigre. "Educação e trabalho da mulher." Formação, June 1946: 27-31.

2388. "Mão-de-obra feminina: O trabalho em tempo parcial." Desenvolvimento y Conjuntura, v. 7 (5), May 1963: 42-50.

2389. Meirellas, Cecilia. "Trabalho feminino no Brasil." O Observador Econômico e Financeiro, July 1939: 93-107.

2390. Pan American Union. "Brazilian Women in the War." Bulletin of the Pan American Union, v. 78, July 1944: 415-416.

2391. Pereira, Luis. "Mulher e trabalho." Educação e Ciências Sociais, v. 8 (15), September 1960: 143-158.

2392. Pires, A. S. "Word With a Brazilian Policewoman." Americas, v. 9, July 1957: 26-27.

2393. "População ativa feminina e o reconhecimiento." Conjuntura Econômica, September 1953: 64-70.

2394. Rabello, Sylvio, et al. "Participação da mulher no mercado de trabalho." Recife: Instituto Joaquim Nabuco de Pesquisas Sociais, 1969.

2395. Russomano, Mozart Victor. "O trabalho da mulher." Trabalho e Seguro Social, v. 24 (85/86), January-February 1950: 57-66.

2396. Saffioti, Heleieth Iara B. "Profissionalização feminina: Professoras primarias e operarias." Mimeo. Araraquara: Faculdade de Filosofía, Ciências, e Letras, 1969.

2397. Suggs, Julia Flanigan. "Women Workers in Brazil." Phylon, v. 7 (1), 1947: 60-67.

2398. Sullerot, Evelyne. "A mulher no trabalho, historia e sociologia." Expressão e Cultura, 1970.

2399. Vasques de Miranda, Glaura. "A educação da mulher brasileira e sua participação nas atividades económicas em 1970." Cadernos de Pesquisa, no. 15, December 1975: 21-36.

2400. _____. "Women in the Labor Force in a Developing Society: The Case of Brazil." Paper presented at the Wellesley Conference on Women and Development, June 1976. Available from Wellesley Center for Research on Women, 828 Washington St., Wellesley, Massachusetts 02181.

E. SOCIAL ASPECTS OF WOMEN'S LABOR

Africa--General

2401. Hansen, Karen Tranberg. "Married Women and Work: Explorations from an Urban Case Study." African Social Research, v. 20, December 1975: 777-799.

2402. Quashie, Angele. "La Femme et le travail." Afrique Nouvelle, v. 20 (1015), 19-25 January 1967.

West Africa

2403. Nigeria. Federal Ministry of Labour. "Report on the Survey on Working Women with Family Responsibilities." Lagos: Federal Ministry of Labour, 1971.

2404. Usoro, Eno J. "The Place of Women in Nigerian Society." African Women, v. 4 (2), June 1961: 27-30.

Central Africa

2405. "Conditions of Work of Women and Children in the Congo (Kinshasa)." International Labour Review, v. 98, October 1968: 357-359.

2406. Schwarz, Alfred. "Illusion d'une émancipation et aliénation réelle de l'ouvrière zaïroise." Canadian Journal of African Studies v. 6 (2), 1972: 183-212.

East Africa

2407. Byangwa, Margaret. "The Muganda Woman's Attitude Towards Work Outside the Home: A Study on the Economic Status of the Married Woman." Sociology Paper, no. 53. Makerere University College, n.d.

2408. Olmstead, Judith V. "Female Fertility, Social Structure and the Economy: A Controlled Comparison of Two South Ethiopian Communities." Ph.D. dissertation, Columbia University, 1974.

2409. Stichter, Sharon B. "Women in the Urban Labor Force in Kenya: Problems and Prospects." Paper presented at the Wellesley Conference on Women and Development, June 1976. Available from Wellesley Center for Research on Women, 828 Washington St., Wellesley, Massachusetts 02181.

Southern Africa

2410. Longmore, L. "Infant Mortality in the Urban Africa. The African Attitude towards It in the Witwatersrand." South African Medical Journal, v. 28 (14), 1954: 295-298.

2411. Wessels, Dina M. "The Employment Potential of Graduate Housewives in the PWV Region — Part I: Part-time Employment." Pretoria: South African Human Sciences Research Council, Institute for Manpower Research, 1972.

2412. _____. "The Employment Potential of Graduate Housewives in the PWV Region — Part II: The Careers of Graduate Housewives." Mimeo. Report No. M-47-1974. Pretoria: South African Human Sciences Research Council, Institute for Manpower Research, 1974.

Latin America--General

2413. Anderson, Mary. "What the Americas Are Doing for the Woman Worker." Bulletin of the Pan American Union, v. 69, July 1935: 521-535.

2414. Bernate de Kanter, M. D. "Summary of the Report on the Economic Status of Working Women in the American Republics." Washington, D.C.: Pan American Union, 1964: 1-61.

2415. Coffee, John M. "Workers and Women in Inter-American Relations." Congressional Record, 1 May 1944.

2416. Elizaga, Juan C. "Participation of Women in the Labor Force of Latin America: Fertility and Other Factors." International Labour Review, v. 109, 1974: 519-538.

2417. Fortín, Geraldo. "Aspectos sociológicos del trabajo femenino." Boletín Documental sobre las Mujeres, v. 1 (1), 1971: 21-31.

2418. International Labour Organization. "Servicios sociales en favor de las trabajadoras madres." Revista Internacional del Trabajo, v. 43, March 1951: 300-317.

2419. Mahoney, T. A. "Factors Determining the Labor Force Participation of Married Women." Latin American Research Review, v. 14, July 1961: 563-577.

2420. Rodríguez, Aida, and Susana Schkolnik. "Chile y Guatemala: Factores que afectan la participación femenina en la actividad económica." Mimeo. Document Series C., no. 156. Santiago: Centro Latinoamericano de Demografía, 1974.

2421. Rothman, Ana María. La participación femenina en actividades económicas en su relación con el nivel de fecundidad en Buenos Aires y México. Santiago: 1967.

2422. Youssef, Nadia H. "Differential Labor Force Participation of Women in Latin American and Middle Eastern Countries: The Influence of Family Characteristics." Social Forces, v. 51, December 1972: 135-153.

Mexico and Central America

2423. Alonso, José Antonio. "La mujer guatemalteca en 1973: De inferioridad a explotación: El trabajo de la mujer casada fuera del hogar en la Ciudad de Guatemala." Estudios Sociales, v. 10, 1976: 15-36.

2424. Alvarez, Elena. Pláticas de las mujeres mexicanas. Mexico City: Ediciones de la Liga de Escritores Revolucionarios, 1924.

2425. Baeres, María. "Estudios analíticos sobre la importancia de la mujer casada en el campo laboral." Revista Mexicana de Trabajo, v. 8 (9-10), September-October 1961: 37-62.

2426. Elu de Leñero, María del Carmen. El trabajo de la mujer en México: Alternativa para el cambio. México City: Ed. IMES, 1975.

2427. Interamerican Regional Organization of Workers. "Los problemas de la mujer trabajadora." Mexico City: Interamerican Regional Organization of Workers, 1956.

2428. O'Connor, Ana Doris. "Informe sobre los estudios verificados en la ciudad de México, D.F., en relación a la oficina investigadora sobre la situación de la mujer y de los menores trabajadores." Revista del Trabajo, v. 3 (11), October-December 1952: 43-90.

2429. Rojas Pérez, Alfonso. "El salario de la mujer y su función social como madre." Revista Mexicana de Trabajo, v. 11 (11/12), November-December 1964: 19-21.

2430. Royer, Fanchón. "Working Women of Mexico." Americas, v. 6 (2), 1949: 167-172.

2431. Ruiz Harrell, R. "Aspectos demográficos, educativos, y laborales de la mujer en México, 1900-1970." Paper presented at the International Women's Year Conference, Mexico City, 1975.

2432. Sierra Padilla, Elena Ernestina. "Algunos de los problemas mas frecuentes de la obra mexicana, vistos a traves del trabajo social." Mexico City: Instituto Marillac, Escuela de Trabajo Social Incorporada a la Universidad Nacional Autónoma de Mexico, 1962.

2433. Stycos, J. Mayone. Margin of Life: Population and Poverty in the Americas. New York: Grossman, 1974. Chapter 7.

2434. Valerio, Adriana de. "La situación de la mujer obrera en Honduras." Pan-America, v. 7 (86), July 1951: 10-11.

Caribbean

2435. Azzize, Vamila. "Luchas de la mujer obrera, 1910-1920." Thesis, University of Puerto Rico, 1974.

2436. Benglesdorf, Carollee, and Alice Hageman. "Emergine From Underdevelopment: Women and Work." Cuba Review, v. 4 (2), 1974: 3-12.

2437. King, Marjorie. "Cuba's Attack on Women's Second Shift, 1974-76." Latin American Perspectives, v. 4 (1-2), Winter-Spring 1977: 106-119.

2438. Quiñones Rodríguez, Carmen F. "Families of Working Mothers in Puerto Rico." Ph.D. dissertation, Ohio State University, 1976.

Andean Region

2439. Angulo, Alejandro, and Ceclia López de Rodríguez. Trabajo y fecundidad de la mujer colombiana. Bogotá: Fundación para la Educación Superior y el Desarrollo, 1975.

2440. Anhuaman R., Martha. "Organización del mercado de trabajo en función de absorción de mano de obra femenina calificada. Thesis, Escuela Superior de Administración Pública, Lima, 1973.

2441. Centro de Estudios de Participación Popular. <u>Situación y aspiraciones de la mujer trabajadora en el Perú.</u> Lima: Ed. del Centro, 1974.

2442. Centro de Estudios Sociales con AITEC. "Efectos del empleo sobre el status de la mujer. Estudios de caso con una muestra de mujeres del barrio las Minas de Baustra, July 1975." Caracas: 1975. Available from CES, Apartado 14.385, Caracas 101, Venezuela.

2443. _____. "The Effects of Employment and Education on the Status of Women in Venezuela. A Progress Report." Paper presented at the 8th World Congress of the Committee on Family Research, International Sociological Association, 1975. Available from CES, Apartado 14.385, Caracas 101, Venezuela.

2444. Ecuador. Instituto Nacional de Previsión. "Condiciones del trabajo de la mujer en el Ecuador." <u>Boletín de Informaciones y de Estudios Social y Economicas,</u> March 1939: 86-88.

2445. Ortíz de Rey, Ada. "El trabajo de la mujer casada." Thesis, Programa Académico de Ciencias Sociales, Pontificia Universidad Católica, Lima, 1973.

2446. Pasco Ramírez, Juana. "Estudio de la madre que trabaja." Thesis, Universidad Nacional Mayor de San Marcos, Lima, 1973.

2447. Torres, Hernando, and Clara González. "La mujer y la delincuencia." <u>Boletín Mensual de Estadística,</u> no. 247, 1972: 81-111.

2448. Zaía Maccán, Sylvana, and Michael Bamberger. "Employment and the Status of Women in Venezuela." <u>Development Digest,</u> v. 13 (3), July 1975: 41-67.

Chile and the Platine

2449. Argentine Republic. Oficina Nacional de la Mujer. "Realidad económica social de la mujer trabajadora." Buenos Aires: Oficina Nacional de la Mujer, 1969.

2450. Bouzón de Terzano, Emilia Beatriz. "El trabajo de la mujer casada." In José I. Cafferata, ed., <u>La familia.</u> Córdoba, Argentina: Taller Editorial de la Universidad Nacional de Córdoba, 1973: 287-307.

2451. Chamorro Greca, Eva. "La madre que sale a trabajar." Revista Universitaria Nacional de Córdoba, v. 10 (1-2), March-June 1969: 241-265.

2452. Covarrubias, Paz, and Mónica Muñoz. "Algunos factores que inciden en la participación laboral de las mujeres de estratos bajos." Santiago: Instituto de Sociología, Universidad Cató lica de Chile, 1972.

2453. del Campo, Guillermina. "Oportunidad y protección en el trabajo." Revista Universitaria Nacional de Córdoba, v. 10 (1-2), March-June 1969: 93-104.

2454. Gregorio Lavié, Lucila de. "Proyección del trabajo femenino en el futuro del país." Revista de Economía Argentina, August 1945: 403-404.

2455. Hollander, Nancy Caro. "Women Workers and the Class Struggle: The Case of Argentina." Latin American Perspectives, v. 4 (1-2), Winter-Spring 1977: 180-193.

2456. International Labour Organization. "Employment of Married Women in Argentina." Industrial and Labour Information, 2 January 1938: 9-10.

2457. Lamperein, Lina Vera. Trabajo femenino. Santiago: Imprenta "El Esfuerzo," 1936.

2458. Leban de Cavia, Lucia N. "Women as Non-Valued Human Resource in the Rural Environment." First Special Issue of Boletín Documental sobre las Mujeres, 1974: 59-64.

2459. Ribeiro, Lucía, and M. Teresita de Barbieri. "La mujer obrera chilena. Una aproximación a su estudio." Cuadernos de la Realidad Nacional, v. 16, 1973: 167-201.

2460. Ventura, Ovidio. "Consecuencias económicas y sociales del trabajo femenino." Revista de Economía Argentina, July 1944: 203-208.

Brazil

2461. Cardone, Marly A. "Mulher casada e contrato de trabalho." Revista Latinoamericana de Trabajo, v. 29 (447), 1965.

2462. Da Silva, Lea Melo. "Family Size and Female Labor Force Participation in Brazil." Ph.D. dissertation, Duke University, 1976.

2463. Durand Ponte, Victor Manuel. "Algunas consideraciones sobre la participación de la mujer de Guanabara en la vida moderna." America Latina, v. 9 (4), October-December 1966: 81-95.

2464. Leite Lopes, José Sergio. "Os salarios das mulheres e sua repercussão sobre a situação da familia da classe trabalhadora." Unpublished manuscript, 1971.

2465. Tudor, Talitha do Carmo. "Trabalho da mulher com encargos de familia." Separata de Juridica, 1970.

2466. Woortmarin, Klaas. "A mulher em situação da classe." America Latina, v. 8 (3), July-September 1965: 62-83.

Chapter IX

WOMEN AND SOCIAL CHANGE

This chapter can serve as a compliment to the preceding chapters through its focus on the social, normative, political, and economic factors that facilitate or hinder change. Entries stress the potential for change and the measurement of actual changes that can be applied to the roles, statuses, and opportunities of women presented by the citations of previous chapters. General topics include migration, adaptation to modern values and ideals, the effects of a changing environment on women's participation, and role conflict resulting from rapid change.

Specific areas of research include the differential impact of adaptive or imposed change (e.g., via development programs) and discussions of the decline in women's status as a consequence of new role concepts introduced into the traditional community or family. Although references often concentrate on the effects of change on women as passive recipients, many articles promote the idea that women can be used as active agents for change, thus effecting change as well as being affected by it.

Africa - General

2467. "African Women on the Ladder." Africa, v. 15, 27 July 1962: 7-8.

2468. "Africa's Food Producers: The Impact of Change on Rural Women." Focus, v. 25, January 1975: 1-7.

2469. Bernheim, M., and E. Bernheim. "New Kind of African Woman!" New York Times Magazine, 7 July 1963: 14-15.

2470. Binet, Jacques. "La Femme et l'évolution de l'afrique." Revue de L'Action Populaire, v. 139, 1959.

2471. Bourgoigne, G. E. Jeune Afrique mobilisable: Les problèmes de la jeunesse désoeuvrée en Afrique noire; développement économique en Afrique noire et coopération de la jeunesse. Paris: Editions Universitaires, 1964.

2472. Boyi, Elisabeth. "La Jeune Fille africaine face au progrès." Documents pour L'Action, v. 19, January-February 1964: 11-18.

2473. Breetveld, J. "New Woman of Africa." Journal of Nursery Education, v. 19, April 1964: 207.

2474. Cheviller, Tugdual Le. "Establir la femme noire d'abord dans ses divits humains." Marchés Coloniaux du Monde, v. 92 (1), August 1947: 1117-1118. Also cited as African Abstracts, v. 2 (4), 1951: 176.

2475. de Hemptinne, C. "Le Femme africaine prend conscience de sa mission." Vivante Afrique, v. 243, March-April 1966: 15-17.

2476. Desanti, Dominique. "La Femme africaine busé le joug." Jeune Afrique, v. 189, 11 June 1964: 29-31.

2477. Dethoor, N. "A quoi rêvent les femmes africaines?" Croissance des Jeunes Nations, v. 50, December 1965: 13-15.

2478. Diarra, F. A. Femmes africaines en devenir. Paris: Editions Anthropos, 1971.

2479. Digby, Margaret, and B. J. Surridge. Agricultural Investment in Developing Countries with Specific Relations to Tropical Africa. London: Plunkett Foundation for Co-operative Studies, 1964.

2480. Dobert, Margarita, and Nwanganga Shields. "Africa's Women: Security in Tradition, Challenge in Change." Africa Report, v. 17 (7), July-August 1972: 14-20.

2481. Gutkind, Peter C. W. "The Poor in Urban Africa: A Prologue to Modernization, Conflict and the Unfinished Revolution." Reprint Series no. 13, Montreal: Centre for Developing Area Studies, McGill University, 1968.

2482. Hafkin, Nancy J., and Edna G. Bay, eds., Women in Africa: Studies in Social and Economic Change. Stanford: Stanford University Press, 1976.

2483. Hill, Adelaide Cromwell. "The Broadening Horizons of African Women." In Africa and the United States: Images and Realities. Washington, D. C.: U. S. National Commission for UNESCO, 1961: 83-90. Also cited as Boston University Graduate Journal, v. 10 (2), December 1961: 37-62.

2484. Holleman, J. F. "The Changing Roles of African Women." In P. Smith, ed., Africa in Transition. London: Reinhardt, 1958: 71-78.

2485. Isaac, S. "Pour la promotion sociale de la femme." African Documents, v. 59, 1962: 216-229.

2486. "Jeune afrique Madame." Jeune Afrique, v. 500, 4 August 1970: Supplément, 27-46.

2487. "Les Jeunes Filles d'Afrique face a leur destin." Afrique Nouvelle, v. 11 (541), 17 December 1957: 8.

2488. Jiagge, A. R. "Changing Roles of Women in Africa." Mimeo. Accra: Court of Appeals, n.d.

2489. Kaberry, Phyliss. "Raising the Status of Women." Times Survey of the British Colonies, December 1950: 11-12.

2490. Kheury N'Dau, Aly. "Vers de nouveaux horizons." Jeune Afrique, v. 712, August 1974: 46-48.

2491. Konka, R. "Crise de la femmê traditionelle africaine." Afrique et Culture, v. 12 (14-15), 1972: 26-30.

2492. Lambo, T. Adeoye. "Socio-Economic Change and Its Influence on the Family, with Special Emphasis on the Role of Women: A Socio-Psychological Evaluation." Ibadan, v. 26, February 1969: 30-35.

2493. Laure, Rosemary. "Emerging Women in Emerging Africa." Marriage, v. 48, March 1966: 38-45.

2494. Lavine, R. A. "Sex Roles and Economic Change in Africa." Ethnology, v. 5 (2), April 1966: 186-193. Also cited in John Middleton, ed., Black Africa: Its Peoples and Their Cultures. New York: Macmillan Co., 1970.

2495. Levin, Michael D. "Family Structure in Bakosi: Social Change in An African Society." Ph.D. dissertation, Princeton University, 1976.

2496. _____."L'Evolution de la femme africaine." L'Afrique en Marche, v. 12-13, 1958: 38-40.

2497. Lippert, Anne. "The Changing Role of Women as Viewed in the Literature of English- and French-Speaking West Africa." Ph.D. dissertation, Indiana University, 1972.

2498. Martin, Pierre. "Evolution de la condition feminine en Afrique." Recherches Internationales, v. 7, March-April 1964: 189-207.

2499. Mazrui, A. A. "Miniskirts and Political Puritanism." Africa Report, v. 13 (7), October 1968: 9-13.

2500. Mennen, William G. "Women in the New Africa." U.S. Department of State Bulletin, no. 1269, 21 October 1963: 636-639.

2501. N'Gassa. "La Promotion sociale de la femme africaine." Nations nouvelles, v. 4, June 1965: 5-11.

2502. Njiiri, Ruth S. "New Roles for Women in Modern Africa." Mimeo. Washington, D.C.: African-American Scholars Council, May 1975.

2503. Raymond, G. Alison. "Woman in Africa: Her Baby Off Her Back: The Sphere of Influence of Women in Africa." Journal of Human Relations, v. 8 (3-4), Spring-Summer 1960: 700-717.

2504. Retif, André. "Promotion de la femme africaine." Etudes, v. 309 (4), April 1961: 16-29.

2505. "The Roles of African Women: Past, Present and Future. Les Roles passés, présents et futurs des femmes africaines." Canadian Journal of African Studies, v. 6 (2), 1972: 143-377.

2506. Roumy, M. "Femme africaine et civilisation moderne." Dialogue et Culture, v. 7 (3), March 1969: 12-15.

2507. du Sacré-Coeur, Marie André, Sister. "Evolution féminine en Afrique noire." Rythmes du Monde, v. 4, October 1947: 46-52.

2508. _____. "Liberty and Dignity of African Women (Address, December 23, 1960)." Vital Speeches, v. 27, 15 March 1961: 331-332.

2509. Scharf, Traute. "L'Evolution de la fonction sociale, économique et politique de la femme en Afrique noire." Afrika, v. 10 (3), 1969: 57-65.

2510. "Supplément féminin, vingt pages interdites aux hommes."

Jeune Afrique, v. 507, 22 September 1970: 29-48.

2511. Tardits, Claude. "Woman against the Lineage." In Porto-Novo, ed., Les Nouvelles génerations entre leurs traditions et l'occident. Paris: Mouton, 1958: 59-76.

2512. Tomo, Paul-Maurice. "L'Evolution de la femme." Europe - France-Outre-mer, v. 47 (483), April 1970: 15-17.

2513. Touré, Sekou. "The Role of Women in the Revolution." Black Scholar, v. 6 (6), March 1975: 32-36.

2514. United Nations. Commission on the Status of Women. United Nations Assistance for the Advancement of Women in Developing Countries. New York: United Nations, 1962. United Nations Document # EC/CN. 6/395.

2515. United Nations Economic Commission for Africa. African Training and Research Centre for Women. "A Path to Progress for African Women." Pamphlet. Addis Ababa: United Nations Economic Commission for Africa, June 1975.

2516. Human Resources Development Division. Women's Programme Unit. "Women of Africa, Today and Tomorrow." Mimeo. Addis Ababa: United Nations Economic Commission for Africa, 1975.

2517. Van Allen, Judith. "Revolutionary Strategies for Change in Africa." Paper presented at the Wellesley Conference on Women and Development, June 1976. Available from Wellesley Center for Research on Women, 828 Washington St., Wellesley, Massachusetts 02181.

2518. Van Hove, J. "La Promotion de la femme africaine." In Libre Blanc. Brussels: L'Academie Royale des Sciences d'Outre-Mer, 1962: 409-412.

2519. Wheeler, Elizabeth Hunting. Women of Modern Africa. New York: Women's African Committee, 1966.

2520. Williams, G. Mennen. "Women in the New Africa: Address, 24 September 1963." U.S. Department of State Bulletin, v. 49, 21 October 1963: 636-639.

2521. Wipper, Audrey, ed. "The Roles of African Women: Past, Present, Future." Canadian Journal of African Studies, v. 6 (2), 1972.

2522. "Women's Place in the African Revolution." Third World, v. 1, December 1972: 33-36.

2523. Women Today: A Journal for Women in Changing Societies. London: Department of Education in Tropical Areas, University of London, Institute of Education, December 1954.

2524. "Women Today (Reports from Africa, the Arab World, Europe, Japan, India, and Latin America.)" Atlas World Press Review, March 1975.

West Africa

2525. Abouet, Henriette and Delphine Yetet. "Un Réveil s'est produit chez la femme." Revue de L'O.A.M.C.E., v. 5, March 1964: 33-37.

2526. Aldous, Joan. "Urbanization, the Extended Family and Kinship Ties in West Africa." In P. L. Van den Berghe, ed., Africa: Social Problems of Change and Conflict. San Francisco: Chandler, 1965: 107-116.

2527. Baker, Tanya, and Mary E. C. Bird. "Urbanization and the Position of Women." Sociological Review, v. 7 (1), July 1959: 99-122.

2528. Bird, Mary E. C. "Social Change in Kinship and Marriage Among the Yourba of West Nigeria." Thesis, Edinburgh University, 1959.

2529. Caldwell, John C. Population Growth and Family Change in Africa: The New Urban Elite in Ghana. New York: Humanities Press, 1968.

2530. Diarra, Fatoumata Agnès. Femmes africaines en devenir: Les femmes zarma du Niger. Paris: Editions Anthropos, 1971.

2531. Dobert, Margarita. "The Changing Status of Women in French-Speaking Africa: Dahomey and Guinea." Mimeo. Washington D.C.: American University, 1970.

2532. Etia, Mme. "Cameroun: La Jeune Fille, la femme évoluent-elles au même rythme que les conditions de vie?" L'Ecole des Parents, v. 1, November 1963: 2-10.

2533. La Femme Tchadienne. Paris: Ecole des Hautes Etudes, 1975.

2534. Gobert, A. "Francir le mur des traditions sclérosées."

Revue de L' O.A.C.E., v. 5, March 1964: 30-33.

2535. Greenstreet, M. "Social Change and Ghanian Women!" Canadian Journal of African Affairs, v. 6 (2), 1972: 351-355.

2536. Klingshirn, Agnes. "The Changing Position of Women in Ghana." Ph.D. inaugural dissertation, University of Marburg, 1971.

2537. Lacroix, C. "La Guinée a l'avant-garde de la promotion féminine." La Vie Africaine, v. 22, February 1962: 30-31.

2538. Little, Kenneth L. "The Changing Position of Women in Sierra Leone Protectorate." Africa, v. 18 (1), January 1948: 1-17. Also cited as American Journal of Sociology, v. 54 (1), July 1948: 10-21.

2539. _____. African Women in Towns: An Aspect of Africa's Social Revolution. London: Cambridge University Press, 1973.

2540. Lombard, J. "Cotonou, ville africaine. Tendances évolutives et réaction des coutûmes traditionelles." Bulletin de L'IFAN, v. 16 (3-4), 1954: 341-377.

2541. M'baye, Annette, and O. Fall. "Promotion de la femme Sénégalaise." Développement et Civilisation, special number, 1962: 67-71.

2542. McCall, Daniel F. "The Effect on Family Structure of Changing Economic Activities of Women in a Gold Coast Town." Ph.D. dissertation, Columbia University, 1956.

2543. Mondah, Agnès. "La Femme dans l'agriculture ivoirienne." Afrique Nouvelle, v. 16 (868), 27 March- 2 April 1964: 14; v. 22 (1133), 24-30 April, 1969: 16+.

2544. O'Connor, George Aquin, Sister. "The Status and Roles of West African Women: A Study in Cultural Change." Ph.D. dissertation, New York University, 1964.

2545. Okonjo, Isabel Kamene. "The Role of Women in Social Change Among the Igbo of Southeastern Nigeria Living West of the River Niger." Ph.D. dissertation, Boston University, 1976.

2546. Ottenberg, Phoebe. "The Changing Economic Position of Women Among the Afikpo Ibo." In W. R. Bascom and M. J. Herskovits, eds., Continuity and Change in African Cultures. Chicago: University of Chicago Press, 1959: 205-223.

2547. Rivière, Claude. "La Promotion de la femme guinéenne." Cahiers d'Etudes Africaines, v. 8, 3 (31): 1968: 406-427.

2548. Senghor, L. S. "L'Evolution de la situation de la femme en A.O.F." Marchés Coloniaux, v. 6 (226), 1950: 541-542.

2549. Smock, A.C. "The Changing Roles and Status of Women in Ghana." In A.C. Smock and J.Z. Giele, eds., Women and Society: An International and Comparative Perspective, 1976.

2550. Sudarkasa, Niara. "Comments on Contemporary West African Migrations, Their Relationship to Development and Their Impact on Women." Paper presented at the Wellesley Conference on Women and Development, June 1976. Available from Wellesley Center for Research on Women, 828 Washington St., Wellesley, Massachusetts 02181.

2551. Taraore, M. "Prêt des femmes en pays soussou (Guinée)." Notes Africaines, v. 29, 1946: 12-13.

2552. The, Marie-Paule de. "Evolution féminine et évolution villageoise chez les Beti du Sud-Cameroun." Bulletin de L'IFAN v. 30 B (4), October 1968: 1533-1565.

2553. "Les Togolaises demandent l'interdiction de la mini-robe." Afrique Nouvelle, v. 1098, 22-28 August 1968: 10.

2554. Uche, Nkem. "Courage to Begin Again--Biafran Women Not Defeated by War." Response, v. 5 (5), May 1973: 14-16.

2555. Uzoma, Adaoha C. "The Changing Position of Married Women of One Ibo Community (Nkwerre) in Township and Village: A Socio-Economic Analysis." Der Ostblock und die Eutwick-lungsländer, v. 44, 1971: 113-150.

2556. Weeks, Dorothy C. Remy. "Adaptive Strategies of Men and Women in Zaria, Nigeria: Industrial Workers and Their Wives." Ph.D. dissertation, University of Michigan, 1973.

2557. Wilson, Elizabeth Ann. "Women in the Changing Pattern of Sierra Leone." Sierra Leone-Trade, Industry, and Travel, v. 4, 1959.

Central Africa

2558. Apthorpe, R., and Clyde J. Mitchell. "The Traditional and Modern Roles and Statuses of Bantu Women in the Two Rhodesias and Nyasaland." In Women's Role in the Development of Tropical and Sub-tropical Countries. Brussels: International Institute of Differing Civilizations, 1959. Appendix y J. C. Mitchell.

2559. Bolamba, A. R. Les Problemes de l'évolution de la femme noire. Elisabethville: L'Essor du Congo, 1949.

2560. Boti, Elisabeth. "Le Jeune fille africaine face au progres." Documents pour L'Action, v. 19, January-February 1964: 11-18.

2561. Colin, Michel. "Quatre heureuses initiatives pour la formation des femmes congolaises." Voix du Congolais, v. 136, July 1957: 522-530.

2562. Comhaire-Sylvain, Suzanne. Femmes de Kinshasa, hier et aujourd'hui. Paris: Mouton, 1968.

2563. "La Corruption des moeurs des femmes dites évoluées." Liaison, v. 58, 1957: 30-34.

2564. de Halleux, B. "Femmme ruandaise, qui deviens-tu?" Vivante, v. 243, March-April 1966: 22-52.

2565. Dutilleux, G. "La Femme détribalisée du centre extra-coutûmier." Bulletin du CEPSI, v. 6 (14), 1950: 106-114.

2566. Fernandes, J.A. Soares. "A mulher africana: Alguns aspectos da sua promoção social em Angola." Estudos Politicos e Sociais, v. 4 (2), 1966: 575-684.

2567. Gerda, Sister. "La Femme ruandaise hier et aujourd'hui." Trait d'Union, v. 44, 957: 11-14.

2568. "How to Appear Evolué (Women in the Congo)." Time, v. 84, 25 September 1964: 33.

2569. Marneffe, J. de. "Foyers sociaux et promotion féminine au Ruanda et au Burundi." Congo-Afrique, v. 6 (9), November 1966: 453-462.

2570. Masangu, J. "L'Evolution de la femme congolaise." Eurafrica, v. 5 (7), August 1961: 13-14.

2571. Mukankiko, A. "La Promotion féminine." Revue de L'O.A.M.C.E., v. 5, March 1964: 49-50.

2572. Petre, M. M. "Promotion féminine dans un centre extracoûtumier d'Afrique centrale." Perspectives de Catholicité, v. 4, 1957: 43-52.

2573. Powdermaker, Hortense. "Social Change through Imagery and Values of Teen-age Africans in Northern Rhodesia." American Anthropologist, v. 58, 1956: 783-813.

2574. "Le Programme d'action sociale de la femme au Ruanda." Servir, v. 25 (1), 1964: 36-37.

2575. Rhodius, Georges. "The Evolution of the Native Woman in the Belgian Congo and Ruanda-Urundi." African Women, v. 1 (3), December 1955: 73-74.

2576. Sohier-Brunard, A. "La Reforme de la dot et la liberté de la femme indigène." Bulletin des Juridictions Indigènes et du Droit Coutûmier Congolais, v. 18 (7), January-February 1950: 217-221.

2577. _____. L'Impréparation de la femme indigène du Congo aux tâches que la vie à notre contact lui impose. Brussels: Librairie Encyclopedique, 1951.

East Africa

2578. Abbott, Susan. "Fulltime Farmers and Weekend Wives: An Analysis of Altering Conjugal Roles." Journal of Marriage and the Family, v. 38, February 1976: 165-174.

2579. Asoyan, B. "Uganda's Women Today." New Times, no. 12, March 1975: 25-26.

2580. Correira, Maximino. "What is Being Done in the East African Territories--Opportunities of Advancement for African Women." East Africa and Rhodesia, v. 27 (1384), 19 April 1951: 893-906.

2581. Habwe, Ruth. "Bigger Role for Women in New Kenya." East African Standard, 28 December 1963: 4.

2582. Hay, Margaret. "Luo Women and Economic Change during the Colonial Period." In E. Bay and N. Hafkin, eds., Women in Africa. Stanford: Stanford University Press, 1976.

2583. "Kenya African Women's Seminar." Women Today, v. 6 (1), December 1963: 5-6.

2584. Kisosonkole, P.E. "La Femme africaine dans l'Ouganda moderne." Way Forum, v. 32, July 1959: 48-51.

2585. Kokuhirwa, Hilda. "Towards the Social and Economic Promotion of Rural Women in Tanzania." Mimeo. Dar-es-Salaam: Institute for Adult Education, 1975.

2586. Maleche, Albert. "A New Status for Women in Kenya." East Africa Journal, v. 9 (6), June 1972: 28-31.

2587. Martins, Judith Alves. "A destribalização da mulher negra em geral com alguns aportamentos sobre a problema em Moçambique." Estudos Ultramarinos, v. 2, 1961: 99-129.

2588. Mbilinyi, Marjorie J. "The 'New Woman' and Traditional Norms in Tanzania." Journal of Modern African Studies, v. 10 (1), May 1972: 57-72.

2589. Neatby, H. "The Contribution of Educated African Women to the Uganda of Today." East and West Review, v. 20 (3), 1954: 67-72.

2590. Obote, M. "Women in a Changing Society." East African Journal, v. 4 (4), July 1967: 29-32.

2591. Oloo, Celina, and Virginia Cone. Kenya Women Look Ahead. Nairobi: East African Literature Bureau, 1965.

2592. Perlman, M. L. "The Changing Status and Role of Women in Toro (Western Uganda)." Cahiers d'Etudes Africaines, v. 6 (24), 1966: 564-591.

2593. Report of the 1964 East African Women's Seminar: East African Women Look Ahead. Nairobi: Regal Press, 1964.

2594. Ricketts, E. "The East African Woman Looks Ahead." African Women, v. 3 (4), June 1960: 73-75.

2595. Shannon, Mary T. "Women's Place in Kikuyu Society: Impact of Modern Ideas in Tribal Life-A Long Term Plan for Female Education." African World, September 1954: 7-10.

2596. Staub, H. "The Changing Role of Women in Tanzania." Rural Life, v. 16 (2), 1971.

2597. Uganda Council of Women. "Uganda Women Look Ahead: Their Place in Home and Community." Kampala: Uganda Council of Women, 1961.

2598. Uku, Skyne. "Obstacles to Social Change among East African Women." Paper presented at the annual meeting of the African Studies Association, San Francisco, October-November 1975.

Southern Africa

2599. Hunter, M. "The Effects of Contact with Europeans on Pondo Women." Africa, v. 6, 1933: 259-276.

2600. Mexeke, C. M. "The Progress of Native Womanhood in South Africa." In J. D. Taylor, ed., Christianity and the Natives of South Africa: A Yearbook of South Africa Missions. Lovedale: Institution Press, 1928: 177-182.

2601. Mayer, Philip, and Iona Mayer. "Women and Children in the Migrant Situation." In Townsmen or Tribesmen. Capetown: Oxford University Press, 1963.

Latin America--General

2602. Elmendorf, Mary Lindsay. "The Role of Women as Agents for Peaceful Social Change." Paper presented at the SID (Society for International Development) Conference, 1971.

2603. Elton, Charlotte. "The Economic Determinants of Female Migration in Latin America." Thesis, University of Sussex, England, 1974.

2604. Enochs, Elisabeth Shirley. "Pan Americanism and the American Woman." Boletín del Instituto Americano del Niño, v. 31 (122), September 1957: 277-286.

2605. Flora, Cornelia Butler. "Women in Latin America: A Force for Tradition or Change." Mimeo. Manhattan, Kansas: Department of Sociology and Anthropology, Kansas State University, 1975.

2606. "The Impact of the International Women's Year Conference on Women in Latin America." IFFP/WHR News Service, v. 3 (4), August 1975.

2607. Jelin, Elizabeth. "Migración a las ciudades y participación en la fuerza del trabajo de las mujeres latinoamericanas: El caso del servicio doméstico." In Estudios Sociales No. 4. Buenos Aires: Centro de Estudios de Estado y Sociedad, 1976.

2608. Pescatello, Ann. "Latin Liberation: Tradition, Ideology, and Social Change in Iberian and Latin American Culture: An Interpretative Essay." In B. Carroll, ed., Liberating Women's History. Urbana, Illinois: University of Illinois Press, forthcoming.

2609. Stolmaker, Charlotte. "Adaptations of Traditional Peasant Practices to Modern Needs." Mimeo. Paper presented at the

Southwestern Antropological Association Meeting, Santa Monica, California, April 1974.

2610. Urquidi, Arturo. "Proyección de la mujer en la sociedad actual." In Estudios de Sociología, no. 8. Buenos Aires: Biblio. Omeba, n.d. (circa 1967).

2611. Villavicencio, Gladys. "Efectos del avance tecnológico sobre la organización de las comunidades indígenas." America Indígena, v. 28 (4), October 1968: 947-962.

2612. "Women and Change: Comparative Perspectives with Emphasis on Cuban Women." Conference held at Boston University, May 1977. Information on papers available from Dr. Oliva Espín, Department of Counselor Education, Boston University, 232 Bay State Rd., Boston, Massachusetts 02215.

2613. "Women in Latin America: Past, Present, Future." America, v. 26, April 1974: 51+.

Mexico and Central America

2614. Abrams, Ira. R. "Cash Crop Farming and Social and Economic Change in a Yucatec Maya Community in Northern British Honduras." Ph.D. dissertation, Harvard University, 1974.

2615. Burke, Melvin. "El sistema de plantación y la proletarización del trabajo agrícola en El Salvador." Estudios Centroamericanos, v. 31 (335-336), September-October 1976: 473-486.

2616. Chinchilla, Norma. "The Changing Role of Women in Guatemala." Paper presented at the Wellesley Conference on Women and Development, June 1976. Available from Wellesley Center for Research on Women, 828 Washington St., Wellesley, Massachusetts 02181.

2617. Elmendorf, Mary Lindsay. "The Mayan Women and Change." Ph. D. dissertation, Union Graduate School, 1972.

2618. _____, Nine Mayan Women: A Village Faces Change." Cambridge: Schenkman Publishing Co., 1975.

2619. _____, "The Mayan Woman and Change." In R. R. Leavitt, ed., Cross-Cultural Perspectives on the Women's Movement and Women's Status. The Hague: Mouton, 1976.

2620. Elu de Leñero, María del Carmen ¿Hacia dónde va la mujer mexicana? Mexico City: Instituto Mexicano de Estudios Sociales, 1969.

2621. Hayner, Norma S. New Patterns in Old Mexico. New Haven, Connecticut: College and University Press, 1966.

2622. Johnson, Allan Griswold. "Modernization and Social Change: Attitudes Toward Women's Roles in Mexico City." Ph.D. dissertation, University of Michigan, 1972.

2623. Korsi de Ripoll, Blanca. "Evolución social de la mujer." Lotería, v. 14 (164), 1969: 34-40.

2624. MacLachlan, Colin M. "Modernization of Female Status in Mexico." Interamerican Review, v. 4 (2), 1974.

2625. Macías, Anna. "Mexican Women in the Social Revolution." Paper presented at the American Historical Association Conference on Latin American History, New York, December 1971. Also cited as "La mujer y la revolución social mexicana." Boletín Documental sobre las Mujeres, v. 3 (4), 1973: 3-14.

2626. "Mujer mexicana en la lucha social." Justicia, v. 28, October 1969: 52+.

2627. Nelson, Cynthia. The Waiting Village: Social Change in Rural Mexico. Boston: Little, Brown and Co., 1971.

2628. Nolasco, Margarita. "Cambio en la tecnología agrícola y población indígena." Anuario Indigenista, v. 28, December 1968: 244-254.

2629. Press, Irwin. Tradition and Adaptation: Life in a Modern Yucatan Maya Village. Westport, Connecticut: Greenwood Press, 1975.

2630. Porras Muñoz, Guillermo. "ESDAI: Oportunidad para la mujer." Istmo, v. 65, December 1969: 29-32.

2631. Ram, B. "Net Internal Migration by Marital Status for Panama: Females 1950-60." Social and Economic Studies, v. 20, 1971: 319-332.

2632. Rengert, Arlene C. "Female and Male Out-Migration in Relation to Socioeconomic Development: An Examination of Some Micro Variables Concerning the Family of Origin in Mexican Villages." Paper presented at the Wellesley Conference on Women and Development, June 1976. Available from Wellesley Center for Research on Women, 828 Washington St., Wellesley, Massachusetts 02181.

2633. Robles de Mendoza, Margarita. La evolución de la mujer en México. Mexico City: Impresas Galas, 1931.

2634. Sámano de López Mateos, Eva, and Adolfo López Mateos. La mujer mexicana en la lucha social. Mexico City: 1958.

2635. Stolmaker, Charlotte. "Examples of Stability and Change from Santa María Atzompa." Paper presented at the Southwestern Anthropological Association Meeting, Tucson, Arizona, 1971.

2636. Young, Kate. "Changing Roles of Women in Two Highland Zapotec Communities." Paper presented at the IV World Congress of Rural Sociology, Poland, 1976.

2637. _____. "The Social Setting of Migration: Factors Affecting Migration From a Sierra Zapotec Village in Oaxaca, Mexico." Master's thesis, University of London, 1976. Chapter 8.

2638. Young, Philip D. Ngawbe: Tradition and Change among the Western Guaymi of Panama. Urbana, Illinois: University of Illinois Press, 1971.

2639. Zavala de Aquino, Carolina. "Estudio sobre valores realizado en una muestra de mujeres guatemaltecas que solicitaron ingresar en la Universidad de San Carlos de Guatemala en los años 1960-63." Thesis, Universidad de San Carlos, 1966.

2640. Zimmerman, Charlotte Benedict. "The Meaning of the Role of Women in a Transition from a Civilization to a Fellaheen Social Order: A Study of Continuity and Change in a Maya Culture." Ph.D. dissertation, St. Louis University, 1960.

Caribbean

2641. Arroyo, Anita. "Presencia de la mujer en la vida cubana." Diario de la Marina. Siglo y Cuatro. Havana: Diario de la Marina, 1955.

2642. Benglesdorf, Carollee, and Alice Hageman. "Emerging From Underdevelopment: Women and Work." Cuba Review, v. 4 (2), 1974: 3-12.

2643. Berman, Joan. "Women in Cuba." Women: A Journal of Liberation, v. 1 (4), Summer 1970: 10-14.

2644. Castro, Fidel. "July 26, 1974." Cuba Review, v. 4 (2), 1974: 35.

2645. _____. This Phenomenon of "Women in the Revolution" is a Revolution in Itself within the Revolution. Havana: 1967.

2646. Chertov, Eva. "Women in Revolutionary Cuba." The Militant, 18 September 1970: 9-11.

2647. Christensen, Edward W. "The Puerto Rican Woman: The Challenge of a Changing Society." Character Potential, v. 7, March 1975: 89-96.

2648. Espín, Oliva M. "La liberación de la mujer cubana." Nuevos Rumbos, v. 2 (3), 1974: 2-11.

2649. García Suárez, Ariel. "La mujer como miembro activo de la nueva sociedad." El Mundo, 15 December 1968: 5.

2650. Gordon, Linda. "Speculations on Women's Liberation in Cuba." Women: A Journal of Liberation, v. 1, Summer 1970: 14+.

2651. Hageman, Alice. "Women: Cuba." IDOC/International Documentation, v. 69, January 1975: 27-31.

2652. Jenness, Linda. "Women and the Cuban Revolution: Speeches by Fidel Castro, Articles by Linda Jenness." Pamphlet. New York: Pathfinder Press, 1970.

2653. Menéndez González, Aldo. "La mujer rebelde." Revolución y Cultura, v. 26, 1974: 46-51.

2654. Olesen, Virginia. "Leads on Old Questions from a New Revolution: Notes on Cuban Women, 1969." Annals of the New York Academy of Science, v. 175, 1970: 781-1065.

2655. Perera, Hilda. "La mujer y el nuevo contexto social en Cuba." Boletín Trimestral de UNESCO, v. 14 (3), Fall 1962: 152-157.

2656. Pico-Vidal de Hernández, Isabel. "La mujer en Puerto Rico." Mimeo. Santurce, P.R.: 1975.

2657. Purcell, Susan Kaufmann. "Modernizing Women for a Modern Society: The Cuban Case." In Ann Pescatello, ed., Female and Male in Latin America: Essays. Pittsburgh: University of Pittsburgh Press, 1973: 257-271.

2658. Ramos, Ana. "La mujer y la revolución en Cuba." Casa de las Americas, v. 10 (65-66), 1971: 56-72.

2659. Randall, Margaret. "Cuban Women Now." Toronto: Canadian Women's Educational Press, 1974.

2660. _____. "Cuban Women Now: Afterword 1974." Toronto: Candian Women's Educational Press, 1974.

2661. _____. Examen de la opresión y la liberación de la mujer. Bogotá: Ed. Barricada, 1973.

2662. _____. La mujer cubana ahora. Havana: Editorial de Ciencias Sociales, Instituto Cubano del Libro, 1972.

2663. _____. Mujeres en la revolución. Mexico City: Siglo Ventjuno Editores, 1972.

2664. _____. "Venceremos: Women in the New Cuba." Canadian Dimension, v. 10 (8), June 1975: 49-55.

2665. _____. "Women in the Cuban Revolution." Women: A Journal of Liberation, v. 3 (4), 1973: 2-4.

2666. Rothkrug, Barbara, and Shari Whitehead. "The Revolution of Cuban Women." In Cuba: 100 Years of Struggle. New York: Cuba Resource Center, 1970.

2667. Sutherland, Elizabeth. The Youngest Revolution. A Personal Report on Cuba. New York: Dial Press, 1969: 169-190.

2668. Torres Hernández, Lázaro. "Presencia de la mujer en la revolución cubana." Bohemia, v. 65, 22 June 1973: 101-106.

2669. "Women Soldiers." Center for Cuban Studies Newsletter, v. 1 (3), 1972: 9-13.

Andean Region

2670. Aguirre Alorriaga, Manuel. "La promoción de la mujer." SIC: Revista Venezolana de Orientación, v. 31 (303), March 1968: 117-118.

2671. Aillón Ríos, Luz. "Un dilema de la mujer boliviana: ¿Madre o profesional?" Estudios Andinos, v. 1 (3), 1970: 55-68.

2672. CODEX. Comité Coordinator de Promoción Femenina. "Organizaciones de promoción femenina." La Paz: Comité Coordinador de Promoción Femenina, 1973.

2673. Cohen, Lucy M. "Colombian Professional Women as Innovators of Culture Change." Ph.D. dissertation, Catholic University of America, 1966.

2674. George, Lya. "Arte, lucha y progreso de la mujer venezolana." Grafos, April 1947: 22+.

2675. Hannot, Tamara. "La Mujer en Venezuela: ¿Nueva imagen o nueva mujer?" In Oficina de Estudios Socioeconómicos, Valores, estructura y sociedad. Caracas: Fondo Editorial Común, 1974: 79-113.

2676. Heyman, Barry Neal. "Urbanization and the Status of Women in Peru." Ph.D. dissertation, University of Wisconsin, 1974.

2677. Instituto Colombiano de Bienestar Familiar. "Evolución del adelanto de la mujer y su integración en el desarrollo." Mimeo. Bogotá: Instituto Colombiano de Bienestar Familiar, 1975.

2678. Poole, Debbie. "Parallelism in Andean Social Structures: The Effects of Social Change upon Women's Status." University of Michigan Papers in Women's Studies, v. 1 (3), 1975: 122-146.

2679. Rubbo, Anna. "The Spread of Rural Capitalism: Its Effects on Black Women in the Cauca Valley, Western Colombia." In R. Reiter, ed., Toward an Anthropology of Women. New York: Monthly Review Press, 1975. Also cited as "La extensión del capitalismo rural: Sus efectos sobre las mujeres negras en el valle del Cauca, Colombia." Estudios Andinos, v. 5 (1), 1976: 119-138.

2680. Schmidt, Steffen W. "Woman's Changing Roles in Colombia." In L. Iglitzin and R. Ross, eds., Women in the World: A Comparative Study. Santa Barbara: ABC Clio Press, 1976.

2681. Watson-Franke, María Barbara. Tradition and Urbanisation: Guajiro-Frauen in der Stadt. Vienna: University of Vienna, 1972

2682. Williamson, Robert C. "Social Class and Orientation to Change: Some Relevant Variables in a Bogotá Sample." Social Forces, v. 46, March 1968: 317-328.

Chile and The Platine

2683. Hilger, Inez M. "Una araucana de los Andes." Mimeo. Santiago: Universidad de Chile, 1970.

2684. Klimpel Alvarado, Felícitas. La mujer chilena: El aporte femenino al progreso de Chile, 1910-1960. Santiago: Ed. Andrés Bellow, 1962.

2685. Lobaczewski, Juan Román A. La mujer del tercer milenio. Buenos Aires: Ed. Fundación Tercer Milenio, 1972.

2686. "La migración de las jóvenes del interior a Buenos Aires, encuesta." Estudios, no. 582, May 1967: 217-227.

2687. Schultz Cazenueva de Mantovani, Fryda. "La mujer en los últimos 30 años." Sur, November-December 1960: 20-29.

2688. Sosa de Newton, Lily. Las argentinas de ayer a hoy. Buenos Aires: Librería y Editorial L.V. Zanetti, 1967.

2689. Thomas, Sandra Carol. "The Women of Chile and Education for a

Contemporary Society: A Study of Chilean Women, Their History and Present Status and the New Demands of a Society in Transition." Ph.D. dissertation, St. Louis University, 1973.

2690. Urbieta Rojas, Pastor. La mujer paraguaya: Esquema historiográfico. Asunción: Colección Paraguay, 1962.

2691. Vidal, Virginia. La emancipación de la mujer. Santiago: Ed. Nacional Quimantú, 1972.

2692. Videla de Plankey, Gabriela. "Las mujeres pobladoras de Chile y el proceso revolucionario." Boletín Documental sobre las Mujeres, v. 4 (4), 1974: 19-24.

Brazil

2693. Alburquerque, María Sabrina, and Zeia Pinho Rezende. "Atividades da Federaçao Brasileira pelo Progresso Femenino." Mimeo. Federação Brasileira pelo Progresso Femenino, 1962.

2694. Berlinck, Manoel Tosta. "Algumas percepções sobre a mudança do papel ocupacional da mulher na cidade de São Paulo." Master's thesis, Fundação Escola de Sociologia e Política de São Paulo, 1964.

2695. Gans, Marjorie; José Pastore; and Eugene A. Wilkening. "La mujer y la modernización de la familia brasileña." Revista Latinoamericana de Sociología, v. 6 (3), 1970: 389-419.

2696. Rosen, Bernard C., and Anita L. La Raia. "Modernity in Women: An Index of Social Change in Brazil." Journal of Marriage and the Family, v. 34 (2), 1972: 353-360.

2697. Smith, Suzanne M.; Eugene A. Wilkening; and José Pastore. "Interaction of Sociological and Ecological Variables Affecting Women's Satisfaction with Brasilia." International Journal of Comparative Sociology, v. 12 (2), June 1971: 114-127.

2698. Vaz da Costa, Rubens. "Migration, Urbanization and the Role of Women in Brazil." Mimeo. 1975.

Editor's Note: See also: Chapter VII, Section A. "General;" and Chapter VIII, Section C, "Feminist Movements."

Chapter X

WOMEN AND DEVELOPMENT

This final chapter compiles references on the integration, participation, involvement, and role of women in the process of development, including a treatment of the roles of women as motivators, leaders, initiators, and labor for development projects. The orientation of much of the research is toward the utilization of women to enhance the implementation of project plans and to ensure that women share in the benefits of development. Likewise, there is considerable mention of the past exclusion of women from both the planning and implementation phases of development and the ultimate detrimental effects this has had on the particular project, on the overall goal of national development, and on the status of women.
   This chapter should be used in conjunction with Appendix A, which brings together general references that speak of the integration of women worldwide or in several geographical regions.
   The citations that deal specifically with the rural area are separated into a subcategory, "Rural Only," as in previous chapters.

Africa--General

2699. "African Conference on the Role of Women in National Development." International Labour Review, v. 104, December 1971: 555-557.

2700. Ahouanmenou, V. "La Femme revendique aujourd'hui sa participation a la construction du monde." Revue de L'O.A.M.C.E., v. 5, March 1964: 29-30.

2701. Binet, Jacques. "La Femme et l'évolution de l'Afrique." Revue de l'Action Populaire, v. 139, June 1960: 747-756.

2702. Carr-Saunders, Alexander. "Women's Role in the Development of Tropical and Sub-Tropical Countries, Economic Aspect." In Women's Role in the Development of Tropical and Sub-Tropical Countries. Brussels: International Institute of Differing Civilizations, 1959.

2703. Dardenne, E. "Le Rôle de la femme dans le développement économique et sociale en Afrique." Paper presented at the New Education Fellowship 6th World Conference, Nice, 1932.

2704. Diop, Fifi. "Le Rôle de nos femmes dans la bataille pour le développement." Afrique Nouvelle, v. 22 (1093), 18-24 July 1968: 11.

2705. Hammond, Dorothy, and Alta Jablow. Women: Their Economic Role in Traditional Societies. Reading, Massachusetts: Addison-Wesley Pub. Co., 1973.

2706. International Federation of University Women. "Africa Today Challenge and Responsibility for the Women of Africa." Report of the Regional Seminar Held at Makerere University College, 1964. London: International Federation of University Women, 1964.

2707. Janelid, Ingrid. The Socio-Economic Role of Farm Women in Agricultural and National Development in West Africa. Rome: FAO, 1971.

2708. Kuoh, T. "Confrontée avec l'évolution de son pays..." Vivante Afrique, v. 239, July-August 1965: 42-45.

2709. Leduc, G. "Structures familiales et développement économique en Afrique intertropicale." Revue Juridique et Politique, v. 21 (1), October-December 1967: 136-146.

2710. Lefaucheux, M. H. "The Contribution of Women to the Economic and Social Development of African Societies." International Labour Review, v. 86 (1), June 1962: 15-30.

2711. Mitchell, J. C. "The Woman's Place in African Advancement." Optima, v. 9 (3), September 1959: 124-131.

2712. Raharosaona, Zaïveline. "La Femme au développement de son pays." Revue de L'O.A.M.C.E., v. 5, March 1964: 42-48.

2713. Regional Meeting on the Role of Women in National Development. Report. Addis Ababa: United Nations Economic Commission for Africa, 1969. U.N. Document # DOK 451 A/a, S2/69.

2714. Retif, André. "Le Rôle de la femme dans le développement des pays tropicaux et subtropicaux (Documents)." Bulletin du CEPSI, v. 51, December 1960: 57-129.

2715. _____. "Role of Women in Urban Development in Africa." Women Today, v. 6 (2), June 1964: 32-33.

2716. Roboff, Farron V., and Hilary L. Renwick. "The Changing Role of Women in the Development of the Sahel." Paper presented at the Annual Meeting of the African Studies Association, Boston, November 1976.

2717. "Role of Women in National Development in African Countries." International Labour Review, v. 101, April 1970: 399-401.

2718. du Sacré-Coeur, Marie André, Sister. Civilisations en marche. Paris: Grasset, 1956.

2719. Salema, María José. "Provinces portugaises d'Afrique." In Women's Role in the Development of Tropical and Sub-Tropical Countries. Brussels: International Institute of Differing Civilizations, 1959.

2720. Soyer-Poskin. "Report on Congo Belge." In Women's Role in the Development of Tropical and Sub-Tropical Countries. Brussels: International Institute of Differing Civilizations, 1959.

2721. Touré, Sékou. "The Role of Women in the Revolution." Black Scholar, v. 6, March 1975: 32-36.

2722. UNICEF (United Nations Children's Fund). Children, Youth, Women and Development Plans in West and Central Africa: Cameroon, Chad, Gabon, Ivory Coast, Mali, Mauritania, Niger, Togo. Abidjan, Ivory Coast: Regional Office for West and Central Africa, 1972.

2723. United Nations. Department of Economic and Social Affairs. "Report of the Regional Seminar for Africa on the Integration of Women in Development, with Special Reference to Population Factors, Addis Ababa, 3-7 June 1974." 2 vols. Mimeo. New York: United Nations, 1975. U.N. Document # ST/ESA/SER.B/6 and Add. 1.

2724. _____. Resolutions. "Africa. Women: Integration in Development." U.N. Document #E/CN/.14/Res/269; E/CN.14/642; ESCOR (59)-suppl 10.

2725. United Nations Economic and Social Council and UNICEF. "Summary of the Report on Women and Girls in National Development. February 1972." U.N. Document #E/ICEF/616/Add3/Annex.

2726. United Nations Economic Commission for Africa (UNECA). "The Data Base for Discussion on the Interrelations between the Integration of Women in Development, Their Situation, and Population Factors in Africa." Paper presented to the Regional

Seminar on the Integration of Women in Development with Special Reference to Population Factors, Addis Ababa, 1974.

2727. _____. "Regional Meeting on the Role of Women in National Development." Addis Ababa: ECA/German Foundation, 1969.

2728. _____. "Report of the Workshop on Urban Problems: The Role of Women in Urban Development." Workshop on Urban Problems, Lagos, 27 November 1963. U.N. Document #E/CN.14/241.

2729. _____. "The Role of Women in Urban Development." Mimeo. Addis Ababa: UNECA, 1963.

2730. _____. "Women and National Development in African Countries." Mimeo. Addis Ababa: UNECA, February 1973.

2731. _____. Human Resources Development Division. "Women: The Neglected Human Resource for African Development." Canadian Journal of African Studies, v. 6 (2), 1972.

2732. _____. _____. African Training and Research Centre for Women. "The Role of Women in Development." Paper presented at the Soroptimist International Convention, Sheffield, England, 27-31 July 1975.

2733. _____. _____. _____. "Women and National Development in African Countries: Some Profound Contradictions." African Studies Review, v. 18 (3), December 1973: 47-70.

2734. _____. _____. _____. "Women in Economic Development: An African Regional Perspective." Mimeo. Paper prepared for the Conference on the African Woman in Economic Development, sponsored by the African-American Scholars Council, Washington, D.C., 1975.

2735. _____. _____. Women's Programme Unit. "The Changing and Contemporary Role of Women in African Development." Mimeo. Addis Ababa: UNECA, 1974.

2736. _____. _____. _____. "The Integration of Women in African Development." Mimeo. Abidjan, Ivory Coast: 1974.

2737. _____. Social Development Section. Women's Programme Unit. "The Role of Women in African Development." Economic Bulletin for Africa, no. M75-1016, 1975.

2738. United Nations Food and Agriculture Organization; United Nations Economic Commission on Africa; and Swedish International Development Authority. "Planning Family Resources for Development (Seminar held in Addis Ababa, March 1972)." In Food and Agricultural Organization, Nutrition Information Series, no. 4, 1972. U.N. Document #ESH: IDS/72/6.

2739. Van Allen, Judith. "Revolutionary Strategies for Change in Africa." Paper presented at the Wellesley Conference on Women and Development, June 1976. Available from Wellesley Center for Research on Women, 828 Washington St., Wellesley, Massachusetts 02181.

2740. "Women in Economic and Social Development in Africa." In Report of the International Conference on Predominant Areas of Women's Activities in the Economic and Social Development of African Countries: Relationship between Training and Labour Market Requirements, Berlin, 6-10 July 1970. Berlin: Deutsche Stiftung für Entwicklungsländer, 1970.

2741. "Women, Jobs, and Development." Afro-Asian Economic Review, v. 15, May-June 1973: 11-15.

Rural Only

2742. Ahmed, Wajik. "Constraints and Requirements to Increase Women's Participation in Integrated Rural Development." Mimeo. Paper presented at the Seminar on the Role of Women in Integrated Rural Development, with Emphasis on Population Problems, Cairo, 1974.

2743. Debelian, L. "The Economic Role of Women with Special Emphasis on the Implementation of Rural Development Schemes in Africa." Paper for FAO/ECA/SIDA Seminar on Home Economics, Development Planning for English-Speaking Countries in Africa, Addis Ababa, 1972. Also cited as: "The Economic Role of Women with Special Emphasis on the Implementation of Rural Development Schemes in Africa." Rome: FAO, 1972. U.N. Document #ES THEP/A/72/8.

2744. FAO (Food and Agriculture Organization). "Women's Groups in Rural Development." Rome: FAO, 1975. Available from UNIPUB, Box 433, Murray Hill Station, New York 10016.

2745. _____, "Women's Leadership in Rural Development." Rome: FAO, 1975. Available from UNIPUB, Box 433, Murray Hill Station, New York 10016.

2746. Lele, Uma. The Design of Rural Development: Lessons From Africa. Baltimore: Johns Hopkins University Press, for the World Bank, 1975.

2747. Pala, Achola O. "The Role of Women in Rural Development: Research Priorities." Discussion Paper No. 203. Nairobi: Institute of Development Studies, University of Nairobi, Kenya, June 1974.

2748. Parsons, Kenneth H. "Customary Land Tenure and the Development of African Agriculture." Land Tenure Center Paper No. 77.

Madison: University of Wisconsin, Land Tenure Center, 1971.

2749. "Traditional Attitudes Toward Women: A Major Constraint on Rural Development." Social Science Conference Paper. Dar-es-Salaam: University of East Africa, 1970.

2750. United Nations Economic Commission for Africa. "Report of the Workshop on Extension of Family and Child Welfare Services Within Community Development Programmes, Accra, 21 November-3 December 1960." Addis Ababa: United Nations, December 1960. U.N. Document # E/CN.14/79; E/CN.14/FCW/3.

2751. _____. "Women-The Neglected Resources for Agrarian Development." Mimeo. July 1972. U.N. Document # ECA/SDHA/AC/2/6.

2752. _____. "The Changing and Contemporary Role of Women in African Development." Addis Ababa: African Training and Research Centre for Women, January 1974.

2753. _____. "The Role of Women in African Development." Paper presented at Mexico City, 1975. New York: United Nations, April 1975. U.N. Document # E/Conf.66/BP/8.

2754. _____. Human Resources Development Division. Women's Programme Unit. "The Role of Women in Population Dynamics Related to Food and Agriculture and Rural Development in Africa." Mimeo. Addis Ababa: United Nations Economic Commission for Africa, 1974.

2755. United Nations Economic Commission for Africa and Food and Agriculture Organization. "The Economic Role of Women With Special Emphasis on the Implementation of Rural Development Schemes in Africa." FAO Nutrition Information Documents Series, no. 4, 1972. U.N. Document # ESN:IDS/72/6.

2756. Weitz, Raanan, ed. "Problem of Peasant Women." In Rural Planning in Developing Countries. Report on the Second Rehovoth Conference, Rehovoth, Israel, August 1963. Cleveland: Western Reserve University Press, 1966.

West Africa

2757. D'Aby, F. J. Amon. "Report on Côte d'Ivoire." In Women's Role in the Development of Tropical and Sub-Tropical Countries. Brussels: International Institute of Differing Civilizations, 1959.

2758. Okigbo, Pius. "Social Consequence of Economic Development in West Africa." Annals of the American Academy of Political and Social Science, no. 305, 1956: 125-133.

2759. Organisation Africaine et Malgache de Coopération Économique. "Colloque sur l'intégration de la femme africaine et malgache au développement, Antsirabe, 24-27 September 1963." Yaoundé: Organisation Africaine et Malgache de Coopération Économique, 1964

2760. Scarbrough, Ellen Mills. "Liberia." In Women's Role in the Development of Tropical and Sub-Tropical Countries. Brussels: International Institute of Differing Civilizations, 1959.

Rural Only

2761. Bellonde, G. "Rural Education and Rural Development Projects in West Africa." Mimeo. Paris: Institut de Recherche et d'Application des Méthodes de Développement, 1974.

2762. Caldwell, John C., et al. "Population and Rural Development Research in West Africa." Rural Africana, v. 8, Spring 1968: 5-60.

2763. Chuta, Enyinna, and Carl Liedholm. "A Progress Report on Research on Rural Small-Scale Industries in Sierra Leone." African Rural Economic Program Paper. East Lansing: Michigan State University, November 1974.

2764. _____. "The Role of Small-Scale Industry in Employment Generation and Rural Development: Initial Research Results from Sierra Leone." African Rural Employment Paper No. 11. East Lansing: Michigan State University, 1975.

2765. Diop, C. "L'Animation féminine." L'O.A.M.C.E., v. 5, March 1964: 50-56.

2766. Du Sautoy, Peter. "Faith That Moves Mountains." The Times Supplement to Ghana, no. 54613, 9 November 1959.

2767. Groote, J. de. "Au Cameroun, animation rural féminine." Monde et Mission, March 1969: 16-21.

2768. Linnhoff, Ursula. "L'Animation rurale des femmes en Afrique francophone-case du Niger." In Report of the International Conference on Predominant Areas of Women's Activities in the Economic and Social Development of African Countries; Relationships between Training and Labour Market Requirements, Berlin, 6-10 July 1970. Berlin: Deutsche Stiftung für Entwicklungslander, 1970:41-44

2769. Melone, Stanislas. La Parenté de la terre dans la stratégie du développement; l'expérience camerounaise, étude critique.

Paris: Klincksieck, 1972.

2770. Schopflin, Ninon. "Difficultés de l'animation féminine rurale en pays Dida." Mimeo. Abidjan, Ivory Coast: Services Communautaires, Projet de Lakota, n.d.

2771. Simmons, Emmy Bartz. "Cultural Assumptions and Women's Roles in Development." Mimeo. Monrovia: Liberian Institute of Public Administration, 1974.

2772. _____. "Economic Research on Women in Rural Development in Northern Nigeria." Overseas Liaison Committee Paper No. 10. Washington, D.C.: Overseas Liaison Committee, September 1976.

2773. Spencer, D. S. C. "African Women in Agricultural Development: A Case Study in Sierra Leone." African Rural Economy Working Paper No. 11. East Lansing: Michigan State University, April 1970.

2774. The, Marie Paule de. Influence des femmes sur l'évolution des structures sociales chez les Beti du Sud Cameroun. Paris: L'École Pratique des Hautes Études, 1965.

2775. _____. "Participation féminine au développement rural dans la region de Bouaké." Centre Africain des Sciences Humaines Appliquées, République de Côte d'Ivoire, Ministere du Plan, September 1968.

Central Africa

2776. Apthorpe, Raymond. "Rhodesia and Nyasaland." In Women's Role in the Development of Tropical and Sub-Tropical Countries. Brussels: International Institute of Differing Civilizations, 1959.

2777. De Noel, L. "A Summary of the Replies Obtained in Answer to a Questionnaire Sent Out in the Belgian Congo." In La Promotion de la femme au Congo et au Ruanda-Urundi. Brussels: Congrès National Colonial, 12th Session, 1956: 325-342.

2778. Naigisiki, Saverio. "Ruanda." In Women's Role in the Development of Tropical and Sub-Tropical Countries. Brussels: International Institute of Differing Civilizations, 1959.

2779. Sa'D Al-Din Fawzi. "The Role of Women in a Developing Sudan." In Women's Role in the Development of Tropical and Sub-Tropical Countries. Brussels: Institute of Differing Civilizations, 1959.

Rural Only

2780. Boismenu, Mlle. de. Projet d'animation féminine rurale dans la préfecture de L'Ouham, République Central Africaine." Processed. Paris: Bureau pour le Développement de la Production Agricole, 1965.

2781. De Decker, H. "L'Animation rurale féminine à Bukavu." Congo Afrique, v. 10 (48), October 1970: 441-453.

2782. Mitchnik, David A. "The Role of Women in Rural Development in Zaire." Mimeo. London: OXFAM, 1972.

2783. Simonart, B. "La Femme dans le developpement communautaire." Antennes, v. 4-5, March 1962: 567-572.

East Africa

2784. Ladner, Joyce. "Tanzanian Women and Nation Building." Black Scholar, v. 3 (4), 1971: 22-28.

2785. Mbilinyi, Marjorie. "Barriers to the Full Participation in the Socialist Transformation of Tanzania." Unpublished paper, University of Dar es Salaam, n.d.

2786. Mboya, T. J. "Woman's Role in National Development." Processed. Keynote address at the Conference Organized by the East African Institute of Social and Cultural Affairs and the National Council of Women of Kenya, Nairobi, 1967.

2787. Nyendwoha, E. S. "Uganda." In Women's Role in the Development of Tropical and Sub-Tropical Countries. Brussels: International Institute of Differing Civilizations, 1959.

2788. Pala, Achola O. "A Preliminary Survey of the Avenues for and Constraints on Women in the Development Process in Kenya." Discussion Paper No. 218. Nairobi: Institute of Development Studies, University of Nairobi, Kenya, March 1975.

2789. "The African Woman Builds the Nation: A Report." National Kenya Women's Seminar. Nairobi: The Regal Press, 1963.

Rural Only

2790. Abbott, Susan. "Women's Importance for Kenyan Rural Development." Community Development Journal, v. 4 (30), October 1975: 179-82.

2791. Berger, Jennifer; Linus Ettyang; and Timothy Gatara. "Women's

Groups in Rural Development." Programmes for Better Family Living Report No. 15. Pokos, Nairobi, Kenya: FAO and the Institute of Adult Studies, 1975.

2792. Chambers, Robert. Managing Rural Development: Ideas and Experiences from East Africa. New York: Africana Publishing Co., 1974.

2793. De Villiers, John. "Community Development in Kenya: New Opportunities for African Women." African World, October 1958: 13.

2794. FAO (Food and Agriculture Organization). "Reaching Rural Families in East Africa." 1973. Available from Home Economics and Social Programmes Service, UN/FAO, Via delle terme di Caracalla, 00100, Rome, Italy.

2795. _____. "Women's Leadership in Rural Development." Programmes for Better Living Report No. 14. Pokos, Nairobi, Kenya: Food and Agriculture Organization and the Institute of Adult Studies, August 1974.

2796. Fuchs-Carsch, Michael. "Planning Donor-Supported Small Farmer Development Projects in Less Developed Countries: Lessons From Ethiopia and Ghana." Ph.D. dissertation, University of Tennessee, 1976.

2797. Heasman, K. "Women and Community Development in Kenya and Uganda." Community Development Journal, v. 4, October 1966: 16-22.

2798. Swedish International Development Authority. "Rural Women in Kenya and Tanzania." Development Digest, v. 13 (3), July 1975: 53-60.

2799. Tadesse, Zenebework. "The Effect of Development Programs on Rural Women in Ethiopia." Paper presented at the Wellesley Conference on Women and Development, June 1976. Available from Wellesley Center for Research on Women, 828 Washington St., Wellesley, Massachusetts 02181.

Southern Africa

2800. Horrell, Muriel. "Union of South Africa." In Women's Role in the Development of Tropical and Sub-Tropical Countries. Brussels: International Institute of Differing Civilizations, 1959.

Rural Only

2801. Wallman, Sandra. Take Out Hunger: Two Case Studies of Rural Development in Basuland. London: Athlone Press, 1969.

Latin America--General

2802. Chaney, Elsa M., and Marianne Schmink. "Las mujeres y la modernización: Acceso a la tecnología." In La mujer en América Latina I. Mexico City: Sepsetentas, 1975. Also (in English) in June Nash and Helen I. Safa, eds., Sex and Class in Latin America. New York: Praeger, 1976: 160-182.

2803. _____, _____, and Gloria Galotti. "Going From Bad to Worse: Women and Modernization." Paper presented at the Conference on Feminine Perspectives in Social Science Research in Latin America, Buenos Aires, 1974.

2804. Elmendorf, Mary Lindsay. "Memo to AID--Suggestions, Recommendations and Resources for Enhancing the Roles of Women in Development in Peru, Chile and Brazil." Washington, D.C.: AID, Department of State, 1974.

2805. Henríquez de Paredes, Querubina; Maritza Izaguirre P.; and Inés Vargas Deleunoy. Participación de la mujer en el desarrollo de América Latina y el Caribe. Santiago: UNICEF, 1975.

2806. Leacock, Eleanor. "Women, Development and Anthropology: Facts and Fictions." Latin American Perspectives, v. 4 (1-2), Winter-Spring 1977: 8-17.

2807. Leitinger, Ilse Abshagen. "Women and Modernization in Lati America." Paper presented at the American Sociological Association annual meeting, San Francisco, August 1975. Also cited as: Foreign Affairs Research Paper No. 22769-P. Washington, D.C.: U.S. Government Printing Office, U.S. Department of State.

2808. Maynard, Betty J. "Economic Development and the Division of Labor in Metropolitan Guatemala, Mexico and the U.S.A." Ph.D. dissertation, University of Texas, 1967.

2809. OAS (Organization of Ameircan States). "Participation of Women in Decisions Concerning Development and Integration." Washington, D.C.: OAS, 18 September 1972. OAS Document # OEA/Ser/6/11/2/16; CIM/INF.7.

2810. Orrego de Figueroa, Teresa. "A Critical Analysis of Latin American Programs to Integrate Women in Development." In Irene

Tinker and Michele Bo Bransen, eds., Women and World Development. Washington, D.C.: Overseas Development Council, 1976: 45-53.

2811. Ortiz de Macaya, Margarita. "'Mujer, desarrollo social y educacional en América Latina.' Excerpts from a speech made at the International Seminar on la Participación de la mujer en el Desarrollo Social y Educacional, Haifa, 1968." Boletín Documental sobre Las Mujeres, v. 0 (1), 1970: 59-62.

2812. "El papel de la mujer en el progreso rural." Informe del Seminario Latinoamericano sobre el Papel de la Mujer en el Progreso Rural, Río de Janeiro, 13-22 August 1956.

2813. UNICEF (United Nations' Children's Fund.) "Latin American Conference on Children and Youth in National Development, Santiago, Chile, 1965. Report. New York: UNICEF, 1966.

2814. _____. "Servicios de apoyo: Mecanismos para la incorporación de la mujer al desarrollo." Santiago, Chile: UNICEF, 1975.

2815. United Nations. Secretariat. "The Participation of Women in the Development of Latin America." Buenos Aires: March 1976. U.N. Document # ESA/SDHA/AC.10/4/Rev.1.

2816. Wolfe, Marshall. "Participation of Women in Development in Latin America." Mimeo. Caracas: Economic Commission for Latin America, April 1975.

Mexico and Central America

2817. Abrams, Ira R. "Cash Crop Farming and Social and Economic Change in a Yucatec Maya Community in Northern British Honduras." Ph.D. dissertation, Harvard University, 1974.

2818. Benito, Carlos A. "Peasants' Response to Modernization Projects in Minifundia Economies." American Journal of Agricultural Economics, v. 58 (2), May 1976: 143-151.

2819. Burgin, Carolyn, et al. Project Report: Azuero Women's Program. Panama City: Peace Corps, 1967.

2820. Chiñas, Beverly L. "Las mujeres zapotecas: Su papel potencial en el desarrollo económico." Paper presented at the annual meeting of the American Anthropological Association, Mexico City, 1974.

2821. Chinchilla, Norma Jean. "Industrialization, Monopology

Capitalism and Women's Work in the U.S. and Guatemala." Paper presented at the Wellesley Conference on Women and Development, June 1976. Available from Wellesley Center for Research on Women, 828 Washington St., Wellesley, Massachusetts 02181.

2822. Coretiño Ruiz, Oralia. "Humanización de la reforma agraria." Thesis, Universidad Nacional Autónoma de México, 1963.

2823. Cruz, Paula, and Mayra Rappacioli. "Report on the Role of Women in the Economic Development of Nicaragua." Washington, D.C.: Agency for International Development, 1975.

2824. Gamio de Alba, Margarita. "The Indian Woman in Latin America." In Women's Role in the Development of Tropical and Sub-Tropical Countries. Brussels: International Institute of Differing Civilizations, 1959.

2825. Heckadon Moreno, Stanley. "Los asentamientos campesinos: Una experiencia panameña en reforma agraria." Guatemala City: UNICEF, 1973.

2826. Partido Nacional Revolucionario (Mexico), Secretaría de Acción Agraria. La redención de la mujer por el ejido. Mexico City: Ed. Especiales para los campesinos, 1934.

2827. Sociedad Panameña de Planificación. "Año Internacional de la mujer, igualdad, desarrollo y paz." Planificación y Cambio Social, v. 2, 1975.

Caribbean

2828. Torriente, Loló de la. "La mujer como factor de progreso en la vida cubana." In Libro de Cuba. Havana: Publicaciones Unidas, 1954.

2829. Velis, Esther. "Situación de la mujer en Cuba en lo referente a su integración al desarrollo con especial referencia a los problemas de población." Mimeo. Caracas: 1975.

2830. "Woman's Role in Country's Economic Development." Translations on Latin America, no. 100, 1968: 101-105.

Andean Region

2831. Carter, William E. "Aymara Communities and the Bolivian Agrarian Reform." Social Science Series no. 24, University of Florida, 1964.

2832. Chesterfield, Ray A., and Kenneth R. Ruddle. "Non Deliberate Education: Venezuelan Campesino Perceptives of Extension Agents and Their Message." In Thomas La Belle, ed., Educational

Alternatives in Latin America: Social Change and Social Stratification. Los Angeles: Latin American Center, University of California at Los Angeles, 1975: 149-168.

2833. Lewis, Mary Gunnell. "Home Demonstrators in Venezuela." Journal of Home Economics, v. 38 (1), January 1946: 1-6.

2834. Ortíz de Castro, Blanca. "Consideraciones sobre la mujer indígena colombiana." América Indígena, v. 32 (4), 1972: 1233-1236.

2835. Mickelwait, Donald R., et al. Women in Rural Development: A Survey of the Roles of Women in Ghana, Lesotho, Kenya, Nigeria, Bolivia, Paraguay and Peru. Boulder: Westview Press, 1976.

2836. Ruddle, Kenneth, and Ray Chesterfield. "The Venezuelan 'Demostradora del hogar': An Example of Women in Nonformal Rural Education." Community Development Journal, v. 9 (2), April 1974: 140+.

2837. Turner, June. "Memo: Suggestions to Enhance the Role and Status of the Rural Women in Bolivia." Washington, D.C.: Agency for International Development, December 1974.

2838. Vásquez Fuller, Gladys. "La mujer indígena frente a los problemas de desarrollo." Paper presented at the V Congreso Indigenista Interamericano, Quito, 1965.

Chile and the Platine

2839. Amadeo, Tomás. "La acción de la mujer en el mejoramiento agrario argentino." Servicio Social, January-February 1942: 8-20.

2840. Rigalt, Francisco. "La mujer rural y el Instituto Nacional de Tecnología Agropecuaria." Revista Universitaria Nacional de Córdoba, v. 10 (1/2), March-June 1969: 217-220.

2841. Stabile, Blanca. La mujer en el desarrollo Nacional. Buenos Aires: Ediciones Arayú, 1961.

Brazil

2842. Barroso, Carmen Lucia de Melo. "A participação da mulher no desenvolvimento cientifico brasileiro." Ciencia e Cultura, v. 27 (6), 1975: 613-620.

2843. De Elia, Carlos Miguel. "Proceso industrial y familia." In

Estudios de Sociología, , V. Buenos Aires: Ed. Bibliográfica Omeba, n.d.: 249-258.

2844. Muraro, Rose Marie. A mulher na construção do mundo futuro. Petropolis: Vozes, 1967.

APPENDICES

APPENDIX A: SUPPLEMENTARY RESEARCH ON WOMEN AND THE DEVELOPMENT PROCESS

1. GENERAL REFERENCES
2. SPECIAL JOURNAL ISSUES RELATED TO THE TOPIC OF WOMEN IN THE DEVELOPMENT PROCESS.

APPENDIX B: SOURCES CONSULTED

1. SOURCES CONSULTED FOR AFRICAN CITATIONS
   a. Bibliographies
   b. Serial Abstracts, Guides, and Indexes
   c. Library Card Catalogs and Acquisition Lists
2. SOURCES CONSULTED FOR LATIN AMERICAN CITATIONS
   a. Bibliographies
   b. Serial Abstracts, Guides, and Indexes
   c. Library Card Catalogs and Acquisition Lists

APPENDIX C: NAME AND PLACE OF PUBLICATION OF SELECTED REFERENCES INCLUDED IN AFRICAN AND LATIN AMERICAN CITATIONS

1. PUBLICATIONS INCLUDED IN AFRICAN CITATIONS
2. PUBLICATIONS INCLUDED IN LATIN AMERICAN CITATIONS

Appendix A

SUPPLEMENTARY RESEARCH ON WOMEN

AND THE DEVELOPMENT PROCESS

The following references are included to provide background information on roles and statuses that are not limited to one specific area. These include classic works, recent publications resulting from International Women's Year conferences and research projects, and the extensive papers and reports of the Agency for International Development and the United Nations. These sources supplement and expand on area-specific sources and may be used to familiarize the user with international trends in the literature on women and the development process.

1. GENERAL REFERENCES

A-1. Agency for International Development, United States Department of State. "Conference on Women in Development." Report. Washington, D.C.: Agency for International Development, October 1975.

A-2. _____. "A Plan for Action for AID Implementation of the Percy Amendment, Section 113 of the Foreign Assistance Act, F. Y. 1974." Washington, D.C.: Agency for International Development, 1974.

A-3. _____. "Participation of Women in Development: A Background Paper on the New Foreign Assistance Act Provision (Percy Amendment)." Washington, D.C.: Agency for International Development, February 1974.

A-4. _____. "Progress Report to Members of the Senior Operations Group." Washington, D.C.: Agency for International Development, June 1976.

A-5. _____. "Women in Development." Pamphlet. Washington, D.C.: Agency for International Development, September 1975.

A-6. _____. "Women's Influence on Development Told." Front Lines, v. 14 (1), 13 November 1975.

A-7. _____. "Workshop on Women in Development." Report. Washington, D.C.: Agency for International Development, May 1975.

A-8. "The Apprenticeship of Women and Girls." International Labour Review, v. 66 (1), July 1952.

A-9. Boserup, Ester. Woman's Role in Economic Development. New York: St. Martin's Press, 1970.

A-10. Boserup, Ester, and Christina Liljencrantz. "Integration of Women in Development: Why, When, How." Pamphlet. New York: United Nations Development Programme, May 1975.

A-11. Boulding, Elise, et al. Handbook of International Data on Women. Boulder: Sage Publications, 1976.

A-12. Bruce, Margaret K. "An Account of United Nations Action to Advance the Status of Women." Annals of the American Academy of Political and Social Science, no. 375, January 1968: 163-175.

A-13. Chabaud, Jacqueline. The Education and Advancement of Women. Paris: UNESCO, 1970. UNESCO Document #LC/1411/C463/x.

A-14. Chaton, Jeanne Henriette. "The UNESCO Long-Range Program for the Advancement of Women." Annals of the American Academy of Political and Social Science, no. 375, January 1968: 145-153.

A-15. Cordell, Magda, and John McHale with Guy Streatfield. Women in World Terms, Facts and Trends. Binghamton: State University of New York, Center for Integrative Studies, 1975.

A-16. De Vries, Margaret G. "Women, Jobs and Development." Finance and Development, v. 4, December 1971: 2-9.

A-17. Germain, Adrienne. "Some Aspects of the Roles of Women in Population and Development." New York: United Nations, 1974. U.N. Document #ESA/SDHA/AC.5/3/Add.1.

A-18. Glancy, Dorothy. "An Around the World View of Women's Roles in Public Affairs." Wellesley, Massachusetts: Wellesley College, Center for Research on Women, 1971.

A-19. Haber, S. "Female Labor Force Participation and Economic Development." Rand Corporation Paper, no. P-1504. Santa Monica, California: Rand Corporation, 1958.

A-20. Huntington, Suellen. "Issues in Woman's Role in Economic Development: Critique and Alternatives." Journal of Marriage and the Family, v. 37, November 1975: 1001-1012.

A-21. International Bank for Reconstruction and Development. "Integrating Women into Development." New York: 1975. Booklet released through the World Bank.

A-22. International Council of Women. "Community Development. Part I: The Participation of Women in Community Development. Part II: The Participation of National Councils of Women in Projects of Development." Paris: International Council of Women, 1967-1970.

A-23. "International Forum on the Role of Women in Population and Development." Available from the Centre for Social Development and Humanitarian Affairs, United Nations, New York 10017. U.N. Document #ST/ESA/SER.B/4, n.d.

A-24. International Labour Organization. "Discrimination in Employment or Occupation on the Basis of Marital Status, Parts I and II." International Labour Review, v. 85, March/April 1962: 262-282; 368-389.

A-25. "Economic Rights and Opportunities for Women. Equal Pay for Equal Work." Progress Report. Geneva: International Labour Organization, 16 November 1966. ILO Document #E/CN.6/468.

A-26. _____. "Equality of Opportunity and Treatment of Women Workers. Report VIII." Geneva: International Labour Organization, 1975.

A-27. _____. "Equal Pay for Work of Equal Value." Report. Geneva: International Labour Organization, 3 December 1968. ILO Document #E/CN.6/519.

A-28. _____. "The Law and Women's Work; a Contribution to the Study of the Status of Women." Geneva: International Labour Organization, 1939.

A-29. _____. "Repercussions of Scientific and Technological Progress on the Conditions of Work and Employment of Women." Report. Geneva: International Labour Organization, 20 January 1970. ILO Document #E/CN.6/539.Add.1, 25 February 1970.

A-30. _____. "Sex Bias in Training." *International Labour Information*, June 1975: 1-2.

A-31. _____. "Women in the Labor Force." *International Labour Review*, v. 77, March 1958: 254-272.

A-32. _____. "Women in the Work Force; The General Picture." *Impact of Science on Society*, v. 25 (2), 1975: 137-145.

A-33. _____. "Women's Wages." *International Labour Review*, v. 81, February 1960: 95-109.

A-34. _____. "Women's Work Under Labor Law: A Survey of Protective Legislation." Geneva: International Labour Organization, 1932.

A-35. _____. *Women Workers in a Changing World*. 2 vols. Geneva: International Labour Organization, 1963-1964.

A-36. _____. "Yearbook of Labor Statistics 1967." Also Supplements, 1969, 1970.

A-37. Johnson, Frances. "Integrating Women into Economic Development." Washington, D.C.: Agency for International Development, 1 March 1974.

A-38. Long, Nira. "Progress Report on Women in Development." Washington, D.C.: Agency for International Development, 1975.

A-39. Mehmet, T. "UNICEF and the Advancement of Women: A Proposal." Mimeo. New York: UNICEF, October 1974. UNICEF Document #E/ICEF/Misc. 232.

A-40. Nash, June C. "Certain Aspects of the Integration of Women in the Development Process: A Point of View." New York: United Nations, 1975. U.N. Document #E/Conf. 66/BP/5.

A-41. O'Barr, Jean F. "The Changing Roles of Women in Developing Societies." Mimeo. Durham, N.C.: Duke University, Comparative Area Studies Program, 1975.

A-42. Planning Assistance, Inc. "Third World Craftswomen and Development." Paper Presented at the International Women's Year Conference, Mexico City, 1975.

A-43. Reid, Elizabeth. "Women at a Standstill. The Need for Radical Change." *International Labour Review*, v. 111 (6), June 1975: 458-468.

A-44. Sanday, Peggy R. "Toward a Theory of the Status of Women." Philadelphia: University of Pennsylvania, Department of Anthropology, n.d.

A-45. Sartin, Pierrette. La promoción de la mujer. Barcelona, Spain: Ed. Labor S.A., 1968.

A-46. Sergio, Lisa. "Women, An Untapped Source of Power in the Fight Against Hunger." Mimeo. Washington, D.C.: 1975.

A-47. Silverstone, Jonathon. "Participation of Women in Development." Washington, D.C.: Agency for International Development, 11 February 1974.

A-48. Sipila, Helvi L. "Women and the United Nations--A Special Message for International Women's Year." Mimeo. New York: United Nations, 1974. Available from the Centre for Social Development and Humanitarian Affairs, United Nations, New York 10017.

A-49. Skonsberg, Else. "The Effect of Aid on Women in Developing Countries." Ceres, 1975.

A-50. Swedish International Development Authority. Women in Developing Countries — Case Studies of Six Countries. Stockholm: Swedish International Development Authority, 1974.

A-51. Tinker, Irene. "The Adverse Impact of Development on Women." In Irene Tinker and Michele Bo Bramsen, eds., Women and World Development. Washington, D.C.: Overseas Development Council, 1976: 22-34.

A-52. _____. "The Widening Gap Between Men and Women at Almost Every Level of Society." International Development Review, v. 16 (4), 1974: 40-42.

A-53. _____, and Michele Bo Bramsen, eds. Women and World Development. Washington, D.C.: Overseas Development Council, 1976.

A-54. United Nations. "Current Trends and Changes in the Status and Roles of Women and Men, and Major Obstacles to be Overcome in the Achievement of Equal Rights, Opportunities and Responsibilities." Paper presented at the International Women's Year Conference, Mexico City, 1975. U.N. Document #E/Conf.66/3 Add. 1,2,3/1975.

A-55. _____. Equal Pay for Equal Work. New York: United Nations, 1960.

A-56. _____. "The Integration of Women in the Development Process as Equal Partners with Men." Paper presented at the International Women's Year Conference, Mexico City, 1975. U.N. Document #E/Conf. 66/4.

A-57. _____. "International Forum on the Role of Women in Population and Development." Report. New York: United Nations, 1974. U.N. Document #ST/ESA/SER.B/4.

A-58. _____. "Participation of Women in Community Development." Report. New York: United Nations, 1972. U.N. Document #E/CN.6/514/Rev.1.

A-59. _____. "Report of the Interregional Meeting of Experts on the Integration of Women in Development." Report. New York: United Nations, June 1972. U.N. Document #ST/SOA/120.

A-60. _____. "Seminar for Accelerating the Participation of Women in Development and Eliminating Sex Discrimination, Ottawa, Canada, September 1974." Report. New York: United Nations, 1975. U.N. Document #ST/ESA/SER.B/7.

A-61. _____. "Seminar on the Effects of Scientific and Technological Developments on the Status of Women, Iasi, Romania, August 1969." Report. New York: United Nations, U.N. Document #ST/TAO/HR/37.

A-62. _____. "Seminar on the Participation of Women in Public Life." New York: United Nations, circa 1959. U.N. Document #ST/TAO/HR/5.

A-63. _____. "Seminar on the Participation of Women in Public Life, Mongolia, August 1965." Report. New York: United Nations, January 1966. U.N. Document #ST/TAO/HR/24.

A-64. _____. "Seminar on the Status of Women in Family Law, Bogotá, December 1963." Report. New York: United Nations, May 1964. U.N. Document #ST/TAO/HR/18.

A-65. _____. "Status of Women and Family Planning." New York: United Nations, 1975. Available from UNIPUB, Box 433, Murray Hill Station, New York 10016.

A-66. _____. "The United Nations and the Status of Women." New York: United Nations, 1964.

A-67. _____. "The United Nations and the Status of Women, Parts I-II." United Nations Review, v. 8 (4), March 1961: 22-27; v. 8 (5), April 1961: 26-32.

A-68. _____. Department of Economic and Social Affairs. "Status of Women and Family Planning: Report of the Special Rapporteur." New York: United Nations, 1975. U.N. Document #E/CN.6/575/Rev.1.

A-69. _____. _____. "Unified Long-Term Program for the Advancement of Women and U.N. Assistance in this Field; Participation of Women in National Economic Social Development." Report of the Secretary General. New York: United Nations, 1969.

A-70. _____. Economic and Social Council. Commission on the Status of Women. "Reports, Sessions 18 Through 25." New York: United Nations, March 1965 through February 1974.

A-71. _____. _____. _____. "Participation of Women in Community Development." New York: United Nations, 1972. U.N. Document #E/CN.6/514/Rev.1.

A-72. _____. _____. _____. "Participation of Women in the Economic and Social Development of their Countries." New York: United Nations, 1970. U.N. Document #E/CN.6/513/Rev.1.

A-73. _____. _____. _____. "Programmes of Concerted International Action to Promote the Advancement of Women and to Increase Their Contribution to the Development of their Countries." New York: United Nations 31 January 1972. U.N. Document #E/CN.6/553/Add.1.

A-74. _____. _____. _____. "Working Group on the Status of Women in Private Law." Report. New York: United Nations, 15 February 1968. UN Document # E/CN.6/L.544.

A-75. _____. Food and Agriculture Organization. "The Contribution of Food Aid to the Improvement of Women's Status." Rome: Food and Agricultural Organization, April 1975. FAO Document #E/Conf.66/BP/12.

A-76. _____. "The Missing Half: Woman 1975." Rome: Food and Agriculture Organization, 1975. Available from UNIPUB, Box 433, Murray Hill Station, New York 10016.

A-77. UNESCO (U.N. Educational, Scientific and Cultural Organization). "Access of Girls to Secondary Education." Report. New York: UNESCO, January 1965. UNESCO Document #E/CN.6/433.

A-78. _____. "Access of Girls and Women to Technical and Vocational Education." Report. New York: UNESCO, January 1968. UNESCO Document #E/CN/.6/498.

A-79. _____. "Access of Women to Education. UNESCO activities in 1965-1966 of Special Interest to Women and Main Activities Proposed for 1967-1968." Report. New York: UNESCO, January 1967. UNESCO Document #E/CN.6/475.

A-80. _____. "The Advancement of Women Through Access to Education." New York: Special Unit, UNESCO, no. 3, 1971.

A-81. _____. "Education and Advancement of Women." New York: UNESCO, 1970. Reprint 1974. Available from UNIPUB, Box 433, Murray Hill Station, New York 10016.

A-82. _____. "Political Role of Women." Paris: UNESCO, 1955.

A-83. _____. "Resources Available to Member States for the Advancement of Women." New York: UNESCO, 1966.

A-84. _____. "Study on Equal Access of Girls and Women to Literacy." Report. New York: UNESCO, February 1975. UNESCO Document #E/CN.6/538; Add. 1, April 1970.

A-85. _____. "U.N. Assistance for the Advancement of Women." New York: UNESCO, 1967.

A-86. _____. "Women and Education in the World Today." Paris: UNESCO, June 1970. UNESCO Document #ED/WS/183.

A-87. UNICEF (United Nations' Children's Fund). Children and Adolescents in the Second Development Decade: Priorities for Action and Planning, New York: UNICEF, April 1973. Chapter 5. UNICEF Document #E/ICEF/627.

A-88. _____. "Helping Women in the Developing Countries." UNICEF News, no. 65, 1975.

A-89. _____. "Inequality of the Sexes in Education is Worldwide--Almost." Mimeo. New York: UNICEF, 1975.

A-90. _____. "Report of the UNICEF Executive Board." New York: UNICEF, April 1973: 23. UNICEF Document #E/ICEF/629.

A-91. _____. "U.N. Assistance for the Advancement of Women." Mimeo. New York: UNICEF, February 1965. UNICEF Document #UNICEF/Misc.100.

A-92. _____. "UNICEF: Consideration of Other Bodies of Interest to UNICEF (on Status of Women.)" New York: UNICEF, 1970. UNICEF Document #E/ICEF/CRP/70/1/Add.3.

A-93. _____. UNICEF Guide List--ISIS: Women and Development. New York: UNICEF, September 1975. UNICEF Document #OSU 6410.

A-94. _____. "Women and Development: the UNICEF Perspective." UNICEF Conference Background Paper, May 1975. U.N. Document #E/Conf.66/BP/15.

A-95. United Nations Secretariat. "Influence of Mass Communication Media on the Formation of a New Attitude towards the Role of Women in Present-Day Society." Report. New York: United Nations, 10 June 1974. U.N. Document #E/CN.6/581.

A-96. United Nations Secretary-General. "The Effect of Resolutions and Recommendations of the Commission (on the Status of Women) on National Legislation." Report. New York: United Nations, 15 January 1966. U.N. Document #E/CN.6/437; Add. 1, 24 January 1966.

A-97. Van Haeften, Roberta K., and Douglas D. Caton. " Strategy for Integrating LDC Rural Women into Their National Economies." Mimeo. Washington: Agency for International Development, May 1974.

A-98. Viscus, Margo. Women and the United Nations. Paris: Ortrud, 1973.

A-99. Ward, Barbara E. "Women and Technology in Developing Countries." Impact of Science on Society, v. 20 (1), 1970: 93-101.

A-100. World Bank. "Integrating Women into Development." Booklet. August 1975.

A-101. Youssef, Nadia H. "Women in Development: Urban Life and Labor." In Irene Tinker and Michele Bo Bramsen, eds., Women and World Development. Washington, D.C.: Overseas Development Council, 1976: 70-77.

Rural Only

A-102. Agricultural Development Council. "Seminar Report on the Role of Rural Women in Development." New York: Agricultural Development Council, October 1975.

A-103. Boserup, Ester. "Women and Their Role in Peasant Society." Mimeo. London: Centre of International and Area Studies, University of London, 1974.

A-104. Boulding, Elise. "Women, Bread and Babies: Directing Aid for 5th World Farmers." Paper. Boulder, Colorado: Institute of Behavioral Sciences, University of Colorado, 1975.

A-105. Development Alternatives, Inc. "A Seven Country Survey on the Roles of Women in Rural Development." Report to the Agency for International Development, December 1974.

A-106. Dhamija, Jasleen. "Handicrafts: A Source of Employment for Women in Developing Rural Economies." International Labour Review, v. 112 (6), December 1975: 459-465.

A-107. Dixon, Ruth B. "The Roles of Rural Women: Female Seclusion, Economic Production and Reproductive Choice." Mimeo. Washington, D.C.: Resources for the Future, 1975.

A-108. Dumont, René. "Development and Mounting Famine: A Role for Women." International Labour Review, v. 111 (6), June 1975: 451-457.

A-109. Jedlicka, Allen. "Diffusion of Technical Innovation: A Case for the Non-Sexist Approach Among Rural Villages." Mimeo. Paper prepared for the Seminar on Women in Development. Sponsored by the American Association for the Advancement of Science, U.N. Development Programme, and the U.N. Institute for Training and Research, Mexico City, 1975.

A-110. Omer, S. "Le rôle des femmes dans le développement communautaire. Sa signification--les difficultés qui s'y opposent." Bulletin du Développement Communautaire, v. 2 (2), 1961: 38-44.

A-111. Palmer, Ingrid. "The Basic Needs Approach to the Integration of Rural Women in Development: Conditions for Success." Paper presented at the Wellesley Conference on Women and Development, June 1976. Available from Wellesley Center for Research on Women, 828 Washington St., Wellesley, Massachusetts 02181.

A-112. Presvelou, C. "Participation of Women in Rural Development Programmes." Rome: Food and Agriculture Organization, 1973. FAO Document #WS/E 5494.

A-113. Smithhills, Jancis. "Agricultural Extension Work Among Rural Women." University of Reading, Agricultural Extension and Rural Development Center, 1972.

A-114. Tryfan, Barbara. "The Role of Rural Women in the Family." Paper presented at the II World Congress of Rural Sociology, 1972.

A-115. UNICEF (United Nations' Children's Fund). "Building New Educational Strategies to Serve Rural Children and Youth." Mimeo. New York: UNICEF March 1974. Chapter 4. UNICEF Document #E/ICEF/C.1304.

A-116. United Nations Economic and Social Council. "Integration of Women in Rural Development." Report of the Secretary General. New York: United Nations, 4 November 1972. U.N. Document #E/CN.5/481.

A-117. UNESCO (U.N. Educational, Scientific and Cultural Organization). "Access of Girls and Women to Education in Rural Areas; A Comparative Study." Paris: UNESCO, 1964. UNESCO Document #ESD/51.

A-118. _____. "Study on the Equality of Access of Girls and Women to Education in the Context of Rural Development." Paris: UNESCO, 1973. UNESCO Document #E/CN/6/566/Rev. 1.

A-119. United Nations. Food and Agricultural Organization. "Programme of Concerted International Action to Promote the Advancement of Women and their Integration in Development. Status of Rural Women, Especially Agricultural Workers." Report. New York: United Nations, 27 December 1973.

A-120. _____. _____. "The Role of Women in Rural Development." Rome: Food and Agricultural Organization, 24 March 1975. FAO Document #E/Conf. 66/BP/11.

A-121. _____. _____. Home Economic Service. "The Role of Women in Food and Agricultural Development." Rome: Food and Agricultural Organization, 1971.

A-122. _____. _____. "Workshops for Trainers in Home Economics and Other Family Oriented Fields, 1973." Available from Home Economics and Social Programmes Service, U.N./FAO, Via delle Terme di Caracalla, 00100, Rome, Italy.

A-123. "Women, Agents of Change." International Women's Year, v. 2 (5), June-July, 1975: 1-9.

2. SPECIAL JOURNAL ISSUES RELATED TO THE TOPIC OF WOMEN IN THE DEVELOPMENT PROCESS

A-124. Actuel Développement (Paris). no. 12, March-April 1976. Partial issue on women.

A-125. American Ethnologist. Special Issue: Sex Roles in Cross-Cultural Perspectives. v. 2 (4), 1975.

A-126. America Indígena. v. 35 (3), July-September 1975. Entire issue on women.

A-127. Atlas World Press Review. Women Today, v. 22 (3), 1975.

A-128. The Black Scholar. v. 4 (6-7), March-April 1973; v. 5 (9), June 1974; v. 6 (6), March 1975.

A-129. Boletín Documental sobre las Mujeres, published by CIDHAL (Comunidad Intercambio y Desarrollo Humano en America Latina), Cuernavaca, Mexico, v. 1+, 1970+.

A-130. Canadian Newsletter of Research on Women. Special Publication no. 3, August 1976. Eichler, Margrit; John Maricki; and Jennifer Newton, "Women: A Bibliography of Special Periodical Issues (1960-1975)."

A-131. The Center Magazine (Center for the Study of Democratic Institutions). v. 7 (3), 1974. Issue entitled "Women Around the World." Available from Box 4068, Santa Barbara, California 93103.

A-132. Ceres: FAO Review on Development, v. 8 (2), March-April 1975. Issue entitled "Women: A Long-Silent Majority."

A-133. Challenge (U.S. Department of Housing and Urban Development). v. 6 (9), September 1975. Special International Women's Year issue.

A-134. Ciencia Interamericana. v. 16 (3-4). Available from Department of Scientific Affairs, OAS, 1725 Eye St., N.W., Washington, D.C. 20006.

A-135. Convergence. v. 8 (1), 1975. Special issue on International Women's Year.

A-136. Cooperation Canada (Canadian International Development Agency). January-February 1975. Special issue on International Women's Year.

A-137. Cuba Review. v. 4 (2), September 1974. Issue on "Women in Transition." Available from Cuba Review, Box 206, Cathedral Station, New York, New York 10025.

A-138. Diálogo Social (Panama). no. 65, 1975. Issue entitled "La Mujer: Año Cero."

A-139. Estudio Andinos. v. 5 (1), 1976. Issue entitled "La mujer en los Andes."

A-140. Futures. v. 7 (5), October 1975. Issue entitled "Women and the future."

A-141. Fichas de ISAL (Montevideo). v. 4 (46), 1973. Special issue entitled "La liberación de la mujer en América Latina."

A-142. Hechos Mundiales (Santiago). v. 5 (58), 1972. Special issue entitled "Liberación Femenina."

A-143. Impact of Science on Society (UNESCO). v. 20 (1), 1970. Issue on "Women in the Age of Science and Technology."

A-144. _____. v. 25 (2), April-June 1975. Issue on "Women in Science: A Man's World."

A-145. Journal of Interamerican Studies and World Affairs. v. 17 (4), Nov. 1975. Special issue on Women.

A-146. Journal of Marriage and the Family. v. 6 (2), 1972. Special cross-cultural issue on women.

A-147. Journal of Social Issues. v. 28 (2), 1972. Special issue entitled "New Perspectives on Women."

A-148. Latin American Perspectives. v. 4 (1-2), Winter-Spring 1977. Issue entitled "Women and the Class Struggle."

A-149. NACLA Latin American and Empire Report. v. 6 (10), 1972. Issue entitled "Women in Struggle."

A-150. _____. v. 9 (6), September 1975. Special issue on "Women's Labor."

A-151. Newsletter on the Status of Women. United Nations, Department of Economic and Social Affairs. Semi-annual (no. 1, September 1950).

A-152. OECD Observer. no. 28, November-December 1975. Issue entitled "Women and Development."

A-153. Pan American Union Bulletin. Various issues contain historical information on suffrage, first women in law and medicine, first Brazilian woman mayor, etc.

A-154. Review of Radical Political Economics. v. 4 (3), July 1972. Special issue entitled "The Political Economics of Women."

A-155. Review of Radical Political Economists (URPE). Forthcoming: Special Issue on women and the economy.

A-156. Revista de Correos y Telecomunicaciones (Buenos Aires). v. 14 (159-160), November-December 1950: 1-96. "Contenido de este número dedicado a la mujer que trabaja."

A-157. Revista de la Universidad Nacional de Córdoba (Córdoba, Argentina). v. 10 (1/2), March-June 1969. Entire issue devoted to women in Latin America.

A-158. Revista Interamericana (Interamerican Review). v. 4 (2), 1974. Special issue entitled "The Latin American Woman: Image and Reality."

A-159. Rural Development Network Bulletin. no. 6, Part 1, July 1976. Special issue on "Women in Rural Development." Available from Overseas Liaison Committee, American Council on Education, 11 Dupont Circle, Washington, D.C. 20036.

A-160. School of Advanced International Studies Review. v. 19 (3), 1975: 1-10. "International Women's Year: A Special Issue."

A-161. Signs: Journal of Women in Culture and Society. Forthcoming, Fall 1977, issue on women and development.

A-162. The UNESCO Courier. (3), March 1975, Issue on International Women's Year.

A-163. _____. August-September 1975. Issue on "Turning Point of Women."

A-164. UNESCO Features. no. 676, 1975; no. 677, 1975; no. 678, 1975. Special issues on International Women's Year.

A-165. UNICEF News. 4 (4), 1974. Issue entitled "Women's Development."

A-166. Women in the World Today (series). 1963-1973. U.S. Department of Labor.

A-167. Women: A Journal of Liberation. v. 3 (4), 1974. Issue entitled "International Women."

A-168. World Health, the Magazine of the World Health Organization. January 1975. Issue on International Women's Year.

Appendix B

SOURCES CONSULTED

1. SOURCES CONSULTED FOR AFRICAN CITATIONS

a. Bibliographies

B-1. African-American Institute. Women's Africa Committee Annual Report. New York: African-American Institute, 1964-1965.

B-2. AID (Agency for International Development). "Women in National Development in Ghana. Study and Annotated Bibliography." Development Assistance Program FY1976-FY1980 Ghana, v. 4, Annex F. Washington, D.C.: April 1975.

B-3. Aguolu, Christian Chukwunedu. Ghana in the Humanities and Social Sciences, 1900-1971. Metuchen, New Jersey: The Scarecrow Press, 1973.

B-4. _____. Nigeria: A Comprehensive Bibliography in the Humanities and Social Sciences, 1900-1971. Boston: G. K. Hall and Company, 1973.

B-5. Blaudin de Thé, Commandant. Essai de Bibliographie du Sahara Français. Paris: Arts et Métiers Graphiques, 1960.

B-6. Boserup, Ester. Woman's Role in Economic Development. London: George Allen and Unwin, Ltd., 1970.

B-7. Brasseur, Paule. Bibliographique Générale du Mali. Dakar: Institut Français d'Afrique Noire, 1964.

B-8. Decalo, Samuel. South-West Africa 1960-1968: An Introductory Bibliography. Occasional Papers in Political Science N-5. Kingston: University of Rhode Island, 1969.

B-9. _____. Tanzania: An Introductory Bibliography. Occasional Papers in Political Science N-4. Kingston: University of Rhode Island, 1968.

B-10. DeLancey, Mark W., and Virginia H. DeLancey. A Bibliography of Cameroon. New York: Africana Publishing Company, 1975.

B-11. Duigan, Peter, ed. United States and Canadian Publications on Africa in 1961. Hoover Bibliographical Series: XIV. Stanford: Hoover Institution on War, Revolution and Peace, 1963.

B-12. _____, ed. United States and Canadian Doctoral Dissertations on Africa. Ann Arbor: Xerox University Microfilms, 1973.

B-13. _____, ed., and Liselotte Hofmann, comp. United States and Canadian Publications in Africa in 1963. Hoover Institution Bibliographical Series: XX. Stanford: Hoover Institution on War, Revolution and Peace, 1965.

B-14. _____, ed., and Hilary Sims, comp. United States and Canadian Publications on Africa in 1962. Hoover Institution Bibliographical Series XV. Stanford: Hoover Institution on War, Revolution and Peace, 1964.

B-15. Glazier, Kenneth M. Africa South of the Sahara. A Select and Annotated Bibliography, 1958-1963. Stanford: Hoover Institution Bibliographical Series: XVI. The Hoover Institution on War, Revolution and Peace, 1964.

B-16. _____. Africa South of the Sahara. A Select and Annotated Bibliography, 1964-1968. Hoover Institution Bibliographical Series: XLII. Stanford: Hoover Institution Press, 1969.

B-17. Harris, John. Books about Nigeria. Ibadan: Ibadan University Press, 1969.

B-18. Hill, R. L. A Bibliography of the Anglo-Egyptian Sudan. London: Oxford University Press, 1939.

B-19. Hofman, Liselotte, comp. United States and Canadian Publications on Africa in 1964. Hoover Bibliographical Series: XXV. Stanford: Hoover Institution on War, Revolution, and Peace, 1966.

B-20. _____, comp. United States and Canadian Publications and Theses on Africa in 1965. Hoover Bibliographical Series: XXXIV. Stanford: Hoover Institution on War, Revolution and Peace, 1967.

B-21. _____, comp. United States and Canadian Publications and Theses on Africa in 1966. Hoover Institution Bibliographical Series: XXXVIII. Stanford: Hoover Institution Press, 1970.

B-22. International African Institute. International African Bibliography/Bibliographic Internationale Africaine. 3 vols. London: International African Institute, 1971-1973.

B-23. _____. Select Annotated Bibliography of Tropical Africa. New York: Twentieth Century Fund, 1956.

B-24. Ita, Nduntuci O. Bibliography of Nigeria: A Survey of Anthropological and Linguistic Writings from the Earliest Times to 1966. London: Frank Cass, 1971.

B-25. Johnson, Albert Frederson. A Bibliography of Ghana, 1930-1961. Evanston: Northwestern University Press, 1964.

B-26. Kafe, Joseph Kofi. Ghana: An Annotated Bibliography of Academic Theses, 1920-1970 in the Commonwealth, The Republic of Ireland and the United States of America. Boston: G.K. Hall and Company, 1973.

B-27. Kratochvil, Laura, and Shauna Shaw. African Women: A Select Bibliography. Cambridge, England: African Studies Centre, 1974.

B-28. Land Tenure Center Library, University of Wisconsin. Rural Development in Africa: A Bibliography. (Part 1: General, Central, East). Number 16 (Supplement), March, 1973; Number 16 (Supplement 2), September, 1974.

B-29. Lele, Uma J. The Design of Rural Development: Lessons from Africa. Baltimore: John Hopkins University Press, 1975.

B-30. Nasri, Abdel Rahman El. A Bibliography of the Sudan, 1938-1958. London: Oxford University Press, 1962.

B-31. Perlman, M., and M. P. Moal. "Analytical Bibliography." In Paulme, Denise, ed., Women of Tropical Africa. Trans. by H. M. Wright. London: Routledge & Kegan Paul, 1963: 231-294.

B-32. Pitcher, G. M., comp. Bibliography of Ghana, 1957-1960. Kumasi (Ghana): Kwame Nkrumah University of Science and Technology, 1962.

B-33. Program of Eastern African Studies, Maxwell School of Citizenship and Public Affairs. A Bibliography on Anthropology and Sociology in Tanzania and East Africa. Compiled by Lucas Kuria and John B. Webster. Occasional Bibliography, no. 4. Syracuse: Syracuse University, 1966.

B-34. _____. A Bibliography on Anthropology and Sociology in Uganda. Compiled by Robert Peckham, Isis Ragheb, Aidan Southall, and John Webster. Occasional Bibliography no. 3, Syracuse: Syracuse University, n.d.

B-35. _____. A Bibliography on Bechuanaland. Compiled by Paulus Mohome and John B. Webster. Occasional Bibliography, no. 5, Syracuse: Syracuse University, 1966.

B-36. _____. A Bibliography on Kenya. Compiled by John B. Webster and others. Eastern African Bibliographical Series, no. 2, Kenya. Syracuse: Syracuse University, 1967.

B-37. _____. A Bibliography on Lesotho. Compiled by John B. Webster and Paulus Mohome. Occasional Bibliography, no. 9. Syracuse: Syracuse University, 1968.

B-38. _____. A Bibliography of Malawi. Compiled by Edward E. Brown, Carol A. Fisher, and John B. Webster. Eastern African Bibliographical Series, no. 1, Malawi. Syracuse: Syracuse University, 1965.

B-39. _____. Education in Kenya Before Independence. An Annotated Bibliography. Compiled by L. A. Martin. Occasional Bibliography no. 15. Syracuse: Syracuse University, 1969.

B-40. _____. A Bibliography on Swaziland. Compiled by John B. Webster and Paulus Mohome. Occasional Bibliography, no. 10. Syracuse: Syracuse University, 1968.

B-41. _____. A Select Bibliography on Traditional and Modern Africa. Compiled by Peter C. W. Gutkind and John B. Webster. Occasional Bibliography, no. 8. Syracuse: Syracuse University, 1968.

B-42. _____. A Select, Preliminary Bibliography on Urbanism in Eastern Africa. Compiled by Barbara A. Skapa. Occasional Bibliography, no. 7. Syracuse: Syracuse University, 1967.

B-43. _____. A Supplement to a Bibliography on Bechuanaland. Compiled by John B. Webster, Paulus Mohome and M. Catherine Todd. Occasional Bibliography, no. 12. Syracuse: Syracuse University, 1968.

B-44. _____. A Supplement to a Bibliography on Malawi. Compiled by John B. Webster and Paulus Mohome. Occasional Bibliography, no. 13, Syracuse: Syracuse University, 1969.

B-45. Rosenberg, Marie Barovic, and Len V. Bergstrom, eds. Women and Society: A Critical Review of the Literature with a Selected Annotated Bibliography. Beverly Hills: Sage Publications, 1975.

B-46. Standing Conference on Library Materials on Africa. Theses in Africa Accepted by Universities in the United Kingdom and Ireland. Cambridge, England: Heffer and Sons, Ltd., 1964.

B-47. _____. United Kingdom Publications and Theses on Africa, 1964. Cambridge, England: Heffer and Sons, Ltd., 1966.

B-48. _____. United Kingdom Publications and Theses on Africa, 1963. Cambridge, England: Heffer and Sons, Ltd., 1966.

B-49. _____. United Kingdom Publications and Theses on Africa, 1965. Cambridge, England: Heffer and Sons, Ltd. 1967.

B-50. _____. United Kingdom Publications and Theses on Africa, 1966. Cambridge, England: Heffer and Sons, Ltd., 1969.

B-51. _____. United Kingdom Publications and Theses on Africa, 1967 and 1968. Edited by Miriam Alman. London: Frank Cass, 1973.

B-52. Solomon, Marvin D., and Warren L. d'Azevedo. A General Bibliography of the Republic of Liberia. Evanston: Northwestern University Working Papers in Social Sciences, no. 1, 1962.

B-53. South African Public Library. A Bibliography of African Bibliographies. (Revised to August 1955). Capetown: South African Public Library, 1955.

B-54. United Nations Economic Commission for Africa." Bibliographies of African Women." Paper presented at the Workshop on Urban Problems, Lagos, September 1963. U.N. Document #E/CN.14/URB/2.

B-55. _____. "Bibliography on Women. Annex K of Report to the Imperial Ethiopian Government of the Exploratory Employment Policy Mission." Mimeo. Geneva: 1973.

B-56. Westfall, Gloria D. "Nigerian Women: A Bibliographical Essay." Africana Journal, v. 5 (2), 1974: 99-138.

b. Serial Abstracts, Guides, and Bibliographies

B-57. African Bibliographic Center. Special Bibliographic Series. v. 1 (1) - v. 6 (3), 1968, esp. v. 6 (2), 1968, entitled "Contemporary African Women: An Introduction, Bibliographical Overview and Guide to Women's Organizations, 1960-1967." New York: Negro Universities Press.

B-58. _____. "Women in Africa." Current Reading List Series, v. 3 (2), 1965.

B-59. African Studies Association. CAMP Catalog. Cooperative African Microfilm Project and Research Liaison Committee. Waltham: African Studies Association, 1972.

B-60. American Journal of Sociology. Cumulative Index v. 1-70 (1895-1965), 1966; Supplementary Index to the Cumulative Index, v. 71-75 (1965-1970), 1971. Chicago: University of Chicago Press.

B-61. Center for Research Libraries. CAMP Catalog, Supplement 1973. Chicago: Center for Research Libraries, 1973.

B-62. _____. CAMP Catalog. Supplement 1974. Chicago: Center for Research Libraries, 1974.

B-63. A Current Bibliography on African Affairs. Series 1, v. 1-3; Series 1, v. 4-6. Westport: Greenwood Periodicals, Inc., 1962, 1963, 1964; 1965, 1966, 1967.

B-64. Dissertation Abstracts International (formerly Dissertation Abstracts), v. 12 (1952) - v. 36 (1975).

B-65. International African Institute. African Abstracts. London: Oxford University Press, v. 1 (1950) - v. 23 (1972).

B-66. An International Bibliography of Sociology/Bibliographic Internationale de Sociologie. Prepared by the International Sociological Association. Paris: UNESCO. v. 1, 1952; v. 9, 1959. International Bibliography of the Social Sciences/ Bibliographic Internationale des Sciences Sociales. Prepared by the International Committee for Social Science Information and Documentation. Chicago: Aldine Publishing Company. v. 10, 1960 - v. 24, 1974.

B-67. Jones, Ruth, comp. African Bibliography Series. Ethnology, Sociology, Linguistics and Related Subjects. West Africa. London: International African Institute, 1958.

B-68. _____, comp. African Bibliography Series. Ethnography, Sociology, Linguistics and Related Subjects. East Africa. London: International African Institute, 1960.

B-69. _____, comp. African Bibliography Series. Ethnography, Sociology, Linguistics and Related Subjects. Southeast Central Africa and Madagascar. London: International African Institute, 1961.

B-70. Library of Congress, General Reference and Bibliography Division, African Section. United States and Canadian Publications on Africa in 1960. Washington: Library of Congress, 1962.

B-71. _____. Africa South of the Sahara. A Selected, Annotated List of Writings. Compiled by Helen F. Conover. Washington: Library of Congress, 1963.

B-72. _____. Sub-Saharan Africa. A Guide to Serials. Washington: Library of Congress, 1970.

B-73. _____. Africa South of the Sahara. Index to Periodical Literature. Boston: G. K. Hall and Company, 1971; 1st supplement, 1973.

B-74. Matthews, Daniel G., ed. Current Themes in African Historical Studies. A Selected Bibliographical Guide to Resources for Research in African History. African Bibliographic Center, Special Bibliographic Series, v. 7 (2), 1970. Westport, Connecticut: Negro Universities Press.

B-75. Public Affairs Information Service. v. 36, 1950 - v. 62, no. 31, 29 May 1976. New York: Public Affairs Information Service.

B-76. Reader's Guide to Periodical Literature, v. 10A (1900) - N.74, 1974.

B-77. Social Sciences Index. v. 1 April 1974-March 1975; v. 2 (1-3), 1975; v. 3 (1), 1976. New York: H. W. Wilson Company. Formerly, Social Sciences and Humanities Index, v. 19 - v. 27, 1965-1974; and formerly International Index. A Guide to Periodical Literature in the Social Sciences and Humanities, v. 1, 1907-1915 - v. 18, April 1964-March 1965.

B-78. Sociological Abstracts, 1953-May 1975 (including supplements). San Diego: United States International University.

B-79. United Nations. United Nations Documents Index (UNDEX), Series A--Subject Index, v. 1 - v. 7:4 (April 1976); Documents Index, v. 1 (1950) - v. 24 (1973).

B-80. Women Studies Abstracts, v. 1 (1972) - v. 4 (1975).

c. Library Card Catalogs and Acquisition Lists

B-81. Boston University, Boston, Massachusetts.

B-82. Brandeis University, Waltham, Massachusetts.

B-83. Melville J. Herskovits Library of African Studies, Northwestern University, Evanston, Illinois.

B-84. Land Tenure Center, University of Wisconsin at Madison.

B-85. University of Michigan, Ann Arbor, including the library of The Center for Research on Economic Development and the Harlan Hatcher Graduate Library.

B-86. University of Texas at Austin.

2. SOURCES CONSULTED FOR LATIN AMERICAN CITATIONS

a. Bibliographies

B-87. Buvinic, Mayra. Women and World Development: An Annotated Bibliography. Washington, D.C.: Overseas Development Council, 1976.

B-88. Elton, Charlotte. "Women in Panama." Revista Panameña de Antropología, v. 1 (1), December 1975.

B-89. Jacobs, Sue Ellen. Women in Perspective: A Guide to Cross-Cultural Studies. Urbana, Illinois: University of Illinois Press, 1974.

B-90. Joyce, Lynda. "Annotated Bibliography of Women in Rural America." Mimeo. University Park: Pennsylvania State University, August 1976.

B-91. Knaster, Meri. Women in Spanish America: An Annotated Bibliography. Boston: G. K. Hall, 1977.

B-92. Land Tenure Center, University of Wisconsin. Agrarian Reform in Latin America: An Annotated Bibliography. Madison: Land Tenure Center, 1974.

B-93. Levenson, Rosaline. "Women in Government and Politics: A Bibliography of American and Foreign Sources." Monticello, Illinois: Council of Planning Librarians Exchange Bibliography no. 491, n.d.

B-94. Pescatello, Ann, ed. Female and Male in Latin America: Essays. Pittsburgh: University of Pittsburgh Press, 1973, pp. 293-334, ("Bibliography").

B-95. Sharma, Prakesh C. "Female Working Roles and Economic Development: A Selected Research Bibliography." Monticello, Illinois: Council of Planning Libraries Exchange Bibliography no. 663, n.d.

B-96. Soeiro, Susan A. "Recent Work on Latin American Women: A Review Essay." Journal of Inter-American Studies and World Affairs, v. 17 (4), November 1975: 497-516.

B-97. UNICEF (United Nations Children's Fund). "Bibliography of UNICEF Documents about Women." New York: UNICEF, 1975.

B-98. United Nations. "Status of Women: A Select Bibliography." New York: United Nations, June 1975. U.N. Document #ST/LIB/SER.B/20.

B-99. Watson, Gayle Hudgens. Colombia, Ecuador, and Venezuela: An Annotated Guide to Reference Materials in the Humanities and Social Sciences. Metuchen, New Jersey: The Scarecrow Press, 1971.

b. Serial Abstracts, Guides, and Indexes

B-100. Abstracts in Anthropology, v. 1-6, 1970-1975.

B-101. Columbus Memorial Library of the Pan American Union. Index to Latin American Periodicals, v. 1-4, 6-9 and 10 (2), 1961-1964, 1966-1969, April-June 1970.

B-102. Comprehensive Dissertation Index, v. 27, 1961-1972 (Law and Political Science); v. 17, 1961-1972 (Social Sciences); v. 3-4, 1974 (Social Sciences); v. 3-4, 1973 (Social Sciences and Humanities).

B-103. Dissertation Abstracts International. v. 31-32, 1971-1972; no. 1-6, 1972; no. 1-12, 1973; no. 1-12, 1974; no. 1-12, 1975; no. 1-12, 1976; also indexes for 1962-69, 1969-1970.

B-104. González, Luis; Guadalupe Monroy; and Susana Uribe. Fuentes de la historia contemporánea de México, vols. 1-3. Mexico City: El Colegio de México, 1961-62.

B-105. Handbook of Latin American Studies. v. 4-38, 1939-1976.

B-106. Hanson, Carl A. Dissertations on Iberian and Latin American History. Troy, New York: Whitston Publishing Company, 1975.

B-107. Institute of Latin American Studies, The University of Texas at Austin. Latin American Research and Publications at The University of Texas at Austin, 1893-1969. Austin: Institute of Latin American Studies, 1971.

B-108. Pan American Union. Index to Latin American Periodical Literature, 1921-1960. 8 vols; 2-vol. supplement, 1961-1965.

B-109. Sable, Martin H. A Guide to Latin American Studies, vols. 1-3. Los Angeles: University of California, 1967.

B-110. Sociological Abstracts. vols. 1-4, 1972-75.

c. Library Card Catalogues and Acquisition Lists

B-111. British Union. Library of the Institute of Latin American Studies, University of London. Latin American Titles, vols. 1-8, 1968-1975.

B-112. Canning House Library. Hispanic Council, vols. 1-4. London: G. K. Hall, 1967.

B-113. Canning House Library. Luzo-Brazilian Council, vol. 1. London: G. K. Hall, 1967.

B-114. Catálogo de la Biblioteca Nacional de Antropología e Historia (México), vols. 1-10. Boston: G. K. Hall, 1972.

B-115. Catholic University of America. Catalog of the Oliveira Lima Library, vols. 1-2. Boston: G. K. Hall, 1970.

B-116. The Hispanic Society of America. Catalogue of the Library, vols. 1-10. Boston: G. K. Hall, 1962, and 4-vol. supplement, 1970.

B-117. Newberry Library. Catalogue of the Greenlee Collection, vols. 1-2. Boston: G. K. Hall, 1970.

B-118. Tulane University Library. Catalog of the Latin American Library, vols. 1-13. Boston: G. K. Hall, 1970-1975.

B-119. University of Florida Libraries. Catalog of the Latin American Collection, vols. 1-13. Boston: G. K. Hall, 1973.

Appendix C

NAME AND PLACE OF PUBLICATION OF SELECTED REFERENCES

INCLUDED IN AFRICAN AND LATIN AMERICAN CITATIONS

1. PUBLICATIONS INCLUDED IN AFRICAN CITATIONS

C-1. Acta Ethnográfica (Budapest)

C-2. Aequatoria (Coquilhatville)

C-3. Africa (London)

C-4. Africa (Rome)

C-5. Africa South (Capetown)

C-6. African Social Research (Lusaka)

C-7. African Studies Review (East Lansing, Michigan)

C-8. African Studies (Johannesburg)

C-9. African Women (London)

C-10. African World (London)

C-11. Afrique (Paris)

C-12. L'Afrique Contemporaine (Paris)

C-13. American Journal of Comparative Law (Berkeley, California)

C-14. Annales Africaines (Dakar)

C-15. Année Sociologique (Paris)

C-16. Antennes (Kinshasa)

C-17. Anthropos (Freiburg)

C-18. Archiv für Völkerkunde (Vienna)

C-19. Assistance aux Maternités et Dispensaires de l'Afrique Centrale. (Brussels)

C-20. Association of American University Women's Journal (Washington, D.C.)

C-21. Bantu Studies (Johannesburg)

C-22. Bingo (Dakar)

C-23. Boletim da Sociedade de Estudios Coloniais de Moçambique (Lourenço-Marques)

C-24. Boletim do Instituto de Investigação Cientifica de Angola (Luanda)

C-25. Bulletin International des Sciences Sociales (Paris)

C-26. Bulletin de la Société de Recherches Congolaises (Brazzaville)

C-27. Bulletin de l'Institut d'Etudes Centrafricaines (Brazzaville)

C-28. Bulletin de l'Union des Femmes Coloniales (Brussels)

C-29. Bulletin de l'Institut Interafricaine du Travail (Brazzaville)

C-30. Bulletin de l'IFAN (Dakar)

C-31. Bulletin des Juridictions Indigènes et du Droit Coutûmier Congolais (Lubumbashi)

C-32. Bulletin du CEPSI (Lubumbashi)

C-33. Boletim do Instituto de Angelo (Luanda)

C-34. Bulletin du Madagascar (Tananarive)

C-35. Bulletin des Séances de l'Académie Royale de Sciences d'Outre-Mer (Brussels)

C-36. Cahiers Centre d'Etudes des Coutûmes (Tananarive)

C-37. Cadicec (Kinshasa)

C-38. Cahiers Economiques et de Liaison des Comités Euroafrique (Paris)

C-39. Cahiers d'Etudes Africaines (Paris)

C-40. Cahiers Ostrom (Paris)

C-41. Cahiers des Auxiliaires Laïques des Missions (Brussels)

C-42. Central African Journal of Medicine (Salisbury)

C-43. Christian Studies and Modern South Africa (Fort Have)

C-44. Civilisations (Brussels)

C-45. Congo (Brussels)

C-46. Congo-Afrique (Kinshasa)

C-47. Congo Mission News (Kinshasa)

C-48. Connaissance de l'Afrique (Paris)

C-49. Construire Ensemble (Bobo-Dioulasso, Upper Volta)

C-50. Continuous (Toronto)

C-51. Coopération et Développement (Paris)

C-52. Le Courier de l'UNESCO (Paris)

C-53. Croissance de Jeunes Nations (Paris)

C-54. Cuadernos de Estudios Africanos (Madrid)

C-55. Développement et Civilisations (Paris)

C-56. Dialogue et Culture (Brussels)

C-57. Diogènes (Paris)

C-58. Documents pour l'Action (Kinshasa)

C-59. East African Journal (Nairobi)

C-60. East Africa and Rhodesia (London)

C-61. Education Africaine (Dakar)

C-62. L'Education Africaine (Senegal)

C-63. L'Enfant en Milieu Tropical (Dakar)

C-64. Estudos Politicos e Sociais (Lisbon)

C-65. Estudos Ultramarinos (Lisbon)

C-66. Etapes (Brussels)

C-67. Ethnographie (Paris)

C-68. Ethnology (Pittsburgh)

C-69. Eurafrica (Brussels)

C-70. Europe-France-Outremer (Paris)

C-71. Echange (Paris)

C-72. Echange et Communication (The Hague)

C-73. Ebur (Abidjan)

C-74. La Femme et le Congo (Brussels)

C-75. Flamingo (Nigeria)

C-76. Forschungen und Fortschritte (Berlin)

C-77. Geographia (Paris)

C-78. Grand Lacs (Namur)

C-79. Hommes et Mondes (Paris)

C-80. ILO Panorama (Geneva)

C-81. Informations Sociales (Geneva)

C-82. Informations Sociales (Paris)

C-83. International African Seminar (Ibadan)

C-84. International Journal of Adult and Youth Education (UNESCO, Paris)

C-85. International Review of Missions (Edinburgh)

C-86. International Science Journal (Paris)

C-87. Journal of Modern African Studies (London)

C-88. Journal of the Centre Islamic Legal Studies (Nigeria)

C-89. Journal of Social Psychology (Johannesburg)

C-90. Journal de la Société des Africanistes (Paris)

C-91. Labor (Brussels)

C-92. Liaison (Brazzaville)

C-93. Manufacturer (Johannesburg)

C-94. Marchés Coloniaux (Paris)

C-95. Marco Polo (Paris)

C-96. Mémoires de l'Académie Royale des Sciences Coloniales (Brussels)

C-97. Mensario Administrativo (Luanda)

C-98. Mercure de France (Paris)

C-99. Missions Catholique (Lyon)

C-100. Monde et Mission (Brussels)

C-101. Native Teachers Journal (Pietermaritsburg, Natal)

C-102. Nada (Salisbury)

C-103. Nations Nouvelles (Yaoundé)

C-104. La Nef (Paris)

C-105. New Times (Moscow)

C-106. Nigeria (Lagos)

C-107. Nigeria Journal of Islam (Ile-Ife)

C-108. Notes Africaines (Dakar)

C-109. La Nouvelle Revue Pédagogique (Tournai, Belgium)

C-110. Odu (Ibadan)

C-111. Onitsha (Nigeria)

C-112. Outlook (Lusaka)

C-113. Outre-mer (Algiers)

C-114. Oversea Quarterly (London)

C-115. Pères Blancs (Paris)

C-116. Perspectives du Catholicité (Brussels)

C-117. Portugal em Africa (Lisbon)

C-118. Primitive Man (Washington, D.C.)

C-119. Problemes Sociaux Congolais (Lubumbashi)

C-120. Remarques Africaines (Brussels)

C-121. Revue de l'Action Populaire (Paris)

C-122. Revue International de l'Education des Adultes et de la Jeunesse (Paris)

C-123. Revue International du Travail (Geneva)

C-124. Review Occident Musulman (Aix-en-Provence)

C-125. Revue de l'Organization Africaine et Malgache de Cooperation économique (Yaoundé)

C-126. La Revue Nouvelle (Brussels)

C-127. Revue de l'Histoire de Colonies (Paris)

C-128. Revue de l'Institut de Sociologie (Brussels)

C-129. Revue Sénégalaise de Droit (Dakar)

C-130. Revue Scientifique (Paris)

C-131. The Rhodes-Livingstone Journal of Problems in British Central Africa (Livingstone)

C-132. Rural Africana (East Lansing, Michigan)

C-133. Rythmes du Monde (Lyon)

C-134. Sacred Heart Messenger (Bronx, N.Y.)

C-135. Sechaba (London)

C-136. Sentiers (Paris)

C-137. Synthéses (Brussels)

C-138. Sudan Society (University of Khartoum)

C-139. Terre Entiére (Paris)

C-140. Today's Health (Chicago)

C-141. Togo-Cameroun (Paris)

C-142. Tropiques (Paris)

C-143. Ultramar (Lisbon)

C-144. UNESCO Chronicle (Paris)

C-145. United Asia (Bombay)

C-146. University Woman (Chicago)

C-147. Vivante Afrique (Namur)

C-148. Voix du Congolais (Kalima)

C-149. West African Journal of Education (Ibadan)

C-150. West African Review (Liverpool)

2. PUBLICATIONS INCLUDED IN LATIN AMERICAN CITATIONS

C-151. Acción Social (Santiago, Chile)

C-152. Allpanchis Phuturinga (Instituto Pastoral Andino, Cuzco)

C-153. América (Havana) Also, a second journal entitled América is published in Quito.

C-154. América Indígena (Mexico City)

C-155. América Latina (Rio de Janeiro) Also, a second journal entitled América Latina is published in Moscow in Russian)

C-156. Américas (Organization of American States, Washington, D.C. English, Portuguese and Spanish)

C-157. Anales de la legislación Boliviana (La Paz)

C-158. Anales de la Universidad Central (Quito)

C-159. Anales de la Universidad de Cuenca (Ecuador)

C-160. Anthropologica (Ottawa)

C-161. Arco; Revista de las Areas Culturales Bolivariana (Bogotá)

C-162. Argentina Austral (Buenos Aires)

C-163. Arquivos Brasileiros de Psicotecnica (Rio de Janeiro)

C-164. Ateneo (San Salvador)

C-165. Banas (São Paulo)

C-166. Boletim do Instituto Joaquim Nabuco de Pesquisas Sociais (Recife)

C-167. Boletin Cultural y Bibliográfico (Bogotá)

C-168. Boletín de la Facultad de Derecho y Ciencias Sociales (Córdoba, Argentina)

C-169. Boletín del Instituto Internacional-Americano de Protección a la Infancia (Montevideo)

C-170. Boletín del Museo Social Argentino (Buenos Aires)

C-171. Boletín Documental sobre las Mujeres   (Cidhal, Cuernavaca)

C-172. Boletín Informativo de la Sociedad de Esposas de Abogados (Panama City)

C-173. Boletín Oficial   (Buenos Aires)

C-174. Boletín Uruguayo de Sociología   (Montevideo)

C-175. Brazil   (New York)

C-176. Brazilian American   (Rio de Janeiro)

C-177. Bulletin of the ICW (Interamerican Commission of Women) (Panamerican Union, Washington, D.C.)

C-178. Bulletin of the Pan American Union   (Washington, D.C.)

C-179. Cadernos Brasileiros   (Rio de Janeiro)

C-180. Cadernos da PVC   (Rio de Janeiro)

C-181. Cadernos de Estudos Rurais e Urbanos   (São Paulo)

C-182. Cadernos de Pesquisa   (Fundação Carlos Chagas, São Paulo)

C-183. Canadian Magazine   (Toronto)

C-184. Carteles   (Havana)

C-185. Casa de las Américas   (Havana)

C-186. Ceres   (Food and Agriculture Organization, United Nations, New York)

C-187. Combate   (San José, Costa Rica)

C-188. Comentario   (Rio de Janeiro)

C-189. Comunidad   (Mexico City)

C-190. Criminalia   (Mexico City)

C-191. Criterio   (Buenos Aires)

C-192. Cromos   (Bogotá)

C-193. Cuadernos   (Paris)

C-194. Cuadernos Americanos (Mexico City)

C-195. Cuadernos Latinoamericanos de Economía Humana (Montevideo)

C-196. Cuban Review (New York)

C-197. La Cultura en Mexico (Mexico City)

C-198. Cultura Politica (Rio de Janeiro)

C-199. Department of State Bulletin (Washington, D.C.)

C-200. Diálogos (Mexico City)

C-201. Digesto Económico (São Paulo)

C-202. Dinámica Social (Buenos Aires)

C-203. Educação e Ciencias Sociais (Rio de Janeiro)

C-204. Educación (Lima)

C-205. Educación Boliviana (La Paz)

C-206. Espejo (Mexico City)

C-207. Estudios (Buenos Aires)

C-208. Estudios Andinos (Pittsburgh)

C-209. Estudios Centroamericanos (San Salvador)

C-210. Estudios de Derecho (Medellín)

C-211. Le Express (Paris)

C-212. La Gaceta (Tegucigalpa)

C-213. Guatemala Indígena (Instituto Indigenista Nacional, Guatemala City)

C-214. Hatun Xaura (Jauja, Peru)

C-215. Hispanic American Historical Review (Durham, North Carolina)

C-216. Humanismo (Havana)

C-217. Iberoamérica (Bahía Blanca, Argentina)

C-218. Industria e Productividade (Rio de Janeiro)

C-219. Industrial and Labour Information (Geneva)

C-220. Industry and Labour (Geneva)

C-221. Inter-American (Washington, D.C.)

C-222. Interamerican Law Review (New Orleans)

C-223. International Labour Review (Geneva)

C-224. Jus Documentação (Rio de Janeiro)

C-225. Justicia (Mexico City)

C-226. Latin American World (London)

C-227. Latinoamérica (Mexico City)

C-228. El Libertador (Quito)

C-229. Lotería (Panama City)

C-230. Mañana (Mexico City)

C-231. María Aestrus, Organo de la Biblioteca del Ministerio de Relaciones Exteriores. (Lima)

C-232. Mexican-American Review (Mexico City)

C-233. Mexican Life (Mexico City)

C-234. Mid-Pacific Magazine (Honolulu)

C-235. Mireya (Bogotá)

C-236. Monthly Labor Review (Washington, D.C.)

C-237. Mundo Hispánico (Madrid)

C-238. Mundo Libre (Mexico City)

C-239. Mundo Nuevo (Paris)

C-240. Negocios Colombo-Americanos (Bogotá)

C-241. New Chile (NACLA, New York)

C-242. Newsletter (Department of State, Washington, D.C.)

C-243. New West Coast Leader (Lima)

C-244. Nicaragua Indígena (Managua)

C-245. Norte. (New York)

C-246. Noticias de la Oficina de Información Obrera y Social (Washington, D.C.)

C-247. Nueva Democracia (New York)

C-248. Nueva Educación (Lima)

C-249. Nueva Era (Panama City)

C-250. Nueva Revista Cubana (Havana)

C-251. La Palabra y el Hombre (Veracruz, Mexico)

C-252. Pan American (New York)

C-253. El Paraguayo (Asunción)

C-254. Peruvian Times (Lima)

C-255. Previsión Social (Quito)

C-256. Progreso y Cultura (Caracas)

C-257. The Progressive (Madison, Wisconsin)

C-258. Punto Crítico (Mexico City)

C-259. Repertorio Americano (San José, Costa Rica)

C-260. La República (Mexico City)

C-261. Review of the River Plate (Buenos Aires)

C-262. Revista Americana de Buenos Aires (Buenos Aires)

C-263. Revista Bimestre Cubana (Havana)

C-264. Revista Bolivariana (Bogotá)

C-265. Revista Brasileira de Estatistica (Rio de Janeiro)

C-266. Revista Brasiliense (São Paulo)

C-267. Revista de Ciencia Política (Rio de Janeiro)

C-268. Revista de Ciencias Jurídicas (San José, Costa Rica)

C-269. Revista de Ciencias Jurídicas y Sociales (Santa Fé, Argentina)

C-270. Revista de Ciencias Psicológicas y Neurológicas (Lima)

C-271. Revista de Ciencias Sociales (Rio Piedras, Puerto Rico)

C-272. Revista de Derecho (La Paz)

C-273. Revista de Derecho Internacional (Havana)

C-274. Revista de Derecho, Jurisprudencia y Administración (Montevideo)

C-275. Revista de Derecho Puertorriqueño (Ponce, Puerto Rico)

C-276. Revista de Derecho y Ciencias Sociales (Concepción, Chile)

C-277. Revista de Historia de América (Mexico City)

C-278. Revista de Indias (Madrid)

C-279. Revista de la Biblioteca Municipal (La Paz)

C-280. Revista de la Universidad del Cauca (Popayán, Colombia)

C-281. Revista de la Universidad de Costa Rica (San José, Costa Rica)

C-282. Revista del Colegio de Abogados (La Plata, Argentina)

C-283. Revista del Foro (Lima)

C-284. Revista del Maestro (Guatemala City)

C-285. Revista del Ministerio de Trabajo y Bienestar Social (Guatemala City)

C-286. Revista del Notariado (Buenos Aires)

C-287. Revista del Pensamiento Centroamericano (Managua)

C-288. Revista do Instituto Histórico e Geográfico Brasileiro (Rio de Janeiro)

C-289. Revista do Ministerio do Trabalho, Industria y Comercio (Rio de Janeiro)

C-290. Revista do Trabalho (Rio de Janeiro)

C-291. Revista Iberoamericana de Seguridad Social (Madrid)

C-292. Revista Internacional y Diplomática (Mexico City)

C-293. Revista Javeriana (Bogotá)

C-294. Revista Jurídica Dominicana (Santo Domingo, República Dominicana)

C-295. Revista La Nación (Buenos Aires)

C-296. Revista Mexicana de Ciencias Políticas y Sociales (Mexico City)

C-297. Revista Mexicana de Trabajo (Mexico City)

C-298. Revista Universitaria Nacional de Córdoba (Also cited as Revista de la Universidad Nacional de Córdoba) (Córdoba, Argentina)

C-299. Revolución (Havana)

C-300. Revolución y Cultura (Havana)

C-301. SIC: Revista Venezolana de Orientación (Caracas)

C-302. Síntese Politica Económica Social (Rio de Janeiro)

C-303. Sociología (São Paulo)

C-304. South Pacific Mail (Valparaíso)

C-305. Sur (Buenos Aires)

C-306. Tierra y Dos Mares (Panama City)

C-307. The UNESCO Courier (New York)

C-308. UNICEF News (New York)

C-309. United Nations Review (New York)

C-310. Universidad de Antioquía (Medellín)

C-311. Universitas (Bogotá)

C-312. Vanguardia (Monterrey)

C-313. Vida Femenina (Buenos Aires)

C-314. Visión (Mexico City)

C-315. La Voz de Atlántida (La Ceiba, Honduras)

C-316. Vozes (Petrópolis, Brazil)

C-317. The Woman Worker (Washington, D.C.)

C-318. Zontian (Chicago)